OXFORD READINGS IN POLITICS
AND GOVERNMENT

THE WEST EUROPEAN PARTY SYSTEM

OXFORD READINGS IN POLITICS
AND GOVERNMENT

General Editors: Vernon Bogdanor and Geoffrey Marshall

The readings in this series are chosen from a variety of journals and other sources to cover major areas or issues in the study of politics, government, and political theory. Each volume contains an introductory essay by the editor and a select guide to further reading.

THE WEST
EUROPEAN
PARTY SYSTEM

EDITED BY

PETER MAIR

OXFORD UNIVERSITY PRESS

1990

Oxford University Press, Walton Street, Oxford OX2 6DP

Oxford New York Toronto
Delhi Bombay Calcutta Madras Karachi
Petaling Jaya Singapore Hong Kong Tokyo
Nairobi Dar es Salaam Cape Town
Melbourne Auckland
and associated companies in
Berlin Ibadan

Oxford is a trade mark of Oxford University Press

Published in the United States
by Oxford University Press, New York

Introduction and compilation © Peter Mair 1990

British Library Cataloguing in Publication Data
The West European party system.— (Oxford readings in
politics and government)
1. Western Europe. Political parties
I. Mair, Peter
324.24
ISBN 0–19–827584–6
ISBN 0–19–827583–8 (pbk.)

Library of Congress Cataloging in Publication Data
The West European party system / edited by Peter Mair.
(Oxford readings in politics and government)
Includes bibliographical references.
1. Political parties—Europe.   2. Europe—Politics and government.
I. Mair, Peter   II. Series.
JN94.A979W45 1990   324.24—dc20   89-27449
ISBN 0–19–827584–6
ISBN 0–19–827583–8 (pbk.)

Photoset by Rowland Phototypesetting Ltd
Bury St Edmunds, Suffolk
Printed in Great Britain
by Biddles Ltd, Guildford and King's Lynn

For Hans Daalder

PREFACE AND
ACKNOWLEDGEMENTS

The study of parties and party systems has always remained a major focus of concern for political scientists. This is nowhere more so than in Western Europe, where the sheer diversity of national experiences can be studied against the homogenizing impact of a shared European culture and historical tradition; indeed, it is this constant interplay between the analysis of individual party systems, on the one hand, and what might almost be termed the European party system, on the other, which has been responsible for much of the most valuable literature in political science in Europe.

In this short collection of readings, I have attempted to do justice to both the quality and the variety of that literature. The explicit focus of the collection is the West European experience as a whole. In no instance have analyses of individual national party systems been included, despite the insights which have been generated by such studies over the years. Moreover, it is the European experience with which all of the writers here, almost without exception, have been primarily concerned. To be sure, all are aware of diversity, all are conscious of the mosaic; but all are also intent on stressing the value of cross-national comparison and the need to understand the shared foundation on which this diversity rests.

All writers, of whatever hue, are understandably conscious of the integrity of their texts. Limitations of space, however, together with a desire to squeeze as much as possible into that limited space, have forced me to ride roughshod over this integrity, and to reproduce these essays in a way which often fails to do justice to the nuances and the elegance of the original argument. Faced with a choice between including a small number of essays, each of which would appear in its entirety, or a larger number, many of which would be edited down, I have opted for the latter course. As such, that which is presented here offers no substitute for a proper reading of the original writings from which these edited selections have been drawn. Rather,

viii   PREFACE AND ACKNOWLEDGEMENTS

these extracts should be seen as an initial guide to those original texts, as well as to other valuable writings which cannot be encompassed within this limited space, and as an introduction to the themes, problems, and dilemmas which have confronted scholars in their attempts to understand parties and party systems in Western Europe.

In the course of preparing this selection, I have benefited from the advice and knowledge of a number of leading scholars in the field, including Stefano Bartolini, Ronald Inglehart, and Giovanni Sartori. Vernon Bogdanor, the general editor of the series of which this volume forms part, and Henry Hardy of Oxford University Press have also proved consistently helpful and accommodating. The bulk of my reading and editing was carried out while I enjoyed a Fellowship in the Netherlands Institute for Advanced Study in the Humanities and Social Sciences, and I would like to thank the Director and the staff for their support. In particular, I would like to pay special thanks to Dinny Young, the NIAS Librarian, who always proved both patient and helpful, even when inundated with requests for some quite arcane material. The year at NIAS also afforded me the welcome opportunity of working again with Hans Daalder, who had initially guided my interest in Western European party systems while we were both at the European University Institute in Florence, and who has also offered me much valuable advice in the preparation of this particular volume. As I began the work of editing, he was celebrating the twenty-fifth anniversary of his appointment as a Professor in the University of Leiden, and in order to mark that occasion, as well as to acknowledge my own debt to someone who still remains one of the leading scholars in the field, I would like to dedicate this collection to him.

P.M.

Wassenaar
January 1989

CONTENTS

INTRODUCTION

PETER MAIR

I. POLITICAL PARTIES AND THE STABILIZATION OF PARTY SYSTEMS

In 1918, in a lecture at the University of Munich, Max Weber addressed himself to the question of 'politics as a vocation'. His theme was the new professionalism of politics, and within that theme he laid particular emphasis on the emergence of the modern mass party. For Weber, the contrast with past political organization was profound:

[T]he most modern forms of party organizations stand in sharp contrast to [the] idyllic state in which circles of notables and, above all, members of parliament rule. These modern forms are the children of democracy, of mass franchise, of the necessity to woo and organize the masses, and develop the utmost unity of direction and the strictest discipline.[1]

Subsequent scholarship was to confirm the pervasiveness of this transformation and its inevitable association with the extension of democratic rights. Mass participation came to mean mass parties, and for many observers, including Schattschneider,[2] it appeared that modern democracy itself was 'unthinkable save in terms of parties'. A brief check-list of the functions normally associated with parties[3] underlines their essential role: parties structure the popular vote, integrate and mobilize the mass of the citizenry; aggregate diverse interests; recruit leaders for public office; and formulate public policy.

---

* indicates a text which is also reproduced in whole or in part as a chapter in this reading.

[1] M. Weber, 'Politics as a Vocation',* in H. H. Gerth and C. Wright Mills (eds.), *From Max Weber: Essays in Sociology* (New York: Oxford University Press, 1946), 102.

[2] E. E. Schattschneider, *Party Government* (New York: Rinehart, 1942), 1.

[3] e.g. Anthony King, 'Political Parties in Western Democracies: Some Sceptical Reflections', *Polity*, 2/2 (1969), 111–41.

Most important of all, within the liberal democracies it is primarily parties which organize modern government, in such a way that, as Wildenmann notes, 'party government is the crucial agency of institutional legitimization'.[4]

At the same time, however, it is impossible to separate the question of the role of parties from that of their legitimacy. The leaders whom parties recruit, the policies which they formulate, and the governments that they seek to control can be legitimized only to the extent that the parties themselves are legitimized: hence the relevance of the mass party. For whatever one can say about the professionalization of politics which came in the wake of mass democracy, it was the popular base of parties which, in the end, was to ensure their legitimacy. Parties reflected the public will and provided the crucial linkage between the citizenry and the state. They did so as mass organizations, for it was as mass organizations that they belonged to the society from which they emanated. In effect, and above all else, the twentieth century has been the century of the mass party.

There are two respects in which this development has been important: first, because of the sheer pervasiveness of the mass party organization in modern democratic politics, second, because of the process of stabilization which resulted from the organizational capacities of the mass party.

The pervasiveness of mass party organization, already noted by Weber, was forcefully underlined in Duverger's pioneering comparative study of parties and party systems.[5] Like Weber, Duverger linked the development of the mass party to the extension of democratic rights, arguing that mass enfranchisement had led to the replacement of caucus-based organizations by branch-based organizations, and of cadre parties by mass parties. Duverger associated this transformation primarily with the left, arguing that the need to secure financial resources

---

[4] Rudolf Wildenmann, 'The Problematic of Party Government', in Francis G. Castles and Rudolf Wildenmann (eds.), *Visions and Realities of Party Government* (Berlin: de Gruyter, 1986), 6.

[5] Maurice Duverger, *Political Parties: Their Organization and Activity in the Modern State** (London: Methuen, 1954). See also Sigmund Neumann, 'Toward a Comparative Study of Political Parties',* in Neumann (ed.), *Modern Political Parties* (Chicago: University of Chicago Press, 1956), 395–421.

made it particularly imperative for socialist parties to develop a mass organization. Parties of the right, on the other hand, which enjoyed the support of wealthy backers and clients, could still afford a more cadre-type organization. Nevertheless, this was not a hard and fast distinction, and Duverger also emphasized the notion of a 'contagion' from the left which could induce the spread of mass party organization right across the political spectrum.

What was even more important, however, was the impact which this had on the stabilization of mass electorates: as Sartori has argued, 'the critical factor in altering the nature of a party system and in bringing about its structural consolidation is the appearance of the mass party'.[6] Through the encapsulation of sections of the mass electorate, and through the inculcation of political identities which proved both solid and enduring, the mass party became the agency by which political behaviour was structured, and by which partisan stability was ensured. Political choice developed into political identity as a result of political organization; in this fashion, the party systems themselves were consolidated.

The critical step was therefore the transition from cadre party to mass party, from loosely based *networks* of like-minded notables to tightly organized, popularly financed mass *organizations*. These latter organizations, through their mass following, closed off the electoral market and stabilized the modern party systems. As Lipset and Rokkan have argued:

the narrowing of the 'support market' brought about through the growth of mass parties . . . left very few openings for new movements. Where the challenge of the emerging working-class parties had been met by concerted efforts of countermobilization through nationwide mass organizations on the liberal and conservative fronts, the leeway for new party formations was particularly small; this was the case whether the threshold of representation was low, as in Scandinavia, or quite high, as in Britain.[7]

---

[6] Giovanni Sartori, 'Political Development and Political Engineering',* *Public Policy*, 17 (1968), 292.

[7] S. M. Lipset and Stein Rokkan, 'Cleavage Structures, Party Systems and Voter Alignments: An Introduction',* in Lipset and Rokkan (eds.), *Party Systems and Voter Alignments* (New York: Free Press, 1967), 51.

The sequence of the process is clear and the logic compelling. The extension of the suffrage incorporates the mass of the citizenry into the political system; mass parties mobilize and integrate these new citizens and inculcate a set of enduring political identities; these political identities, in turn, act as a force for the stabilization of alignments and, in Lipset and Rokkan's familiar terms, for the freezing of party systems. Organization is therefore clearly crucial, for it was only through the independent organizational intervention of the mass party, a party which, in many cases, 'permeated and enveloped other political elites',[8] that these identities could be forged and that these voters could be bonded. It is in this sense, as Sartori has underlined, that 'a freezed party system is simply a party system that intervenes in the political process as an independent *system of channelment*, propelled and maintained by its own laws of inertia'.[9] In sum, the mass party, which has been the creature of mass democracy, acted at the same time to ensure the stabilization of mass democracy.

But while the logic is compelling, it is also contingent. The stability which resulted from the capacity of parties to draw voters firmly into their organizational nets largely depended upon the immediacy of their links with the wider society. To the extent that these links were loosened, and to the extent that the party became more remote from the everyday lives of the citizenry, then the organizational preconditions of such stability would be eroded. To be sure, policy appeals, government performance, and the attraction of particular leaders might help to ensure the maintenance of voter loyalty, but, at the very least, the loosening of organizational ties implied a certain vulnerability.

Just such a sense of vulnerability was to follow from the

[8] Hans Daalder, 'Parties, Elites, and Political Developments in Western Europe',* in Joseph LaPalombara and Myron Weiner (eds.), *Political Parties and Political Development* (Princeton: Princeton University Press, 1966), 58. See also Stein Rokkan, 'Towards a Generalized Concept of *Verzuiling*: A Preliminary Note',* *Political Studies*, 25/4 (1977), 563–70.

[9] G. Sartori, 'The Sociology of Parties: A Critical Review',* in Otto Stammer (ed.), *Party Systems, Party Organisations, and the Politics of the New Masses* (Berlin: Institut fuer Politische Wissenschaft an der Freien Universitaet, 1968), 21.

emergence of what Kirchheimer identified as the 'catch-all party'.[10] While Kirchheimer has proved among the most widely cited of the modern writers on parties and party systems, he has also been subject to a curiously partial reading; for, in taking on board Kirchheimer's prognostications concerning the rise of the catch-all party, most scholars have tended to emphasize the strictly ideological implications of his argument, and have thereby neglected the arguably more crucial organizational developments which were at the heart of the original thesis.[11]

Like Duverger, Kirchheimer was concerned with a contrast between two types of party—what he referred to as the 'mass integration' party, on the one hand, and the new catch-all party, on the other. Moreover, and again like Duverger, he imputed a sequential pattern to the distinction, arguing that the age of the former had passed, and that the West European systems were now faced with the more or less irresistible rise of the catch-all party:

the mass integration party, product of an age with harder class lines and more sharply protruding denominational structures, is transforming itself into a catch-all 'people's' party. Abandoning attempts at the intellectual and moral *encadrement* of the masses, it is turning more fully to the electoral scene, trying to exchange effectiveness in depth for a wider audience and more immediate electoral success.[12]

Kirchheimer then goes on to list five characteristics of the emerging catch-all party. These are 'a drastic reduction of the party's ideological baggage'; a 'further strengthening of top leadership groups'; a 'downgrading of the role of the individual party member'; a 'de-emphasis of the *classe gardée*, specific social-class or denominational clientele, in favour of recruiting

---

[10] Otto Kirchheimer, 'The Transformation of the Western European Party Systems',* in LaPalombara and Weiner (eds.), *Political Parties*, pp. 177–200.

[11] See, e.g., Steven B. Wolinetz, 'The Transformation of Western European Party Systems Revisited',* *West European Politics*, 2/1 (1979), 4–28; Karl Dittrich, 'Testing the Catch-all Thesis: Some Difficulties and Possibilities', in Hans Daalder and Peter Mair (eds.), *Western European Party Systems: Continuity and Change* (London: Sage Publications, 1983), 257–66.

[12] Kirchheimer, 'Transformation of the Western European Party Systems', p. 184.

voters among the population at large'; and a process of 'securing access to a variety of interest groups' (p. 190). Crucially, it is
only the first of these five characteristics which is explicitly
concerned with ideological change. In sum, and above all else,
the catch-all party is an *organizational* phenomenon.

Moreover, the nature of the organizational transformation
involved in the emergence of the catch-all party is also clearly
specified. Kirchheimer depicts a party which has sundered its
close links with the mass electorate and has become essentially
remote from the everyday life of the citizen. This remoteness is
reflected in a shift of internal party power towards the leadership; a loosening of socially specific bonds with sections of the
electorate—be they defined in class terms, denominational
terms, or whatever; and a reduction in the role of ordinary
members.

Thus the catch-all party severs its specific organizational
links with the society of which it is part and begins to operate at
one remove from its constituency. It shifts from being a
'bottom-up' party to being a 'top-down' party, and chooses to
compete on the market rather than attempting to narrow that
market. It builds on conditional support rather than on a sense
of identification. It seeks the endorsement of voters rather than
their encapsulation.

The result is a greater potential for contingent or even
virtually random voting. Thus, it is no accident that the
changes in party organization and style which were noted by
Kirchheimer in the early 1960s were soon succeeded by the
destabilization of the individual party electorates in the late
1960s and 1970s. These latter changes have been well documented, and their sheer suddenness is amply demonstrated by
the juxtaposition in this volume of Rose and Urwin's emphasis
on the evidence of persistence and Pedersen's emphasis on
volatility.[13] For, as parties increasingly tended to operate at one

[13] Richard Rose and Derek Urwin, 'Persistence and Change in Western
Party Systems since 1945',* *Political Studies*, 18/3 (1970), 287–319; Mogens N.
Pedersen, 'The Dynamics of European Party Systems: Changing Patterns of
Electoral Volatility',* *European Journal of Political Research*, 7/1 (1979), 1–26.
See also Wolinetz, 'Transformation of Western European Party Systems
Revisited'; Maria Maguire, 'Is There Still Persistence? Electoral Change in
Western Europe, 1948–1979', in Daalder and Mair (eds.), *Western European*

remove from the society of which they were once part, voters themselves tended to shed their sense of partisan belonging and, as Rose and McAllister put it in a different context, they slowly began to choose.[14] These free-range voters were no longer mobilized by the parties and had ceased to be integrated into the parties. Their horizons widened, their options increased, and, in general, they became more volatile. In effect, as the parties became more remote, the electorate itself became more available. The basis for persistence, which rested on organizational intervention and control, and which thrived on the encapsulation of the mass public, was thereby undermined.

To be sure, the shifting electoral alignments which have characterized Western Europe since the late 1960s cannot simply be explained by reference to the changing organizational style of the traditional parties. As is evident from the variety of arguments presented in the readings in Part III below, there is clearly much more to it than this. Over the past few years, a number of crucial factors have been identified as leading to electoral instability, and a particular emphasis has been laid on the impact of changes in the social structure and the blurring of traditional class boundaries, on the one hand,[15] and on the impact of new value systems and the mobilization of a new post-materialist cleavage, on the other.[16] In addition, while

---

Party Systems, pp. 67–94; Michal Shamir, 'Are Western European Party Systems "Frozen"?', *Comparative Political Studies*, 17/1 (1984), 35–79; Ivor Crewe and David Denver (eds.), *Electoral Change in Western Democracies: Patterns and Sources of Electoral Volatility* (London: Croom Helm, 1985); Stefano Bartolini and Peter Mair, *Identity, Competition, and Electoral Availability: The Stabilization of European Electorates, 1885–1985* (Cambridge: Cambridge University Press, 1990).

[14] Richard Rose and Ian McAllister, *Voters Begin to Choose* (London: Sage Publications, 1986).

[15] Russell J. Dalton, Scott C. Flanagan, and Paul Allen Beck (eds.), *Electoral Change in Advanced Industrial Democracies: Realignment or Dealignment?* (Princeton: Princeton University Press, 1984); S. C. Flanagan and R. J. Dalton, 'Parties Under Stress: Realignment and Dealignment in Advanced Industrial Societies',* *West European Politics*, 7/1 (1984), 7–23.

[16] Ronald Inglehart, *The Silent Revolution: Changing Values and Political Styles among Western Publics** (Princeton: Princeton University Press, 1977); id., 'The Changing Structure of Political Cleavages in Western Society', in Dalton *et al.* (eds.), *Electoral Change*, pp. 25–69; id., 'Value Change in Industrial Societies',* *American Political Science Review*, 81/4 (1987), 1289–303.

unwilling to endorse the sweeping assertions of an 'end of ideology' which characterized much of the writing on political attitudes in the 1960s,[17] it cannot be denied that many of the great issues which once sustained traditional loyalties have now more or less been solved. The struggles of the working class for political rights have been won; the legitimacy of defending the rights of organized religion has also been accepted, as has the legitimacy of the rights of those who reject religious beliefs; a comprehensive welfare state has become the norm in most of the contemporary West European democracies, and such conflicts over welfare rights as do persist tend to be at the margins of the system.[18] The great struggles are over, and as Pizzorno, echoing Kirchheimer, has noted, the situation in most of the Western democracies has become one 'in which no irreducible political identity is at stake and political demands all become negotiable. Interest groups asking for specific policies are the main actors on the political scene whereas the political parties ... tend to lose their programmatic and organizational identity'.[19] That electoral destabilization should then ensue is hardly surprising.

The changes which have been identified in the previous paragraph do, of course, lie largely outwith the control of the parties themselves. Hence the fact that they have been conducive to greater party vulnerability is something which the parties cannot challenge but to which they must adapt. The type of organizational change which was noted earlier, however, is quite another matter, for this does appear to have lain within the control of party. But this surely begs the question: for, to the extent that such organizational change has also acted to encourage electoral destabilization, why then should parties have loosened their societal ties? If electoral vulnerability has

[17] See the survey in Chaim I. Waxman (ed.), *The End of Ideology Debate* (New York: Funk and Wagnalls, 1968).

[18] See Peter Flora, 'Introduction', in Flora (ed.), *Growth to Limits: The Western European Welfare States since World War II*. Vol. 1, *Sweden, Norway, Finland, Denmark* (Berlin: de Gruyter, 1986), pp. v–xxxvi.

[19] Allesandro Pizzorno, 'Interests and Parties in Pluralism',* in Suzanne Berger (ed.), *Organizing Interests in Western Europe: Pluralism, Corporatism, and the Transformation of Politics* (Cambridge: Cambridge University Press, 1981), 272.

been at least the partial consequence of the adoption of a catch-all organizational style, why should the parties have followed this path to begin with?

There are three factors which are important here. First, there are those organizational and institutional developments which, in and of themselves, have facilitated a more catch-all or 'top-down' approach. These include changes in the modes of financing the parties, which have led to a greater reliance on state subventions as against membership subscriptions or other popular forms of finance; the impact of new technologies and of changes in the mass media which have enabled party leaders to appeal directly to voters and which have thereby undermined the need for organizational networks; the increased availability of new marketing techniques, which help to obviate the need for grass-roots liaison as a means of gaining feedback, and so on.

Second, there is the impact of social change on organization itself (as opposed to its impact on issue-concerns, values, etc.—see above), in that the development of a more knowledge-able, well-informed, and competent electorate, together with the undeniable increase in the individualization and atomiza-tion of modern society, have together undermined the sense of collective solidarity which once served as the prerequisite for the traditional mass party. Perhaps ironically, it has sometimes been the very success of the parties which has acted to promote this erosion of collective solidarity. As Einhorn and Logue note in the case of the Social Democrats in Scandinavia, for example,

the principal cause of demobilization was success . . . Social Demo-cratic housing policy moved a good portion of the blue-collar working class out of the densely propulated urban neighborhoods where the party and its organizations had been a way of life; those customs did not move easily to suburbia. Moreover, the centralized mechanisms of the welfare state eliminated the need for solidarity, which had been a crucial characteristic of the labour movement. Previously, solidarity had provided the welfare infrastructure for the working class—trade union benefit societies covering sickness, unemployment, old age and death; housing cooperatives, and the like—but now the need for solidarity and schooling in it were attenuated.[20]

[20] Eric S. Einhorn and John Logue, 'Continuity and Change in the Scandinavian Party Systems', in Steven B. Wolinetz (ed.), *Parties and Party Systems in Liberal Democracies* (London: Routledge, 1988), 180.

Third, it is also possible that the difficulties which we perceive in attempting to puzzle out the reasons for a shift towards attenuated organizational links are not really difficulties at all, but may simply derive from approaching the problem from the wrong end. In this sense, the catch-all or top-down style of party may actually be the norm, while the more encapsulating or solidaristic party may well be the transitory exception. Thus, for example, Pizzorno has hypothesized that

'integration' parties, stable electoral cleavages, and clear alternatives in party programme are more likely to be found in periods of intense social (mainly occupational and geographic) change and of consequent strong pressures by new categories of interests to enter into the political system. If this hypothesis is true, strong parties, with clearly delineated programmes and integrated membership, are a temporary phenomenon. They emerge both to strengthen and to control the access of the new masses into the political system and become redundant once both entry and control are achieved. If they are typical of pluralism, then, they are typical only of its first 'generative' phase, when the big collective actors are admitted to share power into a system of representation.[21]

This argument is also reinforced by a second contention of Pizzorno, that 'in principle, there should be no need for organization . . . to unite the followers of a governmental party'.[22] According to this view, governmental resources, or the promise of such resources, offer incentives to the parties to shed those often unwelcome policy and ideological constraints which are an inevitable side-effect of the maintenance of an active organizational network. To the extent that parties gain greater access to government, then, we might expect them to lay a diminishing emphasis on the need for organization. The importance of this hypothesis is easily indicated by even the most cursory survey of the recent West European experience, for this shows that most of the relevant parties are now governing or potentially-governing parties. In the fifteen-year period from 1970 to 1985, for example, only two West European parties of any notable size remained persistently excluded from government: the British Liberal party, on the one hand, which despite its

[21] Pizzorno, 'Interests and Parties in Pluralism', p. 272.
[22] Ibid. 253.

increasing electoral support remains a very minor party at the parliamentary level; and the Italian *Partito Comunista*, on the other, whose exclusion from government has been tempered by sustained periods in office at the regional level, as well as by a semi-governmental role at national level during the period of the *compromesso storico* in the 1970s. With these qualified exceptions, *all* other European parties of any reasonable electoral size have enjoyed at least one period of incumbency during this fifteen-year span.

Whatever the reasons, however, there is no denying the reality of the shift from mass parties or mass integration parties towards a more catch-all model, a shift which is clearly documented in the writings presented in Part I of this reader. And, as has been argued above, it is also clear that one can identify a link between this transition and the concomitant move from the stabilization of party systems (see Part II) to their subsequent destabilization (see Part III).

2.   THE TRANSFORMATION OF EUROPEAN PARTY SYSTEMS

Ever since a wave of electoral volatility broke over many of the West European party systems in the early 1970s,[23] the literature on European politics has itself has been awash with evocations of change. The contrast with the image of persistence which dominated the writing on parties and party systems in the late 1960s[24] could hardly be sharper. Now, noting the emergence of new political parties, the decline of traditionally dominant alternatives, and a generally pervasive upsurge in electoral instability, the contemporary literature inclines us to a belief that we are witnessing a widespread process of mass political transformation, and that we are confronting the dawn of a wholly new age of mass politics, an age in which cleavages are no longer frozen, traditional social divisions are no longer relevant to politics, and the parties themselves are in decay.

[23] See Pedersen, 'The Dynamics of European Party Systems'.
[24] e.g. Lipset and Rokkan, 'Cleavage Structures, Party Systems and Voter Alignments'; Rose and Urwin, 'Persistence and Change in Western Party Systems since 1945'.

Variations on these themes now form such a major part of the current writing on parties and party systems that a review of the specific interpretations seems hardly necessary at this stage. A number of the discussions are reproduced in Part III of this reader.[25] What does seem appropriate at this point, however, is to sound a note of caution and to introduce a number of important caveats, particularly since the sheer pervasiveness of these emphases on transformation has tended to overwhelm those occasional dissenting voices which still point to the evidence of continuity and persistence. To be sure, there is no denying the extent of contemporary electoral turbulence in Western Europe. Nor can we ignore the importance of the emergence of new political interests and of new modes of political participation.[26] At the same time, however, it is worth emphasizing that even those authors who are prompted by a desire to understand processes of political change nevertheless often end their analyses on a more cautious note. Thus, for example, while emphasizing that 'virtually everywhere among the industrialized democracies, the old order is changing', Dalton *et al.* finally conclude their survey of electoral change by noting: 'despite our emphasis on change, we are struck by the fact that no single author [in *Electoral Change in Advanced Industrial Democracies*] unequivocally states that a new political order has emerged. Most say that change is in the air; a few say that the old order is dead; but none announce the birth of a new political order.'[27] A more recent collection of essays concludes on a similar note: 'Even if change is widespread, it is important not to overstate its extent. Although few party systems have been as constant as they once appeared to be, all exhibit substantial elements of continuity. In each of the countries we

[25] A representative range of the more extended arguments can also be found in Dalton *et al.* (eds.), *Electoral Change*, and Kay Lawson and Peter Merkl (eds.), *When Parties Fail: Emerging Alternative Organizations* (Princeton: Princeton University Press, 1988).

[26] See, e.g., Samuel H. Barnes, Max Kaase, *et al.*, *Political Action: Mass Participation in Five Western Democracies* (Beverly Hills: Sage Publications, 1979).

[27] Russell J. Dalton, Scott C. Flanagan, and Paul Allen Beck, 'Political Forces and Partisan Change', in Dalton *et al.* (eds.), *Electoral Change*, pp. 451, 472.

have considered, established parties not only survive, but also govern.'[28]

Three points are important here. The first of these concerns the point of stability against which the imputed transformation is being measured. Electoral instability is now more pronounced than at any point in the entire post-war period, and is thus seen as marking the end of the process of stabilization which Lipset and Rokkan had identified as crystallizing in the 1920s.[29] In reality, however, as the longer-term perspective demonstrates,[30] electorates in the 1920s and 1930s had also proved remarkably volatile, so much so that the general level of aggregate instability which then prevailed in Europe was substantially more pronounced than that which has characterized elections in the 1970s and 1980s. Indeed, as is evident from this longer-term perspective, the exceptional period, and that which needs to be explained, is not the unstable period of the 1970s and 1980s, but rather the remarkably quiescent period of the 1950s and 1960s. In this sense, if electoral instability is taken as an indicator of the non-frozen character of party systems, then it is not so much that party systems have suddenly thawed; rather, as Shamir concludes, the evidence of the turbulent pre-war electoral history could actually be taken to suggest that they were never frozen to begin with.[31]

The second caveat follows immediately from this, and concerns the interpretation of this electoral instability. One interpretation, as indicated above, would suggest that the evidence of pre-war volatility implies that party systems were never frozen, and that the emphasis of Lipset and Rokkan was misplaced. An alternative interpretation, on the other hand, suggests that for all the evidence of electoral instability, this

[28] Steven B. Wolinetz, 'Party System Change: Past, Present and Future', in Wolinetz (ed.), *Parties and Party Systems*, p. 296.
[29] Lipset and Rokkan, 'Cleavage Structures, Party Systems and Voter Alignments'.
[30] See Bartolini and Mair, *Identity, Competition, and Electoral Availability*. See also Svante Ersson and Jan-Erik Lane, 'Democratic Party Systems in Europe: Dimensions, Change and Stability', *Scandinavian Political Studies*, 5/1 (1982), 67–96, and Shamir, 'Are Western European Party Systems "Frozen"?'
[31] Shamir, 'Are Western European Party Systems "Frozen"?'

does not in itself imply that the Lipset–Rokkan hypothesis is invalid.

The reasoning here is quite simple. While Lipset and Rokkan were concerned with the stabilization of *cleavages* and the party systems which reflected these cleavages, the evidence of electoral change over time is based on measures of the stability/ instability of the votes of *individual parties*.[32] Thus in order for this latter evidence to be seen to counter the Lipset–Rokkan hypothesis, it is necessary to assume a one-to-one correspondence between a cleavage, on the one hand, and an individual party, on the other. In the case of the class cleavage, however, to take just one crucial example, this assumption is clearly invalid, in that the class cleavage boundary divides *blocs* of parties —Socialist and Communist versus Christian Democrat and Liberal, or whatever—rather than individual parties. Hence, any measure of change which operates at the level of the individual party, and which therefore ignores the question of the broader cleavage alignment, cannot distinguish between intra-bloc change, on the one hand, and inter-bloc change, on the other. As such, these measures must be considered as largely inadequate indicators of cleavage persistence *per se*, which, of course, represents the key element in the Lipset– Rokkan freezing hypothesis.[33]

Indeed, when account is taken of the difference between cleavage allies and cleavage opponents, and when the degree of electoral volatility which occurs across the cleavage line is distinguished from that which occurs within each cleavage bloc, it becomes clear that the electoral destabilization of the 1970s and 1980s is much more muted than first appears to be the case. This is certainly true for the class cleavage, for while the degree of electoral interchange and instability within each of the broad class blocs has increased over time, there has actually been a secular *decline* in the levels of interchange across the cleavage boundary, a decline which dates back to the 1920s,

[32] See, e.g., the measures used by Rose and Urwin, 'Persistence and Change in Western Party Systems since 1945', and Pedersen, 'The Dynamics of European Party Systems'.
[33] Peter Mair, 'The Problem of Party System Change', *Journal of Theoretical Politics*, 1/3 (1989), 251–76; Bartolini and Mair, *Identity, Competition, and Electoral Availability*.

that is, precisely to that period in which Lipset and Rokkan located the onset of the freezing process.[34]

The third caveat is perhaps more immediately obvious. As will be apparent from many of the arguments which are included in Part III,[35] much of the emphasis concerning the very question of party system change has been characterized by an electoralist bias, implicitly suggesting that aggregate electoral change is both a necessary and a sufficient indicator of party system change. The possibility that electoral change may be associated with party system stability or, alternatively, the possibility that party system change and adaptation may accompany electoral stability, are therefore largely ignored. If we are to take on board these latter possibilities, it is therefore necessary to go beyond the simple electoral level and to explore evidence of change at the levels of party organization, ideology, and competitive strategy (which, quite appropriately, would imply that it is necessary to incorporate the approach of Kirchheimer).

Once these other dimensions are taken into account, then it is perfectly plausible to conceive of major changes in the party system which can occur notwithstanding a general sense of aggregate electoral stability. Indeed, in certain circumstances, one can even go so far as to argue that such electoral stability is maintained only because of processes of party system adaptation, and only because of change at the level of ideology, organization, and strategy.[36] To be sure, there are no easy answers here. The question of electoral as against other evidence of change is clearly problematic, and it certainly does raise a host of issues which cannot be treated within the limited scope of this brief essay. That said, the evident electoral bias within contemporary accounts of party system change does imply a very limited perspective, and cautions against some of the more apocalyptic interpretations which tend to dominate much of current thinking. In sum, as I have suggested in a recent study of the Irish case, 'precisely because party systems

[34] See Bartolini and Mair, *Identity, Competition, and Electoral Availability*.

[35] And see also Ersson and Lane, 'Democratic Party Systems in Europe', Maguire, 'Is There Still Persistence?', and Shamir, 'Are Western European Party Systems "Frozen"?'

[36] Mair, 'The Problem of Party System Change'.

can be assessed along a number of different dimensions—organizational, ideological and electoral—it is in the end almost impossible to speak of transformation *per se*. Given the number of dimensions involved, party systems may persist as well as change, and . . . they may do so at one and the same time.'[37]

A final suggestion is also in order here, for, in the end, we may be missing the wood for the trees. Our concern is with the transformation and change of party systems, and hence the most appropriate research strategy may well be one which relates evidence of such change, on the one hand, to an understanding of the nature of party systems, on the other, and thus one which distinguishes between change which is of systemic relevance and change which is not of systemic relevance.[38] For, while change at the level of the *party* may be easily identified and explained, it is clear that not all party change will also involve party system change. As Sartori has emphasized, there is little sense in discussing a party system unless we first can define it in terms which go beyond simply the sum of its component parts:

[T]he concept of system is meaningless—for purposes of scientific inquiry—unless (i) the system displays properties that do not belong to a separate consideration of its component elements and (ii) the system results from, and consists of, the patterned interactions of its component parts, thereby implying that such interactions provide the boundaries, or at least the boundedness, of the system . . . a party system is precisely the *system of interactions* resulting from inter-party competition.[39]

If we adopt this perspective, it therefore follows that the concept of system *change* is also meaningless unless it involves elements which go beyond simple party change, and unless it incorporates an emphasis on the transformation of the system of inter-party interactions. In this sense, it may be more useful

[37] Peter Mair, *The Changing Irish Party System: Organisation, Ideology and Electoral Competition* (London: Frances Pinter, 1987), 11.

[38] See, e.g., Gordon Smith, 'A System Perspective on Party System Change', *Journal of Theoretical Politics*, 1/3 (1989), 349–63.

[39] Giovanni Sartori, *Parties and Party Systems: A Framework for Analysis** (Cambridge: Cambridge University Press, 1976), i. 43–4.

to relate the question of party system change to the broader question of the classification and typologization of party systems, and to speak of such change only when it involves a shift from one type of party system to another.

To be sure, such a strategy is both demanding and restrictive, and it may imply an unnecessarily strict conception of party system change. Moreover, since there is also quite a substantial variation in the approaches taken to the classification of party systems (see Part IV), the criteria to be adopted in determining whether or not change is systemic will inevitably vary quite considerably. None the less, though restrictive, such an approach does have the merit of evading the ever-deepening intellectual quagmire which characterizes the present-day debates on the relevance, meaning, and extent of change in contemporary West European party systems.

3. TYPES OF PARTY SYSTEMS

This last point also underlines the importance of devising suitable criteria for distinguishing between different types of party systems. It is the search for such criteria which has stimulated the various writings included in Part IV below, which includes a number of the most important attempts to establish meaningful classifications and typologies of party systems.[40] In most cases, such attempts have begun with the numbers of parties in the different systems, the most familiar distinction being that adopted by Duverger[41] and others which draws a dividing line between 'two-party' systems, on the one hand, and 'multiparty' systems, on the other.[42] Such traditional analyses have also tended to emphasize the supposed merits of the former type, in that the competition between two more or less equivalently sized parties offered the

[40] For an excellent review, see Stefano Bartolini, 'Partiti e Sistemi di Partito', in Gianfranco Pasquino (ed.), *Manuale di Scienza della Politica* (Bologna: Il Mulino, 1986), 231–80.

[41] Duverger, *Political Parties*.

[42] See Peter Mair, 'Types of Party Systems', in Vernon Bogdanor (ed.), *The Blackwell Encyclopaedia of Political Institutions* (Oxford: Blackwell, 1987), 420–2, from which much of what follows is drawn.

prospect of single-party government; alternation in government; policy accountability; and, in particular, the prevalence of centre-seeking electoral strategies. Multiparty systems, on the other hand, offered few of these advantages. In such systems, government formation usually necessitated a coalition of parties and the electorate had little opportunity to influence the process of coalition formation; alternation was not always possible, in that the persistent participation of certain parties was often a *sine qua non* of achieving an effective coalition; centre-seeking strategies were not encouraged, in that a multiplicity of parties stimulated ideological competition; and the coalitions which ensued from this multilateral, competitive, and fragmented pattern of competition were often viewed as being unstable and ineffective. For many scholars, particularly in the 1950s and early 1960s, the contrast between the two types of party system was all too obvious, a contrast epitomized in the differences between the stable and consensual experience of two-party Britain, on the one hand, and the unstable and fraught experiences of multiparty Weimar Germany, Fourth Republic France, and post-war Italy, on the other.

As Daalder has often emphasized, however, and as is evident from the examples just cited, this perspective on the differences between two-party systems and multiparty systems derived mainly from an undue concentration on the experiences of the larger, or pattern states—Britain, France, Germany, and Italy. And, in the wake of the internationalization of political science in Europe, the increased scholarly interest in the experience of the smaller European democracies was soon to demonstrate the superficiality of this traditional classification.[43] Once one moved outside the pattern states, it seemed that many of the European multiparty systems—whether in Belgium, the Netherlands, or Switzerland, or in the Scandinavian countries—proved just as stable and effective as did the two-party British system.

The search for a more effective classification therefore began to move beyond mere numbers. Almond, for example, was to

[43] Hans Daalder, 'The Comparative Study of European Parties and Party Systems: An Overview', in Daalder and Mair, *Western European Party Systems*, pp. 1–28; id., 'Countries in Comparative Politics', *European Journal of Political Research*, 15/1 (1987), 3–21.

lay much weight on the distinction between what he termed
working multiparty systems (e.g. the Scandinavian countries)
and 'non-working' or 'immobilist' multiparty systems (e.g.
France and Italy), [44] and it was an essential dissatisfaction with
the inadequacy of this latter approach which did much to
prompt Lijphart's influential work on consociational democracy.[45] Meanwhile Blondel and Rokkan sought to complement
the question of numbers with that of relative electoral size, the
former distinguishing between two-party and two-and-a-half
party systems, on the one hand, and between multiparty
systems with a dominant party and those without a dominant
party, on the other; the latter distinguishing between 'even
multiparty systems' with three or more parties of equivalent
size, the Scandinavian model with one big party and three or
more small parties, and the 'British–German' model with two
big parties and one small party.[46]

    The most effective and exhaustive typology, however, was
that developed by Sartori, which combined a measure based on
the numbers of parties—or, more correctly, the numbers of
relevant parties—and a measure based on the breadth of the
ideological space of competition.[47] Employing both of these
measures, Sartori was able to distinguish between four principal types of competitive party system: the classic two-party
system; systems of moderate pluralism, which were characterized by limited fragmentation and moderate centripetal competition; systems of polarized pluralism, which were both
highly fragmented and highly polarized in ideological terms;
and predominant-party systems, in which one particular party
usually won an effective majority of the parliamentary seats.

---

[44] Gabriel A. Almond, 'Comparative Political Systems', *Journal of Politics*,
18/3 (1956), 391–409; id., 'A Comparative Study of Interest Groups and the
Political Process', *American Political Science Review*, 52/1 (1958), 270–82. See
also Dankwart W. Rustow, 'Scandinavia: Working Multiparty Systems', in
Neumann, *Modern Political Parties*, pp. 169–93.

[45] Arend Lijphart, 'Typologies of Democratic Systems', *Comparative
Political Studies*, 1/1 (1969), 3–44.

[46] Jean Blondel, 'Party Systems and Patterns of Government in Western
Democracies',* *Canadian Journal of Political Science*, 1/2 (1968), 180–203; Stein
Rokkan, *Citizens, Elections, Parties: Approaches to the Comparative Study of the
Processes of Development** (Oslo: Universitetsforlaget, 1970), 93–6.

[47] Sartori, *Parties and Party Systems*, Vol. 1.

The details of the Sartori framework need not concern us here, as they can be seen in both the original 1976 volume,[48] as well as, in summary form, in the extract in Part IV of this collection. What is relevant to note, however, is that despite some recent supportive criticisms which have sought to qualify the approach,[49] and despite the evident difficulties involved in applying the scheme to the segmented societies,[50] the Sartori approach has now won widespread acceptance within the comparative party literature. In this sense, few if any of the more sophisticated analyses now remain within the terms of reference of the two-party/multiparty distinction; numbers of parties are still seen to be important, but it is the way in which these parties interact which offers the clearest guide towards the understanding of diversity.

4.   SUMMARY OF CONTENTS

The essays in Part I of this reader deal with the development of the mass party, and include Max Weber's initial observations on the professionalization of politics; Duverger's analysis of the shift from what he terms the cadre party towards the mass party, or, as Neumann put it, the shift from the party of individual representation to the party of democratic integration; Kirchheimer's further development of this theme, charting the more recent emergence of the catch-all party; and finally, Pizzorno's speculations concerning the reasons for the survival of party in modern pluralist democracies.

---

[48] For the initial attempts to develop the scheme, see Sartori, 'European Political Parties: The Case of Polarized Pluralism' in LaPalombara and Weiner (eds.), *Political Parties*, pp. 137–76, and id., 'The Typology of Party Systems: Proposals for Improvement', in Erik Allardt and Stein Rokkan (eds.), *Mass Politics: Studies in Political Sociology* (New York: Free Press, 1970), 322–52.

[49] E.g. Hans Daalder, 'In Search of the Centre of European Party Systems', *American Political Science Review*, 78/1 (1984), 92–109; Stefano Bartolini, 'Institutional Constraints and Party Competition in the French Party System', *West European Politics*, 7/4 (1984), 103–27.

[50] E.g. Giacomo Sani and Giovanni Sartori, 'Polarization, Fragmentation and Competition in Western Democracies', in Daalder and Mair (eds.), *Western European Party Systems*, pp. 307–40.

While Part II moves from the development of the mass party to the stabilization of party systems, the various arguments which have been included here nevertheless all share an emphasis on the important structural links between these two processes. Daalder, for example, lays considerable stress on the way in which parties began to permeate other élites in modern mass democracies, and the manner in which they have penetrated 'the mainsprings of political power'. And while the burden of the Lipset and Rokkan analysis lies in the development and stabilization of cleavages, they too emphasize the importance of the intervention of party in the structuring of political alignments. Finally, this aspect is firmly underlined in Rokkan's later essay and, in particular, in Sartori's emphasis on the autonomy of the political and the persuasive power of organization.

In contrast to the essays in Part II, which are concerned with the stabilization of party systems, and most of which date from the 1960s, the literature in Part III deals largely with change and transformation. The single exception is the classic essay by Rose and Urwin, which also dates from the late 1960s, and which is at pains to emphasize stability. Thereafter, and reflecting the emphases in the literature of the late 1970s and 1980s, the theme is change. In the cases of Pedersen and Mair, the emphasis is largely on electoral change, although the contrast between the volatility which is apparent at the level of the individual party (see Pedersen) and the relative stability which is apparent at the level of the blocs of parties (see Mair) should be noted. Wolinetz and Flanagan and Dalton are also concerned with destabilization, and in both cases chart a variety of possible explanations relating to processes of electoral dealignment and realignment. This is also the major thrust of the essays by Inglehart, who emphasizes the transformation of traditional values and charts the emergence and growing importance of what he defines to be a 'post-materialist' generation. Finally, albeit from a different perspective, Lijphart seeks to identify the major ideological dimensions which now underlie contemporary West European party systems.

The final group of readings, in Part IV, concerns the efforts to elaborate meaningful criteria through which to analyse the diversity of European party systems. Much of this literature has

already been surveyed above, and here it suffices to note the
shift of emphasis from numbers of parties alone (Duverger); to
an emphasis on numbers of parties and either patterns of
opposition (Dahl) or electoral weight (Blondel, Rokkan); and
finally to Sartori's emphasis on numbers of parties, or format,
on the one hand, and ideology and patterns of competition, or
mechanics, on the other.

   This is a rich literature which repays close reading. It deals
with questions which are central to an understanding of modern mass democracies, and often reflects a level of scholarship
and intellectual understanding which matches the very best in
political science as a whole. But it must be emphasized that this
is also a voluminous literature, and the essays which have been
included within this reader represent just a small sample of
the themes and problems which have been embraced by
scholarship in the field.

PART I

THE DEVELOPMENT OF THE
MASS PARTY

I

THE ORIGIN OF POLITICAL PARTIES

JOSEPH LAPALOMBARA AND MYRON WEINER

The creation of parties has been a continuous process. The historical graveyards are cluttered with parties which dominated the political scene but which subsequently failed to adapt to new circumstances and therefore died, were absorbed by new more active movements, or withered into small marginal parties. None the less the circumstances under which parties first arise in a developing political system—together with their initial tone and configuration—clearly have an important effect on the kinds of parties which subsequently emerge.

It is customary in the West to associate the development of parties with the rise of parliaments and with the gradual extension of the suffrage. One broad historical formulation of this gradual process is Max Weber's division of party evolution into the stages of aristocratic cliques, small groups of notables, and plebiscitarian democracy.[1] Duverger notes too that parties are related to the evolution of national parliaments and the growth in the size of the electorate. Parties, he suggests, grew out of political assemblies as their members felt the need of a group to act in concert. As the vote was subsequently extended these committees began to organize the electors. Duverger's theory thus postulates stages in party development: First the creation of parliamentary groups, then the organization

Joseph LaPalombara and Myron Weiner, excerpted from 'The Origin and Development of Political Parties' in Joseph LaPalombara and Myron Weiner (eds.), *Political Parties and Political Development*, pp. 3–42. Copyright © 1966 by Princeton University Press and reprinted with their permission.

[1] M. Weber, 'Politics as a Vocation', in Hans Gerth and C. Wright Mills (eds.), *From Max Weber: Essays in Sociology* (New York: Oxford Uniersity Press, 1946), 102–7.

of electoral committees, and finally the establishment of permanent connections between these two elements.[2]

Both Weber and Duverger indicate that the cliques and the élite political clubs, though often the precursors of modern parties, were not political parties as we have been using that term. The famous 'Breton Club', which met in pre-revolutionary France and which later became the nucleus of the Jacobins, was little more than a legislative clique based on a specific geographic region; similarly the political clubs and aristocratic salons that persisted in England into the nineteenth century were essentially makeshift arrangements for electing notables to parliament and, more rarely, for bringing together lawmakers who might share similar views.

To speak of political parties in Europe, then, before the middle of the nineteenth century is to speak very loosely indeed. It is not until the suffrage is broadened and the notables feel the need for some sort of party organization at the local level that we find the first significant prototypes of what we today know as the mass party. Duverger is quite correct in his insistence that it is of great importance to know whether parties were initially created internally or externally. An internally created political party is one that emerges gradually from the activities of the legislators themselves. As the need for creating legislative blocs and of assuring the re-election of members of these blocs is increasingly felt, political organization at the local level or in the electoral constituency occurs. As Duverger observes, such local level organization may be simply the result of the fact that certain legislative blocs or factions share nothing more than origins in the same geographic section of the country. This was the case with legislative groups that emerged in eighteenth-century France; it was similarly and strikingly the case with the first political parties to emerge in Japan in the 1870s and 1880s. Likewise in Italy, which achieved unification late, the first party organizations reflected the geographic proximity of certain legislators who sought co-ordinated action and some

---

[2] Maurice Duverger, *Political Parties* (New York: John Wiley and Sons, Inc., 1955), pp. xxiii–xxxvii. Among the best critiques of Duverger is Aaron B. Wildavsky, 'A Methodological Critique of Duverger's *Political Parties*', *Journal of Politics*, 21 (1959), 303–18.

semblance of local organization as a means of assuring control over governmental policy on the one hand and re-election to office on the other.

The real impetus for the creation of some form of party organization at the local level in the West is generally thought to be the extension of the suffrage. The major steps in the creation of party organization in Great Britain can be clearly associated with the electoral reforms of 1832, 1867, and 1884. Where the suffrage is greatly restricted, local electoral committees are simply not needed; where it is expanded, the need to woo the masses is strongly felt. What was once a struggle limited to an aristocratic élite or small groups of notables now becomes a major drama in which large segments of the citizenry play an active role.

To the extent that entrenched parliamentary groups recognize the implications of an expanded suffrage, an effort to create local electoral committees can be detected. Thus, in much of Europe at least, the modern political party began when a working and continuous relationship was established between such committees and legislative groups. Where the local organization and the local parliamentary connection are established as the result of initiative exercised by those who are already in the legislature or who hold national public office, we can speak of political parties as having been created internally. This is not to imply, of course, that the local units are necessarily simply the creations of the legislators for there are often some local groups which provide the basis for a mass organization. Some striking cases of internally created parties would be the Conservative and Liberal parties in Great Britain and Canada, the Democratic and Republican parties in the United States, the first conservative parties to emerge in Scandinavia in the middle of the last century, the National Liberal and Progressive parties in Bismarckian Germany, the Liberal and Progressive parties in post-Tokugawa Japan, and the Liberal party in nineteenth-century Italy.

Externally created parties are those that emerge outside the legislature and invariably involve some challenge to the ruling group and a demand for representation. Such parties are more recent phenomena; they are invariably associated with an expanded suffrage, strongly articulated secular or religious ideologies, and, in most of the developing areas, nationalistic and anti-colonial movements. Such parties may receive their original organizational impetus from such varied sources as trade unions, co-operatives, university students, intellectuals, religious organizations, veteran associations, and so on. In the West the most notable examples of externally created parties were the many Socialist parties that emerged late in the nineteenth century and the Christian or Christian Democratic parties that were created in the early twentieth century partly in response to the threat of proletarian political movements. The role of the trade unions in the establishment of the British Labour party and of several continental Socialist parties, of agricultural co-operatives in the creation of strong agrarian parties in Scandinavia, of religious organizations in the creation of political parties in Belgium, Austria, Germany, France, and Italy is too well known to require elaboration here. Similarly, most of the political parties now functioning in Africa and Asia were formerly nationalist movements, messianic and chiliastic movements, and caste, religious, or tribal associations that developed outside of and in some instances hostile to whatever parliamentary framework had been created by colonial governments.

Duverger says of the externally created parties that they tend to be more centralized than those that are internally created, more ideologically coherent and disciplined, less subject to influence from the legislative contingents of the parties, and generally less willing to ascribe major importance to or be deferential towards parliament. This may well be the case, and, if so, it would explain in part why many constitutional orders that reflect the values and the relative power alignments of the eighteenth century are clearly threatened by some of the mass parties of external creation and of more recent vintage. It is not merely that the externally created parties are more ideological, more disciplined, or more aggressive in making demands on the system. It is also that, largely as a result of the circumstances under which they arose, they have frequently not developed a vested interest in existing political (and in most instances social or economic) institutions. This observation is equally valid in the developing areas where nationalist movements typically take complete control of the governmental framework when the colonial rulers withdraw from the political system. While Socialist parties in Europe often had to make peace with those who ran the parliamentary framework—or risk civil war—the nationalist movements which took power had as it were a *tabula rasa* on which to operate and could, if they chose, abolish the parliamentary system itself. Nationalist parties often found it relatively easy to establish one-party systems and place extraordinary restrictions on civil liberties precisely because no organized group in the society with any measure of popular support was committed to the maintenance of a competitive framework. The leaders of the governing parties in Africa, in their attempts to establish central authority, or, alternatively, to utilize an opportunity to concentrate power for the purposes of self-aggrandizement, have often banned other political parties and abolished free elections. On the other hand, the Socialist parties of Europe that rejected the parliamentary framework were often ultimately socialized into the democratic constitutional order. The post-Second World War parties, particularly of Austria and Germany, recalled the bitter days of the 1920s and early 1930s when militancy resulted not in the rise of socialism but in the rise of totalitarian regimes; the moderation of parties in these countries today, not to mention their support for the parliamentary order, is in part related to the memories of an earlier unforgettable era.

While some scholars have, as we have seen, stressed the importance of parliament and the expansion of the suffrage as a critical variable in the emergence of parties, others, particularly historians of European intellectual history, have stressed the role of ideology. Thus the emergence of parliaments, adult suffrage, and parties themselves is related to the gradual emergence of democratic ideologies. The notion of popular sovereignty and the earlier medieval notion of tyrannicide are viewed as efforts to restrict autocratic power. R. R. Palmer, in his study of the way in which the 'lower classes' entered the European political process,[3] has forcefully argued that the concepts which justified placing limitations on the authority of kings and the notions which facilitated the creation of parliaments,

---

[3] R. R. Palmer, *The Age of the Democratic Revolution* (Princeton: Princeton University Press, 1959).

the expansion of the suffrage, and the establishment of civil liberties predated these developments. In so far as the emergence of parties, or political organizations or movements which antedate parties, is concerned one can effectively show that a wide variety of ideologies have in fact served as vehicles for their justification. Indeed some parties were created as the instrumentalities of counter ideologies, in sharp disagreement with dominant political values. It has frequently been pointed out, for example, that the republican doctrines which underlay the American constitution did not conceive of parties as an institution of democratic society; similarly British liberal thought of the nineteenth century paid little attention to the parties that were rapidly emerging. Socialist doctrine saw parties as instruments of classes, to wither away along with the state when class struggle came to an end. Indeed most of the mass parties extant in the West would probably not have emerged had there not developed, in addition to an extended suffrage, direct challenges to prevailing ideologies.

2

THE ADVENT OF PLEBISCITARIAN DEMOCRACY

MAX WEBER

In all political associations which are somehow extensive, that
is, associations going beyond the sphere and range of the tasks
of small rural districts where power-holders are periodically
elected, political organization is necessarily managed by men
interested in the management of politics. This is to say that a
relatively small number of men are primarily interested in
political life and hence interested in sharing political power.
They provide themselves with a following through free recruitment, present themselves or their protégés as candidates for
election, collect the financial means, and go out for vote-
grabbing. It is unimaginable how in large associations elections
could function at all without this managerial pattern. In practice this means the division of the citizens with the right to vote
into politically active and politically passive elements. This
difference is based on voluntary attitudes, hence it cannot be
abolished through measures like obligatory voting, or 'occupational status group' representation, or similar measures that
are expressly or actually directed against this state of affairs and
the rule of professional politicians. The active leadership and
their freely recruited following are the necessary elements in the
life of any party. The following, and through it the passive
electorate, are necessary for the election of the leader. But
the structure of parties varies. For instance, the 'parties' of
the medieval cities, such as those of the Guelphs and the

Max Weber, excerpted from 'Politics as a Vocation', from *From Max Weber:
Essays in Sociology*, edited and translated by H. H. Gerth and C. Wright Mills.
Copyright 1946 by Oxford University Press, Inc.; renewed 1973 by Hans H.
Gerth. Reprinted by permission of the publisher. The present title is the
editor's own.

Ghibellines, were purely personal followings. If one considers various things about these medieval parties, one is reminded of Bolshevism and its Soviets. Consider the *Statuta della perta Guelfa*, the confiscations of the Nobili's estates—which originally meant all those families who lived a chivalrous life and who thus qualified for fiefs—consider the exclusion from office-holding and the denial of the right to vote, the inter-local party committees, the strictly military organizations, and the premiums for informers. Then consider Bolshevism with its strictly sieved military and, in Russia especially, informer organizations, the disarmament and denial of the political rights of the 'bourgeois', that is, of the entrepreneur, trader, rentier, clergyman, descendants of the dynasty, police agents, as well as the confiscation policy.

This analogy is still more striking when one considers that, on the one hand, the military organization of the medieval party constituted a pure army of knights organized on the basis of the registered feudal estates and that nobles occupied almost all leading positions, and, on the other hand, that the Soviets have preserved, or rather reintroduced, the highly paid enterpriser, the group wager, the Taylor system, military and workshop discipline, and a search for foreign capital. Hence, in a word, the Soviets have had to accept again absolutely *all* the things that Bolshevism had been fighting as bourgeois class institutions. They have had to do this in order to keep the state and the economy going at all. Moreover, the Soviets have reinstituted the agents of the former Ochrana [Tsarist Secret Police] as the main instrument of their state power. But here we do not have to deal with such organizations for violence, but rather with professional politicians who strive for power through sober and 'peaceful' party campaigns in the market of election votes.

Parties, in the sense usual with us, were at first, for instance in England, pure followings of the aristocracy. If, for any reason whatever, a peer changed his party, everybody dependent upon him likewise changed. Up to the Reform Bill [of 1832], the great noble families and, last but not least, the king controlled the patronage of an immense number of election boroughs. Close to these aristocratic parties were the parties of notables, which develop everywhere with the rising power of the bourgeois.

Under the spiritual leadership of the typical intellectual strata of the Occident, the propertied and cultured circles differentiated themselves into parties and followed them. These parties were formed partly according to class interest, partly according to family traditions, and partly for ideological reasons. Clergymen, teachers, professors, lawyers, doctors, apothecaries, prosperous farmers, manufacturers—in England the whole stratum that considered itself as belonging to the class of gentlemen—formed, at first, occasional associations at most local political clubs. In times of unrest the petty bourgeoisie raised its voice, and once in a while the proletariat, if leaders arose who, however, as a rule did not stem from their midst. In this phase, parties organized as permanent associations between localities do not yet exist in the open country. Only the parliamentary delegates create the cohesion; and the local notables are decisive for the selection of candidates. The election programmes originate partly in the election appeals of the candidates and partly in the meetings of the notables; or, they originate as resolutions of the parliamentary party. Leadership of the clubs is an avocation and an honorific pursuit, as demanded by the occasion.

Where clubs are absent (as is mostly the case), the quite formless management of politics in normal times lies in the hands of the few people constantly interested in it. Only the journalist is a paid professional politician; only the management of the newspaper is a continuous political organization. Besides the newspaper, there is only the parliamentary session. The parliamentary delegates and the parliamentary party leaders know to which local notables one turns if a political action seems desirable. But permanent associations of the parties exist only in the large cities with moderate contributions of the members and periodical conferences and public meetings where the delegate gives account of the parliamentary activities. The party is alive only during election periods.

The members of parliament are interested in the possibility of inter-local electoral compromises, in vigorous and unified programmes endorsed by broad circles, and in a unified agitation throughout the country. In general, these interests form the driving force of a party organization which becomes more and more strict. In principle, however, the nature of a party apparatus as an association of notables remains unchanged. This is so, even though a network of local party affiliations and agents is spread over the whole country, including middle-sized cities. A member of the parliamentary party acts as the leader of the central party office and maintains constant correspondence with the local organizations. Outside of the central bureau, paid officials are still absent; thoroughly 'respectable' people head the local organizations for the sake of the deference which they enjoy anyway. They form the extra-parliamentary 'notables' who exert influence alongside the stratum of political notables who happen to sit in parliament. However, the party correspondence, edited by the party, increasingly provides intellectual nourishment for the press and for the local meetings. Regular contributions of the members become indispensable; a part of these must cover the expenses of headquarters.

Not so long ago most of the German party organizations were still in this stage of development. In France, the first stage of party development was, at least in part, still predominant, and the organization of the members of parliament was quite unstable. In the open country, we find a small number of local notables and programmes drafted by the candidates or set up for them by their patrons in specific campaigns for office. To be sure, these platforms constitute more or less local adaptations to the resolutions and programmes of the members of parliament. This system was only partially punctured. The number of full-time professional politicians was small, consisting in the main of the elected deputies, the few employees of headquarters, and the journalists. In France, the system has also included those job hunters who held 'political office' or, at the moment, strove for one. Politics was formally and by far predominantly an avocation. The number of delegates qualifying for ministerial office was also very restricted and, because of their position as notables, so was the number of election candidates.

However, the number of those who indirectly had a stake in the management of politics, especially a material one, was very large. For, all administrative measures of a ministerial department, and especially all decisions in matters of personnel, were made partly with a view to their influence upon electoral chances. The realization of each and every kind of wish was sought through the local delegate's mediation. For better or for worse the minister had to lend his ear to this delegate, especially if the delegate belonged to the minister's majority. Hence everybody strove for such influence. The single deputy controlled the patronage of office and, in general, any kind of patronage in his election district. In order to be re-elected the deputy, in turn, maintained connections with the local notables.

Now then, the most modern forms of party organizations stand in sharp contrast to this idyllic state in which circles of notables and, above all, members of parliament rule. These modern forms are the children of democracy, of mass franchise, of the necessity to woo and organize the masses, and develop the utmost unity of direction and the strictest discipline. The rule of notables and guidance by members of parliament ceases. 'Professional' politicians *outside* the parliaments take the organization in hand. They do so either as 'entrepreneurs'—the American boss and the English election agent are, in fact, such entrepreneurs—or as officials with a fixed salary. Formally, a fargoing democratization takes place. The parliamentary party no longer creates the authoritative programmes, and the local notables no longer decide the selection of candidates. Rather assemblies of the organized party members select the candidates and delegate members to the assemblies of a higher order. Possibly there are several such conventions leading up to the national convention of the party. Naturally power actually rests in the hands of those who, within the organization, handle the work *continuously*. Otherwise, power rests in the hands of those on whom the organization in its processes depends financially or personally—for instance, on the Maecenases or the directors of powerful political clubs of interested persons (Tammany Hall). It is decisive that this whole apparatus of people—characteristically called a 'machine' in Anglo-Saxon countries —or rather those who direct the machine, keep the members of the parliament in check. They are in a position to impose their will to a rather far-reaching extent, and that is of special significance for the selection of the party leader. The man whom the machine follows now becomes the leader, even over the head of the parliamentary party. In other words, the creation of such machines signifies the advent of *plebiscitarian* democracy.

3

CAUCUS AND BRANCH, CADRE
PARTIES AND MASS PARTIES

MAURICE DUVERGER

A party is not a community but a collection of communities, a union of small groups dispersed throughout the country (branches, caucuses, local associations, etc.) and linked by co-ordinating institutions. The term 'basic elements' is used for these component units of the party organization.

The Caucus. Though this unit might equally well be called a committee, a clique, or a coterie, the English political term 'caucus' will be used here. The first characteristic of the caucus is its limited nature. It consists of a small number of members, and seeks no expansion. It does not indulge in any propaganda with a view to extending its recruitment. Moreover, it does not really admit members, for this limited group is also a closed group; you do not get into it simply because you desire to do so: membership is achieved only by a kind of tacit co-option or by formal nomination. In spite of this numerical weakness the caucus nevertheless wields great power. Its strength does not depend on the number of its members but on their quality. It is a group of notabilities, chosen because of their influence.

Caucuses are an archaic type of political party structure. They form the normal organization of parties under a property qualification franchise, or in a system of universal suffrage that is still in its beginnings. If we except the indirect caucuses, the others do indeed group the traditional social élites. In their composition as well as in their structure (weak collective organization, predominance of individual considerations) they

Maurice Duverger, excerpted from *Political Parties: Their Organization and Activity in the Modern State* (1954), Book I, Chapters 1 and 2. Reprinted by Permission of Methuen & Co. Published in the United States by John Wiley & Sons Inc.

represent the influence of the upper and lower middle class. In Marxist terms they are the normal political expression of the middle class. An attempt to discern pattern would lead one to distinguish two types of caucus in late nineteenth-century Europe: the one, corresponding to the Conservative parties, grouping aristocrats, industrial magnates, bankers, even influential churchmen; the other corresponding to the Liberal or Radical (in the French meaning of the word) parties, being composed of tradespeople and lesser industrialists, civil servants, teachers, lawyers, journalists, and writers.

Normally (under the nineteenth-century property franchise) parties were nothing but federations of caucuses. Further, it is easy to see the relationship between these caucuses and the electoral committees of the period before there were any parties. When these committees were no longer set up *ad hoc* for each contest, but survived the election and acquired a relatively permanent character, they became real party caucuses. It is not always easy to say where the one begins and the other ends.

The coming of universal suffrage did not entail the immediate disappearance of the caucus system in every country. As long as the masses had not been able to form their own trade union or political organizations they acted within the framework already in existence. The caucuses therefore sought a way of influencing them, notably by increasing the number of electoral agents. This represents an effort, sometimes unconscious, to impose old forms on the masses, so as to keep them in a passive role in spite of universal suffrage, in order to limit the political consequences of the latter. Nevertheless, the greater efficiency of recruiting techniques directly adapted to the masses (for example the system of branches) has usually brought about the decline of the caucus.

The Branch. In itself, the term 'branch' designates a basic element which is less decentralized than the caucus: a branch is only part of the whole, and its separate existence is inconceivable: on the other hand the word caucus evokes an autonomous reality, capable of living on its own. As a matter of fact, it will be seen that parties founded on branches are more centralized than those founded on caucuses. But the profound originality of the branch lies in its organization, and not in its connection with the other branches. In this respect, the branch can be described by contrasting each of its characteristics in turn with those of the caucus. The latter is restricted in nature, the branch is extensive and tries to enrol members, to multiply their number, and to increase its total strength. It does not despise quality, but quantity is the most important of considerations. The caucus formed a closed circle into which you could enter only by co-option or as a delegate; the branch is wide open. In practice you only need to wish to belong to be able to do so. Certainly most parties make rules of membership and define entrance requirements, as will be seen later; but these generally remain theoretical, at least in the branch system (this is less true for the cell system). The caucus is a union of notabilities chosen only because of their influence: the branch appeals to the masses.

Moreover it tries to keep in touch with them: which is the reason for its geographical basis being less extensive than that of the caucus. In France, for example, the caucuses function chiefly at *arrondissement* level: the branches are built up within the framework of the *commune*. In the large towns they even tend to multiply and to be based on the *quartier* or ward. Certain parties (but not all) also admit within the branch smaller subdivisions which make possible a closer-knit organization of members: German and Austrian 'block' and tenement units; French Socialist party 'groups'. Nevertheless, a certain mistrust of excessively small subdivisions, as leading to rivalry and disorder, can be seen: thus the constitution of the French Socialist party, when it was united in 1905, affirmed the precedence of the branch over the group by refusing the latter any kind of autonomy. This was a reaction provoked by the disputes between small groups which had weakened the earlier Socialist parties. Finally the permanence of the branch contrasts with the semi-permanent nature of the caucus. Outside the election period the latter lives through a period of hibernation in which its meetings are neither frequent nor regular. On the contrary the activity of the branches, obviously very great at election times, remains important, and above all regular, in the intervals between ballots. Socialist branches generally meet every month or every fortnight. Moreover the character of the meeting is not the same as that of the caucus: it deals not only with election tactics, but also with political education. Party speakers come to talk of problems to the branch members; their lecture is usually followed by a discussion. It is true that experience has shown that meetings have a strong tendency to wander on to petty local and electoral matters; but usually the parties make praiseworthy efforts to counter this tendency and to ensure an adequate place for discussions of doctrine and of general questions.

The branch is a Socialist invention. The Socialist parties which became organized on a purely political basis and direct structure naturally chose it as the fundamental unit in their activities. Certain Socialist indirect parties adopted it too: for example the initial group of the Belgian Workers' party was the local 'Workers' Guild', which brought together the members of Trade Unions, Co-operatives, and Friendly Societies, a great number of members belonging simultaneously to several organizations: such an organization makes the party less indirect in character, and more like a direct party having many 'ancillary organizations' aimed at strengthening the bonds of membership. The choice of the branch by Socialist parties was perfectly natural. They were the first to try and organize the masses, to give them a political education, and to recruit from them the working-class élites. The branch corresponded to this triple requirement. In contrast to the caucus, the middle-class organ of political expression, it seemed the normal organ of political expression for the masses. But these masses did not all accept Socialism: consequently, various middle-class parties tried to attract them in their direction by the very methods that were making the working-class parties so successful. In many countries the parties of the Centre and even of the Right changed their organization and replaced the caucus by the branch as a basic element. Almost all the new parties have followed these tactics, but many old parties as well: this is an interesting example of contagious organization.

Cadre Parties and Mass Parties. The distinction between cadre and mass parties is not based upon their dimensions, upon the number of their members: the difference involved is not one of size but of structure. Consider, for example, the French Socialist party: in its eyes the recruiting of members is a fundamental activity, both from the political and the financial standpoints. In the first place, the party aims at the political education of the working class, at picking out from it an élite capable of taking over the government and the administration of the country: the members are therefore the very substance of the party, the stuff of its activity. Without members, the party would be like a teacher without pupils. Secondly, from the financial point of view, the party is essentially based upon the subscriptions paid by its members: the first duty of the branch is to ensure that they are regularly collected. In this way, the party gathers the funds required for its work of political education and for its day-to-day activity; in the same way it is enabled to finance electioneering: the financial and the political are here at one. This last point is fundamental: every electoral campaign represents considerable expense. The mass-party technique in effect replaces the capitalist financing of electioneering by democratic financing. Instead of appealing to a few big private donors, industrialists, bankers, or important merchants, for funds to meet campaign expenses—which makes the candidate (and the person elected) dependent on them—the mass party spreads the burden over the largest possible number of members, each of whom contributes a modest sum. This invention of the mass party is comparable with that of National Defence Bonds in 1914: before then Treasury Bonds were issued in large denominations and taken up by a few great banks which loaned to the state: in 1914 came the brilliant idea of issuing many more small bonds to be taken up by as many members of the public as possible. In the same way, it is characteristic of the mass party that it appeals to the public: to the paying public who make it possible for the electoral campaign to be free from capitalist pressures; to the listening, active public which receives a political education and learns how to intervene in the life of the state.

The cadre party corresponds to a different conception: the grouping of notabilities for the preparation of elections, conducting campaigns, and maintaining contact with the candidates. Influential persons, in the first place, whose name, prestige, or connections can provide a backing for the candidate and secure him votes; experts, in the second place, who know how to handle the electors and how to organize a campaign; last of all financiers, who can bring the sinews of war. Quality is the most important factor: extent of prestige, skill in technique, size of fortune. What the mass party secures by numbers, the cadre party achieves by selection. Adherence to it has therefore quite a different meaning: it is a completely personal act, based upon the aptitudes or the peculiar circumstances of a man; it is determined strictly by individual qualities. It is an act that is restricted to a few; it is dependent upon rigid and exclusive selection. If we define a member as one who signs an undertaking to the party and thereafter regularly pays his subscription, then cadre parties have no members. Some do make a show of recruiting after the contagious pattern of mass parties, but this is not to be taken seriously. The problem of the number of members belonging to the French Radical Socialist party is susceptible of no precise answer, simply because the problem itself is meaningless. The members of the Radical party cannot be counted, because the Radical party recruits no members, strictly speaking: it is a cadre party. American parties and the majority of European moderate and Conservative parties belong to the same category.

This distinction, though clear in theory, is not always easy to make in practice. As we have just noted, cadre parties sometimes admit ordinary members in imitation of mass parties. In fact, the practice is fairly widespread: there are few purely cadre parties. The others are not in practice far removed from them, but their outward form is likely to mislead the observer who must look beyond the official clauses laid down in the constitution or the declarations of the leaders. The absence of any system of registration of members or of any regular collection of subscriptions is a fairly reliable criterion; no true membership is conceivable in their absence, as we shall see. The vagueness of the figures put out can also be considered presumptive evidence: in 1950, the Turkish Democratic party claimed before the elections that it had 'three or four million members'. Obviously, it was referring to supporters; in actual fact, it was essentially a cadre party. In the same way, the distinction seems contradicted by the existence of indirect parties: mass parties which have no personal members. Consider the example of the Labour party: it was founded in 1900 to make it financially possible for working-class candidates to contest elections; from the financial point of view, the system is a mass-party system, election costs being met by trade unions, collectively. But this collective membership remains quite different from individual membership: it involves no true political enrolment and no personal pledge to the party. This profoundly alters the nature of the party and of membership, as we shall attempt to show in detail later. On the other hand, let us take the example of American parties in states which operate the system of 'closed primaries' with registration of electors; they resemble mass parties from the political point of view. Participation in the primary, with the registration and pledges it involves, may be considered as an act of membership. Moreover, activity connected with the nomination of candidates presented at elections by a party constitutes one of the activities typical of party membership. But, in this particular instance, this is the sole activity: there is no activity which at all resembles the branch meetings of the mass parties. More particularly there is no regular system of subscription to provide for the financing of the party and of election campaigns: from the financial point of view these are clearly examples of the cadre party. All things considered, the indirect party and the American party with closed primaries should be classified as semi-mass parties, though these examples must not be held to constitute a third category distinct from the two others because of their heterogeneous nature.

The distinction between cadre and mass parties corresponds to a difference in social and political substructure. In the beginning, it coincided on the whole with the replacement of a limited franchise by universal suffrage. In electoral systems based on a property qualification, which were the rule in the nineteenth century, parties obviously took on the form of cadre parties: there could be no question of enrolling the masses at a time when they had no political influence. Moreover, capitalist financing of elections appeared natural. Indeed, it has survived the property franchise. In point of fact, the coming of universal suffrage did not immediately lead to the arrival of true mass parties. The cadre parties simply attempted to make their organization more flexible by pretending to open their ranks to the masses. The Birmingham caucus system in the British Liberal party, the Primrose League in the Conservative party, the institution of primaries in America, correspond to this first stage. The problem was how to give the masses some scope for political activity and how to confer on the notabilities composing the caucus the air of having been popularly invested. In the first two cases some approach was made towards the mass party: there existed a system of formal membership as well as a periodic subscription. But the real life of the party was lived independently of the members: the Primrose League, an organization distinct from the party proper, aimed at social mixing; the primaries are limited to the nomination of candidates; the Birmingham caucus alone with its local branch foreshadowed a true mass party, but it proved to be no more than a passing experiment. The political and financial bases of the mass party were lacking. There was no question of rescuing candidates and elections from the clutches of capitalist finance, nor of educating the masses and making direct use in political life of their activity. The question was rather how to use the political and financial strength of the masses as an ancillary force. The first step had been taken, but only the first step.

The introduction of universal suffrage led almost everywhere (the United States excepted) to the development of Socialist parties which made the decisive transition, not always, however, at once. In France, for example, the first Socialist groups were not very different from the middle-class parties; registration of members, collection of subscriptions, autonomous financing of elections, developed only slowly. Development was even slower in Italy and in politically less-developed countries. Yet, at the outbreak of the 1914–18 War, the European Socialist parties constituted great human communities profoundly different from the earlier cadre parties. A notable example is the German Social Democratic party which, with more than a million members and an annual budget of nearly two million marks, constituted a veritable state more powerful than some national states. It was the Marxist conception of the class party that led to such massive structures: if the party is the political expression of a class it must naturally seek to rally the whole of the class, to form it politically, to pick out the élites capable of leadership and administration. This effort of organization also made it possible to free the working class from the tutelage of middle-class parties: in order to put up independent working-class candidates at elections it was necessary to become independent of capitalist financing (except perhaps as a makeweight, the roles being reversed) and this was possible only with collective finances. To establish, in opposition to the middle-class political press, a working-class political press, it was necessary to collect funds and organize the distribution of the newspaper. Only a mass party could make these things possible.

This explains why the distinction between cadre and mass parties also corresponds approximately with the distinction between Right and Left, Middle-class and Workers' parties. The middle-class Right had no need, financial or political, to seek the organized support of the masses: it already had its élites, its personages, and its financial backers. It considered its own political education to be adequate. For these reasons, until the coming of Fascism, attempts to create mass Conservative parties have generally failed. The instinctive repugnance felt by the middle class for regimentation and collective action also played some part in the failures, just as the opposite tendency amongst the working class favoured mass organization in Socialist parties. It would not be out of place to reiterate at this point some earlier observations. Nothing less than the development of Communism or of revolutionary tactics was required before the middle classes, realizing that cadre parties were inadequate, were to make serious attempts to create mass parties: in 1932, the National Socialist party had reached a membership of 800,000. This however really signified its breach with democracy. Under the electoral and parliamentary system cadre parties have generally been found sufficient by the Right; in the struggle against the electoral and parliamentary system mass parties of the Fascist type have rarely shown the balance and stability of proletarian parties. They tend, moreover, as we shall see, to lose their pure mass-party characteristics.

Finally this distinction between cadre parties and mass parties coincides with differences arising out of the various kinds of party organization. Cadre parties correspond to the caucus parties, decentralized and weakly knit; mass parties to parties based on branches, more centralized and more firmly knit.

4

THE PARTY OF DEMOCRATIC
INTEGRATION

SIGMUND NEUMANN

Modern parties have steadily enlarged their scope and power within the political community and have consequently changed their own functions and character. In place of a *party of individual representation*, our contemporary society increasingly shows a *party of social integration*.

This shift must be seen within the context of our changing society and its underlying philosophy. Three major stages can be observed in its development. Modern parties originated with the drive of a rising, self-conscious middle class that fought for liberation from the shackles of a feudal society and for representation to check monarchical absolutism. While the French Revolution officially proclaimed the end of this first phase of modern social development, the successful emancipation of rational man from the bonds of the *ancien régime* and its caste system proved to be only a transitional second stage. The individual, set free, was soon striving at reintegration into a new society. In fact, since the middle of the nineteenth century diverse claims for such a new orientation have been raised, promising to stop the fragmentation of a *laissez-faire* society. The first and lasting challenge of rising socialism, the emergence and appeal of political irrationalism, and an awakening social liberalism gave contrasting answers to this key issue of our century. The dislocations caused by the sweeping industrialization, radical urbanization, and international migration, by world wars and total revolutions, gave substance to a planned search for a new social order. We are still in the midst of this third phase. It constitutes the crisis of modern society.

Sigmund Neumann, excerpted from 'Toward a Comparative Study of Political Parties', in Sigmund Neumann (ed.), *Modern Political Parties* (1956), pp. 395–421, © 1956 by The University of Chicago. All rights reserved.

It is against this background of crisis that a new concept of party is evolving. Its emergence and persistence, in fact, may well depend on the momentous character of social crisis. The well-balanced communities of the Scandinavian states and the Anglo-American world seem to be least affected by this new type, while it has found its most complete expression within nations in the grip of revolutions. The islands of social equilibrium, however, have shrunk, and the party of integration has no doubt become a salient feature of our contemporary landscape.

The *party of individual representation* is characteristic of a society with a restricted political domain and only a limited degree of participation. Its membership activity is, for all practical purposes, limited to balloting, and the party organization (if existent at all) is dormant between election periods. Its main function is the selection of representatives, who, once chosen, are possessed of an absolutely 'free mandate' and are in every respect responsible only to their own consciences. This conception of an ephemeral party as a mere electoral committee does not correspond to the political reality and practice of the modern mass democracy, a fact which in many countries has been recognized (though often most reluctantly) in the crucial controversy over party discipline and even in numerous court decisions codifying party regulations, responsibilities, and prerogatives. The fundamental concept of party, however, has hardly been challenged within democratic thinking.

Under the cover of such a persistent framework and rarely perceived even by circumspect political observers, a new type of party has emerged—the *party of integration*. The claim with which this party approaches its adherents is incomparably greater than that of the party of individual representation. It demands not only permanent dues-paying membership (which may be found to a smaller extent within the loose party of representation too) but, above all, an increasing influence over all spheres of the individual's daily life.

The first example of such a new party was presented by the continental Socialists. Their organization has been jokingly characterized as extending from the cradle to the grave, from the workers' infant-care association to the atheists' cremation society; yet such a description articulates the intrinsic difference from the liberal party of representation, with its principle of 'free recruitment' among a socially uncommitted, free-floating electorate (the bulk of which, in reality, may not be so independent). The following of the new movement is, indeed, much more clearly circumscribed by its permanent membership, the definite class alignment of its voting population, and its far-flung participation in overall social affairs. The party can count on its adherents; it has taken over a good part of their social existence.

Despite such extensive organization and intensified ties of its partisans, the Socialist party (and in an even more limited way the Catholic movement and other democratic parties of integration) include only a small active core among its wider circle of mere dues-paying members and its even greater number of mere voters. In fact, this differentiation is at the base of the much-disputed 'oligarchical' tendencies of modern mass parties which permit a relatively small group to decide the political fate of the disinterested and apathetic majority. Still, what is important is that the party in modern mass democracies has generally taken on an ever increasing area of commitments and responsibilities assuring the individual's share in society and incorporating him into the community. This is no mere usurpation of power by the politicians but the natural consequence of the extension of the public domain and the constantly increasing governmental functions in a reintegrated twentieth-century society.

In this sense the phenomenon of the *party of democratic integration* has become a matter of record. This fact makes it more imperative to recognize its basic variance from the *party of total integration*, which has found its prototype in Bolshevism, Fascism, and National Socialism. This all-inclusive party demands the citizen's unconditional surrender. It denies not only the relative freedom of choice among the voters and followers but also any possibility of coalition and compromise among parties. It can perceive nothing but total seizure and exercise of power, undisputed acceptance of the party line, and monolithic rule. The rise of this absolutist police state decrees the end of democracy, of constitutionalism, of communal self-government, of Western man and his inalienable rights, of political parties.

This radical juxtaposition should forewarn the responsible

student of modern mass society against the threat of party petrifaction, but such a mortal peril cannot be met simply by a denial of the extended functions of modern parties and of their radically changing character—for the choice is not between the absolute state and the absolute individual or between autocracy or anarchy, as the great simplifiers and political demagogues make us believe. On the contrary, constructive thinking must concentrate on the much more difficult and urgent task of devising political institutions that allow for a new adjustment between the integrated society and the free individual. It is within such a realistic delineation of the fundamental prerequisites, present-day responsibilities, and necessary safeguards of a democratic society that the sociology of modern parties must be re-examined.

5

THE CATCH-ALL PARTY

OTTO KIRCHHEIMER

I. THE ANTEBELLUM MASS INTEGRATION PARTY

Socialist parties around the turn of the century exercised an
important socializing function in regard to their members.
They facilitated the transition from agrarian to industrial
society in many ways. They subjected a considerable number of
people hitherto living only as isolated individuals to voluntarily
accepted discipline operating in close connection with expectations of a future total transformation of society. But this
discipline had its roots in the alienation of these parties from the
pre-World War I political system whose demise they wanted to
guarantee and speed up by impressing the population as a
whole with their exemplary attitudes.

During and soon after the First World War the other participants in the political game showed that they were not yet
willing to honour the claims of the working-class mass parties
—claims based on the formal rules of democracy. This discov-
ery was one of the primary reasons why the social integration
into the industrial system through the working-class organizations did not advance to the state of a comparable political
integration. Participation in the war, the long quarrels over the
financial incidence of war burdens, the ravages of inflation, the
rise of Bolshevist parties and a Soviet system actively competing for mass loyalty with the existing political mass organizations in most European countries, and finally the effect of the
depression setting in at the end of the decade—all these were

Otto Kirchheimer, excerpted from 'The Transformation of the Western
European Party Systems', in Joseph LaPalombara and Myron Weiner (eds.),
Political Parties and Political Development, pp. 177–200. Copyright © 1966 by
Princeton University Press and reprinted with their permission.

much more effective agents in the politicization of the masses than their participation in occasional elections, their fight for the extension of suffrage (Belgium, Britain, Germany), or even their *encadrement* in political parties and trade union organizations. But politicization is not tantamount to political integration; integration presupposes a general willingness by a society to offer and accept full-fledged political partnership of all citizens without reservations. The consequences of integration into the class-mass party depended on the responses of other forces in the existing political system; in some cases those responses were so negative as to lead to delayed integration into the political system or to make for its disintegration.

Now we come to the other side of this failure to progress from integration into the proletarian mass party and industrial society at large to integration into the political system proper. This is the failure of bourgeois parties to advance from parties of individual representation to parties of integration, a failure already noted in France. The two tendencies, the failure of the integration of proletarian mass parties into the official political system and the failure of the bourgeois parties to advance to the stage of integration parties, condition each other. An exception, if only a partial one, is that of denominational parties such as the German Centre or Don Sturzo's *Partito Popolare*. These parties to a certain extent fulfilled both functions: social integration into industrial society and political integration within the existing political system. Yet their denominational nature gave such parties a fortress-type character seriously restricting their growth potential.

With these partial exceptions, bourgeois parties showed no capacity to change from clubs for parliamentary representation into agencies for mass politics able to bargain with the integration-type mass parties according to the laws of the political market. There was only a limited incentive for intensive bourgeois party organization. Access to the favours of the state, even after formal democratization, remained reserved via educational and other class privileges. What the bourgeoisie lacked in numbers it could make good by strategic relations with the army and the bureaucracy.

Not all bourgeois groups accepted the need for transformation to integration parties. As long as such groups had other means of access to the state apparatus they might find it convenient to delay setting up counterparts to existing mass parties while still using the state apparatus for keeping mass integration parties from becoming fully effective in the political market. Yet after the Second World War the acceptance of the law of the political market became inevitable in the major Western European countries. This change in turn found its echo in the changing structure of political parties.

2. THE POST-WAR CATCH-ALL PARTY

Following the Second World War, the old-style bourgeois party of individual representation became the exception. While some of the species continue to survive, they do not determine the nature of the party system any longer. By the same token, the mass integration party, product of an age with harder class lines and more sharply protruding denominational structures, is transforming itself into a catch-all 'people's' party. Abandoning attempts at the intellectual and moral *encadrement* of the masses, it is turning more fully to the electoral scene, trying to exchange effectiveness in depth for a wider audience and more immediate electoral success. The narrower political task and the immediate electoral goal differ sharply from the former all-embracing concerns; today the latter are seen as counter-productive since they deter segments of a potential nationwide clientele.

For the class-mass parties we may roughly distinguish three stages in this process of transformation. There is first the period of gathering strength lasting to the beginning of the First World War; then comes their first governmental experience in the 1920s and 1930s (MacDonald, Weimar Republic, *Front Populaire*), unsatisfactory if measured both against the expectations of the class-mass party followers or leaders and suggesting the need for a broader basis of consensus in the political system. This period is followed by the present more or less advanced stages in the catch-all grouping, with some of the parties still trying to hold their special working-class clientele and at the same time embracing a variety of other clienteles.

Can we find some rules according to which this transformation is taking place, singling out factors which advance or delay or arrest it? We might think of the current rate of economic development as the most important determinant; but if it were so important, France would certainly be ahead of Great Britain and, for that matter, also of the United States, still the classical example of an all-pervasive catch-all party system. What about the impact of the continuity or discontinuity of the political system? If this were so important, Germany and Great Britain would appear at opposite ends of the spectrum rather than showing a similar speed of transformation. We must then be satisfied to make some comments on the general trend and to note special limiting factors.

In some instances the catch-all performance meets definite limits in the traditional framework of society. The all-pervasive denominational background of the Italian *Democrazia Cristiana* means from the outset that the party cannot successfully appeal to the anticlerical elements of the population. Otherwise nothing prevents the party from phrasing its appeals so as to maximize its chances of catching more of those numerous elements which are not disturbed by the party's clerical ties. The solidary element of its doctrinal core has long been successfully employed to attract a socially diversified clientele.

Or take the case of two other major European parties, the German SPD (Social Democratic party) and the British Labour party. It is unlikely that either of them is able to make any concession to the specific desires of real estate interests or independent operators of agricultural properties while at the same time maintaining credibility with the masses of the urban population. Fortunately, however, there is enough community of interest between wage-and-salary earning urban or suburban white- and blue-collar workers and civil servants to designate them all as strategic objects of simultaneous appeals. Thus tradition and the pattern of social and professional stratification may set limits and offer potential audiences to the party's appeal.

If the party cannot hope to catch all categories of voters, it may have a reasonable expectation of catching more voters in all those categories whose interests do not adamantly conflict. Minor differences between group claims, such as between white-collar and manual labour groups, might be smoothed over by vigorous emphasis on programmes which benefit both sections alike, for example, some cushioning against the shocks of automation.

Even more important is the heavy concentration on issues which are scarcely liable to meet resistance in the community. National societal goals transcending group interests offer the best sales prospect for the party intent on establishing or enlarging an appeal previously limited to specific sections of the population. The party which propagates most aggressively, for example, enlarged educational facilities may hear faint rumblings over the excessive cost or the danger to the quality of education from élites previously enjoying educational privileges. Yet the party's stock with any other family may be influenced only by how much more quickly and aggressively it took up the new national priority than its major competitor and how well its propaganda linked the individual family's future with the enlarged educational structures. To that extent its potential clientele is almost limitless. The catch-all of a given category performance turns virtually into an unlimited catch-all performance.

The last remark already transcends the group-interest confines. On the one hand, in such developed societies as I am dealing with, thanks to general levels of economic well-being and security and to existing welfare schemes universalized by the state or enshrined in collective bargaining, many individuals no longer need such protection as they once sought from the state. On the other hand, many have become aware of the number and complexity of the general factors on which their future well-being depends. This change of priorities and pre-occupation may lead them to examine political offerings less under the aspect of their own particular claims than under that of the political leader's ability to meet general future contingencies. Among the major present-day parties, it is the French UNR (National Republican Union), a latecomer, that speculates most clearly on the possibility of its channelling such less specialized needs to which its patron saint de Gaulle constantly appeals into its own version of the catch-all party. Its assumed asset would rest in a doctrine of national purpose and unity vague and flexible enough to allow the most variegated interpretation and yet—at least as long as the General continues to function—attractive enough to serve as a convenient rallying point for many groups and isolated individuals.

While the UNR thus manipulates ideology for maximum general appeal, we have noted that ideology in the case of the *Democrazia Cristiana* is a slightly limiting factor. The UNR ideology in principle excludes no one. The Christian Democratic ideology by definition excludes the non-believers, or at least the seriously non-believing voter. It pays for the ties of religious solidarity and the advantages of supporting organizations by repelling some millions of voters. The catch-all parties in Europe appear at a time of de-ideologization which has substantially contributed to their rise and spread. De-ideologization in the political field involves the transfer of ideology from partnership in a clearly visible political goal structure into one of many sufficient but by no means necessary motivational forces operative in the voters' choice. The German and Austrian Social Democratic parties in the last two decades most clearly exhibit the politics of de-ideologization. The example of the German Christian Democratic Union (CDU) is less clear only because there was less to de-ideologize. In the CDU, ideology was from the outset only a general background atmosphere, both all-embracing and conveniently vague enough to allow recruiting among Catholic and Protestant denominations.

As a rule, only major parties can become successful catch-all parties. Neither a small, strictly regional party such as the South Tyrolian Peoples' party nor a party built around the espousal of harsh and limited ideological claims, like the Dutch Calvinists; or transitory group claims, such as the German Refugees; or a specific professional category's claims, such as the Swedish Agrarians; or a limited-action programme, such as the Danish single-tax Justice party can aspire to a catch-all performance. Its *raison d'être* is the defence of a specific clientele or the lobbying for a limited reform clearly delineated to allow for a restricted appeal, perhaps intense, but excluding a wider impact or—once the original job is terminated—excluding a life-saving transformation.

Nor is the catch-all performance in vogue or even sought among the majority of the larger parties in small democracies. Securely entrenched, often enjoying majority status for decades—as the Norwegian and Swedish Social Democratic parties—and accustomed to a large amount of interparty co-operation,[1] such parties have no incentive to change their form of recruitment or their appeal to well-defined social groups. With fewer factors intervening and therefore more clearly foreseeable results of political actions and decisions, it seems easier to stabilize political relations on the basis of strictly circumscribed competition (Switzerland, for instance) than to change over to the more aleatory form of catch-all competition.

Conversion to catch-all parties constitutes a competitive phenomenon. A party is apt to accommodate to its competitor's successful style because of hope of benefits or fear of losses on election day. Conversely, the more a party convinces itself that a competitor's favourable results were due only to some non-repetitive circumstances, and that the competitor's capacity of overcoming internal dissension is a temporary phenomenon, the smaller the over-all conversion chance and the greater the inclination to hold fast to a loyal—though limited—clientele.

To evaluate the impact of these changes I have found it useful to list the functions which European parties exercised during earlier decades (late in the nineteenth and early in the twentieth centuries) and to compare them with the present situation. Parties have functioned as channels for integrating individuals and groups into the existing political order, or as instruments for modifying or altogether replacing that order (integration–disintegration). Parties have attempted to determine political-action preferences and influence other participants in the political process into accepting them. Parties have nominated

---

[1] Ulf Torgersen, 'The Trend Towards Political Consensus: The Case of Norway', in Stein Rokkan (ed.), *Approaches to the Study of Political Participation* (Bergen: Christian Michelsen Institute, 1962); and Stein Rokkan and Henry Valen, 'Regional Contrasts in Norwegian Politics' (1963, mimeographed), esp. p. 29. For both weighty historical and contemporary reasons the Austrian Social Democratic party forms a partial exception to the rule of less clear-cut transformation tendencies among major class-mass parties in smaller countries. It is becoming an eager and rather successful member of the catch-all club. For the most adequate treatment see K. L. Shell, *The Transformation of Austrian Socialism* (New York: State University of New York Press, 1962).

public office-holders and presented them to the public at large for confirmation.

The so-called 'expressive function'[2] of the party, if not belonging to a category by itself, nevertheless warrants a special word. Its high tide belongs to the era of the nineteenth-century constitutionalism when a more clear-cut separation existed between opinion formation-and-expression and the business of government. At that time the internally created parliamentary parties expressed opinions and criticism widely shared among the educated minority of the population. They pressed these opinions on their governments. But as the governments largely rested on an independent social and con-stitutional basis, they could if necessary hold out against the promptings of parliamentary factions and clubs. Full democra-tization merged the opinion-expressing and the governmental business in the same political parties and put them in the seat either of government or an alternative government. But it has left the expressive function of the party in a more ambiguous state. For electoral reasons, the democratic catch-all party, intent on spreading as wide as possible a net over a potential clientele, must continue to express widely felt popular con-cerns. Yet, bent on continuing in power or moving into gov-ernmental power, it performs this expressive function subject to manifold restrictions and changing tactical considerations. The party would atrophy if it were no longer able to function as a relay between the population and governmental structure, taking up grievances, ideas, and problems developed in a more searching and systematic fashion elsewhere in the body politic. Yet the caution it must give its present or prospective gov-ernmental role requires modulation and restraint. The very nature of today's catch-all party forbids an option between these two performances. It requires a constant shift between the party's critical role and its role as establishment support, a shift hard to perform but still harder to avoid.

In order to leave a maximum imprint on the polity a party has to exercise all of the first three functions. Without the ability

[2] Cf. Sartori's paper, 'European Political Parties: The Case of Polarized Pluralism' [in G. LaPalombara and M. Weiner (eds.), *Political Parties and Political Development* (Princeton: Princeton University Press, 1966)].

to integrate people into the community the party could not compel other power-holders to listen to its clarions. The party influences other power centres to the extent that people are willing to follow its leadership. Conversely, people are willing to listen to the party because the party is the carrier of messages—here called action preferences—that are at least partially in accord with the images, desires, hopes, and fears of the electorate. Nominations for public office serve to tie together all these purposes; they may further the realization of action preferences if they elicit positive response from voters or from other power-holders. The nominations concretize the party's image with the public at large, on which confidence the party's effective functioning depends.

Now we can discuss the presence or absence of these three functions in Western society today. Under present conditions of spreading secular and mass consumer-goods orientation, with shifting and less obtrusive class lines, the former class-mass parties and denominational mass parties are both under pressure to become catch-all peoples' parties. The same applies to those few remnants of former bourgeois parties of individual representation which aspire to a secure future as political organizations independent of the vagaries of electoral laws and the tactical moves of their mass-party competitors.[3] This change involves: (a) Drastic reduction of the party's ideological baggage. In France's SFIO, for example, ideological remnants serve at best as scant cover for what has become known as 'Molletisme', the absolute reign of short-term tactical considerations. (b) Further strengthening of top leadership groups, whose actions and omissions are now judged from the viewpoint of their contribution to the efficiency of the entire social system rather than identification with the goals of their particular organization. (c) Downgrading of the role of the individual party member, a role considered a historical relic which may

[3] Liberal parties without sharply profiled programme or clientele may, however, make such conversion attempts. Val Lorwin draws my attention to the excellent example of a former bourgeois party, the Belgian Liberal party, which became in 1961 the 'Party of Liberty and Progress', de-emphasizing anticlericalism and appealing to the right wing of the Social Christian party, worried about this party's governmental alliance with the Socialists.

obscure the newly built-up catch-all party image.[4] (*d*) De-emphasis of the *classe gardée*, specific social-class or denominational clientele, in favour of recruiting voters among the population at large. (*e*) Securing access to a variety of interest groups. The financial reasons are obvious, but they are not the most important where official financing is available, as in Germany, or where access to the most important media of communication is fairly open, as in England and Germany. The chief reason is to secure electoral support via interest-group intercession.

From this fairly universal development the sometimes considerable remnants of two old class-mass parties, the French and the Italian Communist parties, are excluding themselves. These parties are in part ossified, in part solidified by a combination of official rejection and legitimate sectional grievances. In this situation the ceremonial invocation of the rapidly fading background of a remote and inapplicable revolutionary experience has not yet been completely abandoned as a part of political strategy. What is the position of such opposition parties of the older class-mass type, which still jealously try to hold an exclusive loyalty of their members, while not admitted nor fully ready to share in the hostile state power? Such parties face the same difficulties in recruiting and holding intensity of membership interest as other political organizations. Yet, in contrast to their competitors working within the confines of the existing political order, they cannot make a virtue out of necessity and adapt themselves fully to the new style of catch-all peoples' party. This conservatism does not cost them the confidence of their regular corps of voters. On the other hand, the continued renewal of confidence on election day does not involve an intimate enough bond to utilize as a basis for major political operations.

The attitudes of regular voters—in contrast to those of members and activists—attest to the extent of incongruency between full-fledged participation in the social processes of a consumer-goods oriented society and the old political style which rested on the primordial need for sweeping political

[4] See also A. Pizzorno, 'The Individualistic Mobilization of Europe', in *Daedalus* (Winter 1964), pp. 199, 217.

change. The latter option has gone out of fashion in Western countries and has been carefully eliminated from the expectations, calculations, and symbols of the catch-all mass party. The incongruency may rest on the total absence of any connection between general social-cultural behaviour and political style. In this sense electoral choice may rest on family tradition or empathy with the political underdog without thereby becoming part of a coherent personality structure. Or the choice may be made in the expectation that it will have no influence on the course of political development; it is then an act of either adjusting to or, as the case may be, signing out of the existing political system rather than a manifestation of signing up somewhere else.

6

PARTIES IN PLURALISM

ALESSANDRO PIZZORNO

It has been frequently observed that despite the wide range of parties in the parliaments of the representative democracies they tend increasingly to say the same things to their electorate. Tingsten in 1955 backed up this observation with systematic data, and recently J. C. Thomas, in a thorough enquiry into party programmes presented in the parliaments of eleven countries,[1] has shown that over the past forty to sixty years the average differences among party positions on ten principal programmatic themes have constantly decreased. Likewise diminished is the intensity with which reforms are advocated in these programmes: 'There has been a dramatic narrowing of the scope of domestic political conflict between parties in western nations. The limit of this narrowing is just short of zero, like in American parties.'[2] Observations on the marketing style of latter-day electoral campaigns, on the way the various parties compete to represent the same social groups and hence the development of what Kirchheimer called the 'catch-all' parties, constitute less systematic but nevertheless telling proofs of the same phenomenon.

Is this phenomenon restricted to programme 'enunciations', or does it reflect a deeper lack of political alternatives, some

Alessandro Pizzorno, excerpted from 'Interests and Parties in Pluralism', in Suzanne Berger (ed.), *Organizing Interests in Western Europe: Pluralism, Corporatism, and the Transformation of Politics* (1981), pp. 247–84. Reprinted by permission of Cambridge University Press.

[1] J. C. Thomas, *The Decline of Ideology in Western Political Parties* (London: Sage Publications, 1975). It should be remembered that Thomas's data go only until the early sixties. The countries analysed are Australia, Austria, Canada, England, France, Germany, Italy, Japan, New Zealand, Sweden, USSR, USA.

[2] Ibid. 46.

impracticability of real options in pluralist regimes? Is the
trend it delineates a secular one, or does it show a cyclical
pattern? And does it represent a decisive alteration of the
pluralist machinery? I shall try to discuss these three questions,
being aware of the fact that a definitive answer is not possible at
the current state of our knowledge.

1. Are political alternatives only illusory in pluralistic
regimes? It is possible that although party programmes tend to
converge, real party policies, when parties are in government,
do not. Certain research and common-sense observation would
tell us, for example, that Social Democratic parties pursue
policies favouring full employment, whereas liberal and conservative parties pursue policies aiming at reducing inflation at
the expense of unemployment. Neither common-sense observation nor the current state of the research is convincing on this
point. In fact, the relevant data should be analysed on three
levels: What the parties say, what the parties try to do, what the
effective outcome of their policies is. On the third level,
obviously so many other factors and constraints (foreign and
internal) are operating, that we may not reach any well-tested
conclusion. On the second level, what the parties try to do when
in government depends at least as much on the pressures they
receive and the evaluation of the needs for coalitions, compromises, and so on with other social and political forces, as from
the need to identify with the programme submitted to the
electors. For the first level, the declarations about their own
intentions obviously depend on the evaluation of their effects on
the electors, given the constraints of maintaining some distinction from the other parties. But distinctions can also be secured
through either general ideological construction, not requiring
detailed programme specification, or techniques of image
building, leading the electors to identify with personal or group
characteristics more than with policy orientation.

The distinction between the first (what the parties say) and
the second level (how they operate) suggests a corresponding
distinction in political languages. To the first level corresponds
the open, exoteric, generally programmatic language, formulated with electoral goals in mind. Here different speakers are
hardly distinguishable. To the second level corresponds an
esoteric, subtle, allusive language, directed at the public of

those who represent interests and understand the allusions that escape others. At this second level the messages aim at negotiating alliances, working out exchanges, and prospecting demands and supports. Here the specialized public can easily tell one speaker from the others.[3] Alternatives are real for specialists, they are illusory, or fragmented in thousands of contradictory measures, for the general public.

2. Are we witnessing a secular trend towards programmatic convergence as Thomas's findings tend to suggest? Several observations invite us rather to consider a possible cyclical hypothesis. Until about World War I, with variations from country to country, the trend was towards differentiation. The cause of this was clearly to be ascribed to the 'new entries' (Socialist and Catholic parties) into parliament. (In fact, the United States did not experience any differentiation.) Elsewhere, new 'external' parties (in Duverger's sense) representing interests that had formerly been excluded, forced their entry into parliament. Their first need was to affirm their separate identities, hence to emphasize the differences between themselves and the older parties constituting the 'system'. As a consequence, their programmes were 'radical' and their goals non-negotiable. Once taken inside and recognized and accepted by the others, they felt a lesser need to affirm their identities. The continual interaction with the other actors within the system, the awareness in general of the constraints that limit the achievement of any political goal, the need to appeal to the marginal voter, discourage excessive differentiation—hence the phenomenon of convergence. We can confidently conclude, therefore, that, *ceteris paribus*, new entries result in more programme differentiation, whereas a lack of

---

[3] This distinction between the first and the second level is similar to the one G. Sartori draws between *visible* and *invisible* politics in *Parties and Party Systems* (Cambridge: Cambridge University Press, 1976, p. 143), even if it can hardly be maintained that the second level of action is 'invisible', because it is still performed through public language, although specially codified. I would not agree, however, with the statement that 'the lesser the ideological bent . . . the greater the (relative) proximity and convertibility between rhetoric and feasibility, between image selling and deeds'. 'Non-ideological' image selling may be as distant from real action as the most abstract ideology.

new entries, that is, a long permanence of the same subjects in a system, produces convergence.

This also helps to throw light on the famous dispute over the 'end of ideology'. If ideology means differentiated proposals for long-term goals, there is no doubt that the political forces are more inclined to abandon this kind of message the longer they stay in parliament. But this message is not likewise abandoned by the 'social forces', the collective subjects outside parliament. On the contrary, it is probable that, in certain periods at least, the less ideological are the messages (i.e. proposals of long-term goals) issued by the parties pursuing governmental power, the greater will be the number of producers of ideology outside the parliamentary system. These are not bound by the rules of the political game in the same ways as those inside and hence can propose programmes, the realism of which need not be immediately verified.

If the process of programme convergence approaches the point where all distinctions are cancelled, the electors become unable to choose for want of separate identities, and participation in political life approaches meaninglessness, except when professionally motivated. The old parties will then be either exposed to schisms or threatened by new entries. A more or less durable revamping of the ideological stance, hence of the identity, of a party may then be the most convenient response. The Thatcher case in the United Kingdom, followed by the organizational reform in the Labour party, which has increased the power of the 'ideological core' of its supporters, can be considered an example of how separate identities need to be restated when policy constraints have blurred all distinctions. There is another suggestion here that the convergence/divergence path of parties' programmes may follow a cyclical pattern.

A different way out from this impasse may be to shift to personalities for the task of representing alternatives. Choice among parties, ideologies, and programmes—or among sub-cultural memberships—is then replaced by choice among images of personalities in which the electors are asked to put their trust. (US politics come closer to this idea type.) Here the choice is dissimilar from the choice between programmes—and more similar to the choice between ideologies—in that it is not binding on the specific policy of the elected, and therefore allows the governing groups to adopt very similar policies even if their images are distinct enough to make a choice possible. The deep factors generating programme convergence are hence not interfered with.

3. The third question is the most relevant to our general theme. Does this decline in distinction among party programmes signify a relevant alteration of the pluralist system?

To answer this question, we first consider another aspect of the evolution of the political parties: the weakening of their function of 'social integration'. Parties no longer represent or do not represent to the same extent (Austrian parties and the Communist party in Italy being the main partly deviant cases) a source of social integration for their followers. Neither are electoral cleavages as stable as they had been for the more than sixty years since they were formed as a reflection of class and religious differences at the end of the last century.[4] The European electorate—as well as the American—has become more fluid, and shifts in preference from one election to the next have become increasingly frequent.[5] It is not easy to judge the depth of such a change and its causes today, but we may at least say that it is linked with the long-term decline in the programmatic function and the integrational function of the parties. A general explanatory hypothesis can be offered that 'integration' parties, stable electoral cleavages, and clear alternatives in party programme are more likely to be found in periods of intense social (mainly occupational and geographic) change and of consequent strong pressures by new categories of interests to enter into the political system.

If this hypothesis is true, strong parties, with clearly delineated programmes and integrated membership, are a temporary phenomenon. They emerge both to strengthen and to control the access of the new masses into the political system and become redundant once both entry and control are achieved. If they are typical of pluralism, then, they are typical

[4] S. M. Lipset and S. Rokkan, 'Cleavage Structures, Party Systems and Voter Alignments: An Introduction', in Lipset and Rokkan (eds.), *Party Systems and Voter Alignments* (New York: Free Press, 1967), 1–64.
[5] S. B. Wolinetz, 'Stabilità e mutamento nei sistemi partitici dell'Europa Occidentale', *Rivista Italiana di Scienza Politica* 1 (1978), 3–56.

only of its first 'generative' phase, when the big collective actors are admitted to share power into a system of representation; they still tend to control their followers as whole persons, not just to represent them in specific roles. Typically, there is no pluralist 'political market' in this phase, no crosscutting of memberships. Although this 'integrated' form of representation seems characteristic of the working-class parties, that is, of the parties organizing a class that is excluded from the individualistic access to multiple public roles, after World War I, and in certain cases even before, in more than one country, bourgeois parties and movements organized themselves in the same 'integrated', almost totalitarian, way.

This phase may last longer in certain countries (Italy, France, Austria) and be almost non-existent in others (e.g. United States), but sooner or later it makes place for a situation in which no irreducible political identity is at stake and political demands all become negotiable. Interest groups asking for specific policies are the main actors on the political scene whereas the political parties, in their effort to represent multiple interests in order to conquer the marginal voter, as well as to have the support of as many interest groups as possible, tend to lose their programmatic and organizational identity.

The analysis that we have been conducting until now should give us the clue to explain how this phase of pluralism has come about. We can summarize the main factors responsible for the change as follows.

The acceptance of the rule of electoral choice tends to bring parties to resemble each other more and more, to rub this distinctiveness out. The growing economic interdependence, both national and international, strengthens the veto powers of international and private national actors, restricting the autonomy of the central authorities of the system, their capacity of pursuing long-term policies and of achieving a unitary will to modify society according to some overall programme. This obviously makes the tools for the elaboration of coherent programmes obsolete. Because political decisions are entirely the outcome of negotiations between separate interests, political parties have to adapt their structure to the needs of the real actors, the interest groups.

Not all political decisions, however, are the outcome of

negotiations between private interests. Even in a pluralist polity, a level of decisions escapes the pluralist procedures of representation because it deals with problems of the system as a whole in its relationship with the other systems on the international scene. Here is the domain of *arcana imperii*: Decisions are secret, secluded, momentous. Neither interest organizations nor political parties are the fittest structures to intervene in forming the decision, but small groups of power-holders, or of persons informally related to them are. (This does *not* mean that all decisions of foreign policy pertain to this level; a large part is the outcome of negotiations among all sorts of interests.)

A dualistic structure of power seems therefore to constitute the natural outcome of pluralistic regimes: a caesaristic, secluded level of decisions and an effectively pluralistic, polyarchical, negotiated one. On both levels a contradictory logic is at work. At the caesaristic level the contradiction is between the 'absolute' unitary nature of the decisions to be taken and the dependence of the incumbent on the multiformity of public opinions. On the polyarchical level the tension is between the trend towards an institutional (corporative) definition of the interests to be represented and recognized and the continuous surge of new issues and the aggregations of interests around them. On neither level do the political parties seem the most appropriate instruments.

A third level of 'nonpower' should be added to these two levels of power, where the 'excluded' interests are located: those of the population that is going in and out of the labour market, enjoying no security, belonging to no union or party or other association, without real contact with any structure of political representation, voting or not out of mechanical allegiances. Political parties could probably be interested in this stratum of the population, but the cost of mobilizing it would be too high for them.

FIVE HYPOTHESES TO EXPLAIN THE SURVIVAL OF POLITICAL PARTIES

One question is now open: if they appear redundant, how is the persistence of political parties in representative regimes to be explained? Obviously, we could surmise that political parties are structures born in response to the initial needs of these regimes and now outdated. The particularistic interests that have in time built up around these structures would be sufficient to justify their survival, considering their reliance on the institutionally guaranteed monopoly over the selection of political personnel. But this would not explain those cases in which the party system was interrupted and later reestablished. Although not a prerequisite, the presence of at least one party does in fact seem to be closely associated with all types of government in advanced industrial societies. Four hypotheses can be put together from the existing literature to explain this fact.

1. The hypothesis of *illusory choice*. Because the principle of popular sovereignty implies that the people must somehow choose, the parties are there to permit them to do so. The principle of popular sovereignty might be merely ideological were it not for the fact that it actually makes governing society easier, for the illusion of being able to choose their governors prevents the population from opposing the regime. Thus parties last because they help maintain consent, which they do by constituting conditions of choice. Although choice would exist even if there were only individual representation without organized parties, parties offer more or less stable collective identities as the basis of choice. Indeed, here we might use the concept of *illusorische Gemeinschaft*, which Marx used for the state. Just as the state takes the place of religion to offer the illusion of a community within which conflicts of particular interests are eliminated, so the parties offer the same illusion, once the state can no longer do so (its possibilities of doing so have been undermined by the very struggles of the ideological mass parties). The party appears as a collective body within which particularistic interests disappear. This fosters the illusion of being able to choose rulers and also to choose them according to general criteria shared by a solidary and stable collectivity rather than for individual utilities.

This hypothesis has two parts, one on the plurality of parties, hence the *illusion of choice*, and the other on the parties as a collective body, hence the *illusion of community*. The force of the hypothesis may correspondingly be summed up in two formulas. (1) If the illusion of choice were to disappear, an important instrument of consent would be lost and thus it would be more difficult to govern society. (2) If the illusion of community were to disappear, the members of a population would be reduced to judging public affairs according to criteria of individual utility, and there would be no way that was not arbitrary of passing from individual criteria to criteria capable of defining collective utility. This would also make government more difficult, and hence the need for parties.

The objections to these hypotheses are the following. The illusion of choice cannot be considered an indispensable instrument of government because many advanced industrial societies have only one party (and even if the repression in these countries seems to be harsher, it does not necessarily cost more than it does in multiparty countries). The illusion of community, on the other hand, is very strong within ideological parties in opposition, where obviously it does not aid but rather hinders governmental action. The illusion of community is also strong in parties governing with opposition. But here it is bound to be confused with the illusion that the state itself is a community immune from fundamental conflicts of interests, and this illusion should be sufficient to induce the population to consent to state action. Hence where this is their only function, parties should disappear.

2. The hypothesis of *cohesiveness*. The upper-level bureaucrats and also the political personnel deriving from their ranks are bound to have a sectoral view of government. The goals they pursue are those of administrative efficiency rather than those derived from a certain view of society in general. Furthermore, they remain attached to the administrative environment from which they came. This makes it difficult for them to govern impartially. To overcome this, the political personnel in government would have to be made up of a cohesive group of individuals, who know each other, are able to communicate easily, and have some end in common so that they would consider administrative efficiency as a means rather than as an end. This would make them something close to a party, a social body that can guarantee internal homogeneity and easy communication. In a party, though, these are bound to have developed in the struggle against other parties.

The hypothesis make public virtues (cohesiveness and co-ordination of purposes) derive from private vices (cliquishness or complicity between the members of a group who want to overpower another group).

The objections arise from the observations we have made earlier. If in fact the programmatic function in the party weakens, there will be little to distinguish the party's political personnel from the bureaucrats in the various administrative sectors. The inferior specific competence of the former will no longer be compensated by a vision of general goals built up in party action. And if the function of social integration and cultural formation gets weaker in the parties and no synthesis or mediation takes place among the various interests represented, the individuals that move from party to governmental positions will lack a common vision and will be no more able to communicate among themselves than any other group of individuals can. Thus if parties' only function were the formation of a governing group that is organic and has common goals, their presence would not be justified.

3. The hypothesis of *responsible polling*. The representatives are in a position to carry out a survey of the electorate and thus to transmit information useful for government. It is true that any good public opinion research organization can do better surveys as far as reliability is concerned than can the representatives of the people; these latter, however, carry them out with 'responsibility'; that is, if their information is not adequate, they may be punished by their electorate. But polls of this sort are bound to be vague and erratic. Even if they were efficient, there would still be no need for parties but only for individual representatives.

4. The *reduction-of-complexity* hypothesis. Political parties reduce the excess of problems that the state would have to address if all the demands of society reached it directly. That is, they reduce the number of options that the executive organs have to consider. At the same time, because the public recognizes itself in the parties, at least partially, such a reduction of options appears acceptable. Consequently, the parties, on the one hand, facilitate the choice for the electors inasmuch as they present them with large, general problems on which to decide; on the other hand, they facilitate administrative decisions in

that they reduce the area of what is considered politically possible.

But this 'screening' function, as we have seen, can be performed also by interest organization. Moreover, how does one explain the long-term historical tendency towards programmatic convergence that makes general choices illusory? And how does one explain that in many of the most advanced industrial countries such as the United States the parties are less well aggregated than in other, 'simpler' societies? In what sense can one say that the work of political parties serves to sustain and to legitimize the decisions of the government? Certain parties sustain them; others oppose them. A parliament of individual representatives is sufficient to define a majority and a minority; organized parties are not required.

5. Each of the four hypotheses that I have reconstructed to understand the reasons for the survival of the political parties in spite of the loss of their most obvious functions appears inadequate in itself, although they all contain insights. A fifth hypothesis may be put forward. We should first consider the specific role of party politicians in the decision-making process. They seem legitimated to take part in it so long as they enjoy the trust of others. Because the same is true also for representatives of special interests, one might infer that what is special about the party politicians' position is that they present themselves as potential representatives of general interests. But this is hardly plausible. We shall argue rather that the party politician acts to guarantee the currency that is exchanged on the political market.

In other words, if representatives of private interests want to obtain a particular measure, they can offer in exchange to the decision-maker those resources they control (money, favours, votes, etc.). This kind of exchange is limited to two actors and to rather short-run effects. If long-term political transactions involving a large number of actors are to be made possible, a class of identifiable mediators becomes necessary; durable trust in them will act as a guarantee for the deferral of payments. The party, with its durable structure and public exposure, is a sort of guarantee of political mediation, a kind of 'political credit' institution, made possible by a continual verification of the available credit, through the electoral process.

If creation and preservation of political trust is to be considered the ultimate function of political parties in a representative regime, we may conclude, as previously indicated, that political parties are thriving when other bases for trust (religious, ethnic, associational, local, etc.) are lacking or politically dormant, and citizens are in need of stable structures to which they can trustfully refer to orient themselves not only in their utilization of political machineries but also in their acquisition of new social identities. Parties decay when these conditions do not obtain.

PART II

THE STABILIZATION OF
PARTY SYSTEMS

7

STRUCTURING THE PARTY SYSTEM

GIOVANNI SARTORI

[T]he critical factor in altering the nature of a party system and in bringing about its structural consolidation is the appearance of the mass party. This does not mean that only the mass party brings about the nationalization of politics, but that the two are closely intertwined. It is necessary, then, to pin down the notion of the mass party. At the same time, a comparison between the parties of notables and the mass party provides by itself a telling explanatory clue.

The pre-mass parties—of the élite or notability variety— are typically fragile if not evanescent parties; they reflect a 'coalition linkage', at best a confederal linkage, among self-sufficient units, i.e. among notables or popular leaders elected in their own right. Therefore the élite-notability parties amount to loose, if not to shifting systems of alliances. In other words, in the pre-mass stage the leaders stand above the party: in a very literal sense, the party consists of the leaders. In contrast to the coalition party, the mass party is a linkage party; not only is it a suprapersonal entity that stands above its leaders, but the party consists of its organizational linkage. In a very real sense, the linkage *is* the party.

Therefore the mass party is not merely a party having masses of people behind it, a mass-based party. A mass following accounts for the success of the party, not for its nature. The mass party is a solid and very real (not evanescent) party, qualified by at least the following two traits: (1) the development of a stable and extensive (even if merely skeletal) organization throughout the country, and (2) the fact that it presents itself to the electorate as an abstract entity

Giovanni Sartori, excerpted from 'Political Development and Political Engineering', from *Public Policy*, 17 (1968), 261–98. Reprinted by permission.

(ideologically or programmatically qualified) that allows stable identifications.

The fact that the mass party proposes itself as an object of stable identification, thereby undermining purely personal and personalized loyalties, points to the crucial, although often neglected condition that the mass party stage cannot be entered until an adequate spread of literacy allows 'capacity for abstraction'. This is not to say, to be sure, that in largely pre-literate societies mass movements and mass phenomena do not occur. Of course they do, especially when the mass media come into play. This is to say, then, that mass movements and mass-followed parties should not be confused with mass parties, and that the former are not conducive to the latter (no matter how much mobilizing pressure is exerted from above) until the literacy-abstraction requirement that severs personalized identifications is satisfied. It is also to suggest that the correlation between literacy and democracy becomes meaningful, and crucial, when the structuring of a party system is under way. The trumps are played at that moment; subsequent events are largely shaped by the kind of mass party that seizes the opportunity at this stage of the process.

Reverting to the point, the link between the two occurrences —the appearance of the mass party, on the one hand, and the structural consolidation and nationalization of the party system as a whole, on the other hand—can be highlighted by the following hypothesis:

Hypothesis: With the appearance of one or two mass parties a situation of party atomization cannot endure, for either the pre-existing élites meet the challenge by coalescing into more solid parties, or the parties of notabilities are swept away and survive, at best, as marginal parties.

This is the same as saying that the party system becomes structured in response to the rise of one or two mass parties. Alternatively, a system becomes structured because it consists of mass parties. This latter outcome presupposes a plurality system, however; under systems of PR the mass party generally plays a catalystic role. The notion of structured party systems does not imply, therefore, that all of the parties should have a mass following. It does mean, however, that the boneless coalition party either disappears or merely survives at the periphery of the political system. A structured party system can be defined, therefore, as a state of the system in which the major parties become 'solid' and more 'real' than the personalities. Naturally some parties will be far more solid than others: Differences in cohesion, discipline, and organization will remain very great. Yet when the pace is set by mass parties, the destiny of the fragile élite party is sealed.

8

THE 'REACH' OF THE PARTY SYSTEM

HANS DAALDER

Partly as a consequence of historical factors European parties have differed greatly in the extent to which they have permeated and enveloped other political élites. In some countries the role of parties has become all pervasive; in others the parties have penetrated far less successfully to the mainsprings of political power. Substantial differences are also encountered in the extent to which parties have become true integrating agencies between political élites on the national and on the local scene. In this section the 'reach' of a party system is briefly analysed along the following three dimensions: the extent of involvement of traditional political élites in the party system; the measure of absorption of new political claimants; and the degree of 'homogenization' which parties provide between national and local political élites.

Party Systems and Traditional Élites

In European societies the relationship of traditionally powerful political élites and the party system seems to have taken one of three forms: they have participated from the outset, slowly learning to share power with newer groups; they have participated in the party system but only half-heartedly and with reactionary intentions; or they have stayed outside altogether, seeking to maintain their influence through other power structures (notably the military, the bureaucracy, business, or the Church). The precise developments depended greatly on the way parties originated and the specific nature and extent of the democratizing process.

As we have noted, some European parties were in many ways the outcome of earlier institutionalized conflict on the élite level; factions hardened increasingly into substantial political organizations as these conflicts spread from the élites downward into an ever widening circle of political actors. Though older élites were eventually confronted with new parties outside their control, they never came in immediate conflict with the party system. This facilitated the transition from oligarchical to polyarchical forms of government.

In other European countries parties were first established in opposition to autocratic regimes that forbade or at least restricted the scope of party conflict. Eventually in these countries too older élites found it necessary to participate in electoral processes. But parties established under their auspices tended to remain little more than outward appearances, democratic figleaves, so to speak, for entrenched power positions that had their real basis elsewhere. Consequently right-wing parties in various European countries came to assume basically different attitudes towards the rules of the game of democratic party politics. The acceptance of the substance of democratic ideals and practices is still the clearest criterion with which to distinguish Scandinavian or British Conservatives from, say, the right in France, Weimar Germany, or present-day Italy. In the latter the constant presence of potentially or actually antidemocratic parties within the party system has hindered the effective working of democratic politics; it has narrowed the range of democratic rule; it has caused disillusionment to spread to other potentially more democratic groups; and it finally eroded the very existence of democratic regimes.

The 'reach' of the party system over against other traditional political élites is revealed most clearly in its relation to the permanent bureaucracy. Bureaucracies have been far more responsive to the party system in some countries than in others. Much has depended on historical relations and the specific characteristics of the ensuing party system.

Thus it was of profound significance whether an articulated party system developed before, after, or concurrently with the rise of a bureaucracy. In France and Germany powerful bureaucracies were built up as social control-mechanisms long before non-bureaucratic social groups had learned to use the weapon of political organization to secure influence. Ever since, parties have had difficulty in obtaining full control, and to this day bureaucracies have tended to enjoy a distinct political existence. In Britain, on the other hand, the build-up of a modern civil service occurred after non-official social groups were securely in political control; ever since, the civil service has loyally accepted control by party ministers. Many other European countries would seem to fall between these two cases. State bureaucracies developed earlier than in Britain, but non-state groups were strong enough to make their weight felt simultaneously, and ultimately to prevent them from becoming uncontrollable elements in the body politics. To use a somewhat simple metaphor, the British Civil Service was from the outset below party; the French and German bureaucracies were to a very real extent above it; in other cases parties and bureaucracies tended to be on one line. In systems where certain parties tended for long to have a hegemonic position they often staffed the bureaucracies after their own image; thus Liberal dominance made the Dutch bureaucracy long a Liberal perquisite, and in somewhat similar fashion the *Democrazia Cristiana* is at present heavily represented in the Italian bureaucracy. Alternation between parties could lead to an attempt to take the bureaucracy out of politics (as in Britain), but also to competitive politicization by rival parties. Coalition politics has often led to a careful distribution of administrative 'fiefs' to rival parties, as in present-day Austria and Belgium, or to balanced appointments of rival partisans not only at the ministerial level but also in *cabinets du ministre*, or even in established administrative posts. Generally speaking, bureaucratic traditions, fortified by political and legal doctrines, have prevented such devices from degenerating into the full excesses of the American nineteenth-century spoils system. Contrary to traditional belief, they have worked not too badly in those systems in which the party system itself was reasonably cohesive and effective. In a segmented society like the Netherlands, carefully balanced political appointments would even seem to have smoothed the relations among the parties and between politicians and bureaucrats. They have given parties the certainty that their views were taken into consideration at the beginnings of policy formation and in the details of policy execution; they have provided officials with a new avenue by which to obtain political support for administrative concerns; they have thus acted as brokers between officials and politicians and between various parties, softening political conflict in the process.

The Party System and New Claimants

As in their relation towards older élites, party systems have differed in their responsiveness to the claims of new groups seeking political representation. In European history the outs at the lower end of the scale have been either lower-class groups (notably the working classes and the peasantry) or religious protesters (e.g. Dutch Calvinists and Catholics, English Non-conformists, the Norwegian Left). Again, the relation between these new claimants and the party system took any of three forms: their absorption into a pre-existing party system which gradually came to widen its appeal; the formation of special parties; or their continued exclusion from the party system.

Robert Dahl[1] has suggested in the case of the United States that the non-appearance of a special working-class party was due to a considerable extent to the fact that representative government and a wide franchise were introduced before an urbanized proletariat came to exert new demands on the system. Hence parties and political techniques suitable to the operation of parties were evolved in time to grapple with this new challenge and to accommodate labour in the existing system. In contrast, in Britain representative government came early, the urban proletariat next, and general suffrage only at the end. While developments were such as to keep new rising groups within the constitutional order, the existing parties were not elastic enough to accommodate the rising demands of the working classes. In Germany, urbanization and the general suffrage preceded representative government, thus sterilizing political party activity into necessarily ineffective attitudes.

---

[1] See R. A. Dahl (ed.), *Political Oppositions in Western Democracies* (New Haven: Yale University Press, 1966), ch. 13.

With somewhat similar ideas in mind, Stein Rokkan has asked for further study of the interesting relationship between franchise extension, special electoral arrangements (such as weighting of votes, privatization of electoral preferences, proportional representation versus other electoral systems), and the mobilization of new groups into the political system.[2] These studies must then be further related, I suggest, to such factors as the earlier élite-setting, and the extent of disparity between political and social and economic development (also in their regional variations) to account for the measure of actual involvement of the out-groups in one political framework.

Generally speaking, then, not the establishment of special parties representative of the lesser groups of society but only their psychological identification with the political order and the responsiveness of that order, in turn, to new demands can serve as the true measure of the relation between the party system and new claimants. A responsive political order may ensure an effective political participation of new claimants without the establishment of special parties. Special parties, on the other hand, can both integrate and isolate according to the reaction of other parts of a party system. Thus Dutch Calvinists and Catholics established highly segmented political and social organizations but jointly rose to power and in the process ensured the integration of their clienteles into the political system, actually making it more integrated, responsive, and democratized.[3] The same cannot be said, it seems to me, of the Norwegian Christians or of various parties composed of nationality interests in the Austrian–Hungarian Empire. The uncritical use of the term 'fragmentation', thus, does not bring the analysis much further if attention is not paid at the same time to the question whether a division of a political system into a number of quite distinct spiritual and political groups ultimately means the break-up of one society, or rather the growing of roots of very different groupings in one constitutional order. To use Sartori's terms, seemingly fragmented

---

[2] See his 'Mass Suffrage, Secret Voting and Political Participation', *European Journal of Sociology*, 2 (1961), 132–52.

[3] See H. Daalder, 'The Netherlands: Opposition in a Segmented Society', in Dahl, *Political Oppositions*, ch. 6.

systems can in practice be centrifugal or centripetal, and only exact sociological analysis can reveal which is ultimately the case.

Just as older élites in certain cases stayed outside (if not above) the party system, so various groups of society remained outside or below it even after the general franchise was introduced. As suggested earlier, one cause may have been a disparity between a strong politicization of the working classes and the granting to them of the means of effective political action. In the Latin countries anarchism and syndicalism were strengthened by the acute feeling that party and parliamentary activity could achieve little in practice. Vested interests may so continue to dominate the parliamentary scene that even their nominal voters may feel manipulated rather than active participants. This has been for long true of Italy, for instance, and still is to a lesser extent of most European countries.

If we combine the first and the second paragraph of this section, the 'reach' of a party system in relation to various groups in the society might be visualized as follows. Most removed (though not necessarily antagonistic) would be those political groups which are outside or below the system altogether; by definition they are politically unorganized. Following them are conscious anti-system groups that reject the existing political order but have some measure of group identification (e.g. the syndicalists, even though they rejected party organization and put their trust in spontaneous rather than institutional leaders). A somewhat closer participation is found among those who organize in political anti-system parties but with the deliberate aim of participating in order to destroy; in practice, however, the very act of participation tends to create certain vested interests in the system (cf. Robert de Jouvenel's famous dictum that there is more in common between two deputies one of whom is a revolutionary than between two revolutionaries one of whom is a deputy). Anti-system parties may therefore show a wide range between outright rejection and near-acceptance, and their influence may become so great that their presence becomes a significant variable within the system. Somewhat further on the road to involvement are those isolationist parties that have no chance to gain even part-power but continue to organize definite subcultural groups that wish their voices to be heard (even if with little chance of their being taken into account). Next in the scale would come opposition parties that effectively compete for office, proximity to power being the criterion with which to measure real involvement. Here again there is considerable scope of variation; whereas some are natural 'outs', others are semi-government supporters. Finally come governing parties, tied most closely to the existing system, the extent of their dominance being the measure of their effective control. A simplified representation of this scheme is given in Figure 8.1.

Party Systems: The Centre and Local Realities

The central-local axis provides yet another dimension by which to measure the permeation of party systems. Increased interaction between the centre and the localities greatly affected the formation and organization of parties. Generally speaking, a two-way process took place: political forces in the centre sought to extend their political bases by mobilizing political support over wider geographic areas, while political groups in the periphery organized to promote regional interests with the centre.

This two-way movement resulted in very different situations. In some cases, a fundamental nationalization of politics led to a far-reaching 'homogenization' between politics at the centre and in regional areas; such a movement was facilitated by the absence of strong economic or cultural regional cleavages, by good communications, and by the entry of issues that helped to nationalize politics (e.g. class). In other cases ethnic, linguistic, religious, or geographic barriers prevented such an osmosis from taking place. Politicization tended to strengthen centrifugal rather than centripetal tendencies (separatist political movements like that of the Irish in nineteenth-century Britain, or of nationality groupings in the Austrian–Hungarian Empire, forming their logical extreme). In yet different cases politics at the centre and in the localities tended to remain highly differentiated spheres, with only minimal linkages between them. Although this did not threaten national existence, it complicated national politics. Again, a comparison between Britain and France offers an instructive contrast.

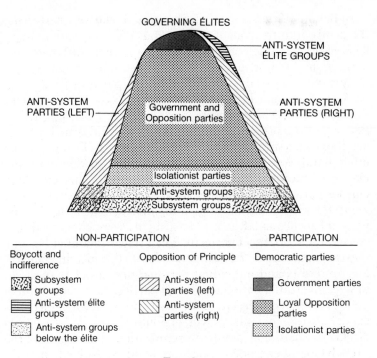

Fig. 8.1.

The area of effective democratic party government is restricted to that of the Government and loyal opposition parties—hence the 'reach' of a democratic party system is measured by its total proportion of the political pyramid. This proportion is very different in various European societies: while in some it is nearly coterminous with the whole (England, Sweden) in others it occupies only a relatively small area (present-day Italy, Weimar Germany, French Fourth Republic). Proportions are far from stable moreover. On the one hand, isolationist and anti-system parties may gradually be domesticated into the system (e.g. the Nenni Socialists). On the other hand, increasing opposition to the system (as measured by a proportionate increase in the strength of anti-system groups and anti-system parties), and mounting indifference (as apparent in an increase of subsystem groups) may narrow the area of democratic politics. Anti-system parties may seek deliberate involvement to discredit democratic politics and thus to increase both anti-system and subsystem groups. This is the reasoning behind traditional Communist tactics and seems to reflect fairly accurately the situation in France before 1958, when anti-system parties, anti-system groups, and political malaise made the area of Democratic politics shrink to such an extent as to make it practically ineffective.

In Britain leaders and labels penetrated relatively early from the centre into the constituencies, thus drawing national and local élites into one reasonably unified system. Although certain regional sentiments and interests continued to have some importance, to this day providing British parties with distinct pockets of regional strength, they were not such as to fragment the decision-making process at the centre. The essence of British politics is therefore national politics, and British parties are above all national political organizations. In France, on the other hand, local concerns long continued to dominate the choice of national parliamentary personnel. This caused a curious paradox: provided the local representative showed due respect for local sensitivities and interests, he was, on the national scene, as far as his constituents were concerned to a considerable extent a free agent. The French Chamber became therefore very much '*La Maison sans Fenêtres*', a meeting place of local interests and individual personalities rather than of cohesive, integrated national political parties. Nationalization of politics occurred therefore more easily on the level of ideological debate than of political will, of political oratory rather than of effective national political organization. For the rest, the French Chamber tended to be more highly sensitive to interest groups (pressuring MPs in their local base) than to issues of more national importance. This accentuated the cleavage between the French bureaucracy (feeling itself the self-appointed guardian of France in a truly Parisian way) and the Chamber, stronger in resisting the executive than in dominating it, more ready to veto than to formulate national policies.

The 'homogenization' of politics between the centre and the localities is therefore an important factor in the politics of both. An effective linkage helps to legitimize the national political order. Where links are absent, alienation is likely to ensue. The character of the party system is an important variable in this process. Parties can be agencies of both integration and disintegration. They assist national integration if they serve as genuine brokers between disparate regional or social interests (without losing their national existence in the process). They are likely to strengthen centrifugal forces, on the other hand, if they become the passive tools of sectional interests. Paradoxically, synthetic unifiers who seek to identify their own sectional interests with that of the one and indivisible nation can contribute as much to such disintegrating tendencies as those who deny the existence of one political community from over-particularistic concerns.

THE CLEAVAGE LINES OF THE PARTY SYSTEM

European countries reveal considerable differences according to the character and the intensity of the cleavage lines that form the basis for political conflict and political organization. These differences are partly due to objective differences in social structure; certain social cleavages did exist in some countries but not in others (e.g. ethnic diversity). They depend further on the circumstance of whether and to what extent particular cleavages were effectively politicized; factors such as religion or class have been much more exploited in some political systems than in others. Finally, considerable variations also exist in the persistence of cleavage lines in the party system. Whereas some issues have been of only passing importance and have subsequently fallen out of the political domain, others have remained characteristic dividing lines long after their original *raisons d'être* have been forgotten. In this way the particular history of past political controversy has continued to exercise a substantial influence on political loyalties and on the way in which new issues are focused and processed. Therefore only careful historical, sociological, and political analysis can do full justice to the distinct qualities of any given political system. It follows that it is much easier to categorize a number of cleavages that seem to have been historically important in European political development than to evaluate their importance for political stability or effective decision-making.

In early days David Hume considered 'factions from interest' and 'factions from affection' as the most normal cases, proclaiming, unlike Burke, the rise of a new category of 'factions from principle': 'the most extraordinary and unaccountable phenomenon that has yet appeared in human affairs.'[4]

---

[4] See David Hume, *Political Essays*, ed. Charles W. Hendel (New York: Bobbs-Merrill, 1953), 80–1.

Generally speaking, the most important dividing lines in Europe have tended to be: class or sectional interest (the landed versus the moneyed interests; parties representative of sections of industry or commerce, labour, or agriculture); religion (Modernists versus Fundamentalists, Catholics versus Protestants, Clericals versus Anticlericals, Anglicans versus Nonconformists); geographic conflict (town versus country, centre versus periphery); nationality or nationalism (ethnic minority parties, extreme-nationalist movements, and parties having their real allegiance to another national state, etc.); and regime (status quo parties versus reform parties, revolutionary, or counter-revolutionary parties).

The difficulty of qualitative analysis of the importance of cleavage structures comes out in the exaggerated attention paid to quasi-mechanical factors, such as the number of cleavages, or whether they run parallel to or cut across one another. Both English and American literature seem to be based often on the a priori notion that the political universe is by nature dualistic, so that two-party systems are the self-evident political norm. This view is reinforced by Duverger's analysis, which attempts to reduce the explanation also of multiparty systems to a 'superposition of dualisms',[5] to the non-coincidence of dividing lines in the body politic. While 'bargaining parties' in a dualist system are likely to ensure both stability and the orderly solution of successive issues, so the standard argument goes, a multiparty system leads perforce to fragmentation and *immobilisme*.

This view is based on a slender empirical basis. Britain and the United States have two parties, their politics are apparently satisfactory to the theorist, *ergo* a two-party system is good. In contrast, France, Weimar Germany, and Italy had many parties, their politics were unsatisfactory, hence a multiparty system is a lesser if not an outright degenerated form. This type of reasoning then leads to the curious term of 'working multiparty systems'[6]—phenomena that are apparently somewhat akin to 'the boneless wonder' of Barnum's Circus. Such a view

---

[5] M. Duverger, *Political Parties* (London: Methuen, 1954), 229 ff.

[6] Cf. Gabriel A. Almond, in *The Politics of the Developing Areas* (Princeton: Princeton University Press, 1960).

testifies to an insufficient awareness of the political experience of a host of smaller European countries (such as Belgium, the Netherlands, Denmark, or Switzerland) that have successfully governed themselves for generations under complex multi-party systems. Would it not be possible on the basis of the politics of these countries as confidently (but equally subjectively) to assert that the best political system is one in which all important social groupings have occasion to have themselves politically represented in separate parties, which can then use the forum of parliament and coalition government to reach the politics of compromise?

The confusion is clearly revealed by our tendency to hold two conflicting theories with equal conviction. On the one hand, we argue that politics is best served by a constant dualistic regrouping of political forces in distinct majority–minority positions. On the other hand, we hold with equal conviction that a political system can quickly be brought to the breaking-point if a number of cleavages come to run parallel to one another—for instance, if conflicts about religion, nationality, and class each make for the same division of society. Whereas we point at one time to the crisscrossing of cleavage lines as the main source of political inefficiency, we assert at another moment that only adequate cross-pressures, which offset tendencies towards increased polarization, can make for a working political community. It is to this variable that we look to explain why Flemish and Walloons, why Capital and Labour, why Clericals and Anticlericals can continue to co-operate in feasible political systems. I suggest that this paradox cannot be explained unless new variables are also taken into account.

Of crucial importance are not only the severity and incidence of conflicts but also the attitudes political élites take towards the need to solve them by compromise rather than combat. Such attitudes are deeply rooted in political culture, itself the product of complex historical factors that differ greatly from one country to another. Traditional leadership styles, the traumatic memory of past conflicts (which may either perpetuate conflict, or cause parties to draw together), a realistic sense of what can be reached through political action and what not, the presence of substantial or imaginary common interests, the extent to which party leaders are more tolerant than their followers and

are yet able to carry them along—all are important. Unfortunately they are evasive of systematic analysis except in a
specific context.

9

CLEAVAGE STRUCTURES, PARTY SYSTEMS, AND VOTER ALIGNMENTS

SEYMOUR MARTIN LIPSET AND STEIN ROKKAN

Whatever the structure of the polity, parties have served as essential agencies of mobilization and as such have helped to integrate local communities into the nation or the broader federation. This was true of the earliest competitive party systems, and it is eminently true of the single-party nations of the post-colonial era. In his insightful analysis of the formation of the American party system, William Chambers has assembled a wide range of indications of the integrative role of the first national parties, the Federalists and the Democratic-Republicans: they were the first genuinely national organizations; they represented the first successful efforts to pull Americans out of their local community and their state and to give them roles in the national polity.[1] Analyses of parties in the new nations of the twentieth century arrive at similar conclusions. Ruth Schachter has shown how the African single-party organizations have been used by the political leaders to 'awaken a wider national sense of community' and to create ties of communication and co-operation across territorial and ethnic populations.[2]

In competitive party systems this process of integration can be analysed at two levels: on the one hand, each party establishes a network of cross-local communication channels and in

Seymour Martin Lipset and Stein Rokkan, abridged with permission of The Free Press, a Division of Macmillan, Inc., from pp. 1–64, *Party Systems and Voter Alignments: Cross-National Perspectives* edited by Seymour Martin Lipset and Stein Rokkan. Copyright © 1967 by The Free Press.

[1] W. Chambers, *Parties in a New Nation* (New York: Oxford University Press, 1963), 80.
[2] R. Schachter, 'Single-Party Systems in West Africa', *American Political Science Review*, 55 (1961), 301.

that way helps to strengthen national identities; on the other, its very competitiveness helps to set the national system of government *above* any particular set of office-holders. This cuts both ways: the citizens are encouraged to distinguish between their loyalty to the total political system and their attitudes to the sets of competing politicians, and the contenders for power will, at least if they have some chance of gaining office, have some interest in maintaining this attachment of all citizens to the polity and its rules of alternation. In a monolithic polity citizens are not encouraged to distinguish between the system and current office-holders. The citizenry tends to identify the polity with the policies of particular leaders, and the power-holders habitually exploit the established national loyalties to rally support for themselves. In such societies any attack on the political leaders or on the dominant party tends to turn into an attack on the political system itself. Quarrels over particular policies or particular incumbencies immediately raise fundamental issues of system survival. In a competitive party system opponents of the current governing team may well be accused of weakening the state or betraying the traditions of the nation, but the continued existence of the political system is not in jeopardy. A competitive party system protects the nation against the discontents of its citizens: grievances and attacks are deflected from the overall system and directed towards the current set of power-holders.[3]

Sociologists such as E. A. Ross and Georg Simmel[4] have analysed the integrative role of institutionalized conflicts within political systems. The establishment of regular channels for the expression of conflicting interests has helped to stabilize the structure of a great number of nation-states. The effective equalization of the status of different denominations has helped to take much of the brunt off the earlier conflicts over religious issues. The extension of the suffrage and the enforcement of the

---

[3] For a general analysis of this process, see S. M. Lipset *et al.*, *Union Democracy* (New York: Free Press, 1956), 268–9.

[4] E. A. Ross, *The Principles of Sociology* (New York: Century, 1920), 164–5; G. Simmel, *Soziologie* (Berlin: Duncker & Humblot, 1923 and 1958), ch. 4. See the translation in *Conflict and the Web of Group Affiliates* (New York: Free Press, 1964).

freedom of political expression also helped to strengthen the legitimacy of the nation-state. The opening up of channels for the expression of manifest or latent conflicts between the established and the underprivileged classes may have brought many systems out of equilibrium in the earlier phase but tended to strengthen the body politic over time.

This conflict-integration dialectic is of central concern in current research on the comparative sociology of political parties. In this [essay] the emphasis will be on *conflicts and their translation into party systems*. This does not mean that we shall neglect the integrative functions of parties. We have simply chosen to start out from the latent or manifest strains and cleavages and will deal with trends towards compromise and reconciliation against the background of the initial conflicts. Our concern in this introductory discussion is with parties as *alliances in conflicts over policies and value commitments within the larger body politic*. For the sociologist, parties exert a double fascination. They help to crystallize and make explicit the conflicting interests, the latent strains and contrasts in the existing social structure, and they force subjects and citizens to ally themselves across structural cleavage lines and to set up priorities among their commitments to established or prospective roles in the system. Parties have an *expressive* function; they develop a rhetoric for the translation of contrasts in the social and the cultural structure into demands and pressures for action or inaction. But they also have *instrumental* and *representative* functions: they force the spokesmen for the many contrasting interests and outlooks to strike bargains, to stagger demands, and to aggregate pressures. Small parties may content themselves with expressive functions, but no party can hope to gain decisive influence on the affairs of a community without some willingness to cut across existing cleavages to establish common fronts with potential enemies and opponents. This was true at the early stage of embryonic party formations around cliques and clubs of *notables* and legislators, but the need for such broad alliances became even more pronounced with the extension of the rights of participation to new strata of the citizenry.

Most of the parties aspiring to majority positions in the West are conglomerates of groups differing on wide ranges of issues, but still united in their greater hostility to their competitors in the other camps. Conflicts and controversies can arise out of a great variety of relationships in the social structure, but only a few of these tend to polarize the politics of any given system. There is a *hierarchy of cleavage bases* in each system and these orders of political primacy not only vary among polities, but also tend to undergo changes over time. Such differences and changes in the political weight of sociocultural cleavages set fundamental problems for comparative research: When is region, language, or ethnicity most likely to prove polarizing? When will class take the primacy and when will denominational commitments and religious identities prove equally important cleavage bases? Which sets of circumstances are most likely to favour accommodations of such oppositions *within* parties and in which circumstances are they more apt to constitute issues *between* the parties? Which types of alliances tend to maximize the strain on the polity and which ones help to integrate it? Questions such as these will be on the agenda of comparative political sociology for years to come. There is no dearth of hypotheses, but so far very little in the way of systematic analysis across several systems. It has often been suggested that systems will come under much heavier strain if the main lines of cleavage are over morals and the nature of human destiny than if they concern such mundane and negotiable matters as the prices of commodities, the rights of debtors and creditors, wages and profits, and the ownership of property. However, this does not take us very far; what we want to know is when the one type of cleavage will prove more salient than the other, what kind of alliances they have produced and what consequences these constellations of forces have had for consensus-building within the nation-state. We do not pretend to find clear-cut answers, but we have tried to move the analysis one step further. We shall start out with a review of a variety of *logically possible* sources of strains and oppositions in social structures and shall then proceed to an inventory of the *empirically extant examples of political expressions of each set of conflicts*. We have not tried to present a comprehensive scheme of analysis in this context but would like to point to one possible line of approach.

Dimensions of Cleavage: A Possible Model

Our suggestion is that the crucial cleavages and their political expressions can be ordered within the two-dimensional space [shown in Fig. 9.1].

In this model the *l–g* line represents a *territorial* dimension of the national cleavage structure and the *a–i* line a *functional* dimension.

At the *l* end of the territorial axis we would find strictly local oppositions to encroachments of the aspiring or the dominant national élites and their bureaucracies: the typical reactions of peripheral regions, linguistic minorities, and culturally threatened populations to the pressures of the centralizing, standardizing, and 'rationalizing' machinery of the nation-state. At the *g* end of the axis we would find conflicts not between territorial units *within* the system but over the control, the organization, the goals, and the policy options of the system *as a whole*. These might be nothing more than direct struggles among competing élites for central power, but they might also reflect deeper differences in conceptions of nationhood, over domestic priorities and over external strategies.

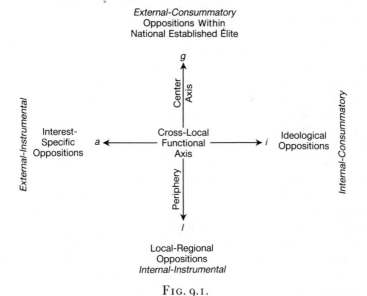

FIG. 9.1.

Conflicts along the *a–i* axis *cut across* the territorial units of the nation. They produce alliances of similarly situated or similarly oriented subjects and households over wide ranges of localities and tend to undermine the inherited solidarity of the established territorial communities. At the *a* end of this dimension we would find the typical conflict over short-term or long-term allocations of resources, products, and benefits in the economy: conflicts between producers and buyers, between workers and employers, between borrowers and lenders, between tenants and owners, between contributors and beneficiaries. At this end the alignments are specific and the conflicts tend to be solved through rational bargaining and the establishment of universalistic rules of allocation. The farther we move toward the *i* end of the axis, the more diffuse the criteria of alignment, the more intensive the identification with the 'we' group, and the more uncompromising the rejection of the 'they' group. At the *i* end of the dimension we find the typical 'friend–foe' oppositions of tight-knit religious or ideological movements to the surrounding community. The conflict is no longer over specific gains or losses but over conceptions of moral right and over the interpretation of history and human destiny; membership is no longer a matter of multiple affiliation in many directions, but a diffuse '24-hour' commitment incompatible with other ties within the community; and communication is no longer kept flowing freely over the cleavage lines but restricted and regulated to protect the movement against impurities and the seeds of compromise.

Historically documented cleavages rarely fall at the poles of the two axes: a concrete conflict is rarely exclusively territorial or exclusively functional but will feed on strains in both directions. The model essentially serves as a *grid* in the comparative analysis of political systems: the task is to locate the alliances behind given parties at given times within this two-dimensional space. The axes are not easily quantifiable, and they may not satisfy any criteria of strict scalability; nevertheless, they seem heuristically useful in attempts such as ours at linking up empirical variations in political structures with current conceptualizations in sociological theory.

A few concrete illustrations of party developments may help to clarify the distinctions in our model.

In Britain, the first nation-state to recognize the legitimacy of party oppositions, the initial conflicts were essentially of the types we have located at the *l* end of the vertical axis. The heads of independent landed families in the counties opposed the powers and the decisions of the government and the adminis-tration in London. The opposition between the 'Country party' of knights and squires and the 'Court and Treasury party' of the Whig magnates and the 'placemen' was primarily territorial. The animosities of the Tories were not necessarily directed against the predominance of London in the affairs of the nation, but they were certainly aroused by the high-handed manipu-lations of the influential office-holders in the administration and their powerful allies in the boroughs. The conflict was not over general policies but over patronage and places. The gentry did not get their share of the *quid pro quo* exchanges of local influence against governmental offices and never established a clear-cut common front against the central power-holders. 'Toryism about 1750 was primarily the opposition of the local rulers to central authority and vanished wherever members of that class entered the orbit of Government.'[5]

Such particularistic, kin-centred, 'ins–outs' oppositions are common in the early phases of nation-building: the electoral clienteles are small, undifferentiated, and easily controlled, and the stakes to be gained or lost in public life tend to be personal and concrete rather than collective and general.

Purely territorial oppositions rarely survive extensions of the suffrage. Much will depend, of course, on the timing of the crucial steps in the building of the nation: territorial unifi-cation, the establishment of legitimate government and the monopolization of the agencies of violence, the take-off towards industrialization and economic growth, the development of popular education, and the entry of the lower classes into organized politics. Early democratization will not necessarily generate clear-cut divisions on functional lines. The initial result of a widening of the suffrage will often be an accentuation of the contrasts between the countryside and the urban centres and between the orthodox-fundamentalist beliefs of the

[5] Lewis Namier, *England in the Age of the American Revolution* (London: Macmillan, 1930), quoted from the 2nd edn. (1961), 183.

peasantry and the small-town citizens and the secularism fostered in the larger cities and the metropolis. In the United States, the cleavages were typically cultural and religious. The struggles between the Jeffersonians and the Federalists, the Jacksonians and the Whigs, the Democrats and the Republicans centred on contrasting conceptions of public morality and pitted Puritans and other Protestants against Deists, Freemasons, and immigrant Catholics and Jews. The accelerating influx of lower-class immigrants into the metropolitan areas and the centres of industry accentuated the contrasts between the rural and the urban cultural environments and between the backward and the advanced states of the Union. Such cumulations of territorial and cultural cleavages in the early phases of democratization can be documented for country after country. In Norway, all freehold and most leasehold peasants were given the vote as early as in 1814, but took several decades to mobilize in opposition to the King's officials and the dominance of the cities in the national economy. The crucial cleavages brought out into the open in the seventies were essentially territorial and cultural: the provinces were pitted against the capital; the increasingly estate-conscious peasants defended their traditions and their culture against the standards forced on them by the bureaucracy and the urban bourgeoisie. Interestingly, the extension of the suffrage to the landless labourers in the countryside and the propertyless workers in the cities did not bring about an immediate polarization of the polity on class lines. Issues of language, religion, and morality kept up the territorial oppositions in the system and cut across issues between the poorer and the better-off strata of the population. There were significant variations, however, between localities and between religions: the initial 'politics of cultural defence' survived the extension of the suffrage in the egalitarian communities of the South and the West, but lost to straight class politics in the economically backward, hierarchically organized communities of the North. The developments in the South and West of Norway find interesting parallels in the 'Celtic fringe' of Britain. In these areas, particularly in Wales, opposition to the territorial, cultural, and economic dominance of the English offered a basis for communitywide support for the Liberals and retarded the development of straight class

politics, even in the coalfields. The sudden upsure of Socialist strength in the northern periphery of Norway parallels
the spectacular victory of the Finnish working-class party at the
first election under universal suffrage: the fishermen and the
crofters of the Norwegian North backed a distinct lower-class
party as soon as they got the vote, and so did the Finnish rural
proletariat. In terms of our abstract model the politics of the
western peripheries of Norway and Britain has its focus at the
lower end of the l–g axis, whereas the politics of the backward
districts of Finland and the Norwegian North represent alliance
formations closer to g and at varying points of the a–i axis. In the
one case the decisive criterion of alignment is *commitment to the
locality and its dominant culture*: you vote with your community
and its leaders irrespective of your economic position. In the
other the criterion is *commitment to a class and its collective interests*:
you vote with others in the same position as yourself whatever
their localities, and you are willing to do so even if this brings
you into opposition with members of your community. We
rarely find one criterion of alignment completely dominant.
There will be deviants from straight territorial voting just as
often as from straight class voting. But we often find marked
differences between regions in the *weight* of the one or the other
criterion of alignment. Here ecological analyses of electoral
records and census data for the early phases of mobilization
may help us to map such variations in greater detail and to
pinpoint factors strengthening the dominance of territorial politics and factors accelerating the process of class polarization.

The Two Revolutions: The National and the Industrial

Territorial oppositions set limits to the process of nation-
building; pushed to their extreme they lead to war, secession,
possibly even population transfers. Functional oppositions can
only develop after some initial consolidation of the national
territory. They emerge with increasing interaction and communication across the localities and the regions, and they
spread through a process of 'social mobilization'.[6] The growing

---

[6] For a definition of this concept and a specification of possible indicators,
see Karl Deutsch, 'Social Mobilization and Political Development', *American
Political Science Review*, 55 (1961), 493–514.

nation-state developed a wide range of agencies of unification and standardization and gradually penetrated the bastions of 'primordial' local culture. So did the organizations of the Church, sometimes in close co-operation with the secular administrators, often in opposition to and competition with the officers of the state. And so did the many autonomous agencies of economic development and growth, the networks of traders and merchants, of bankers and financiers, of artisans and industrial entrepreneurs.

The early growth of the national bureaucracy tended to produce essentially territorial oppositions, but the subsequent widening of the scope of governmental activities and the acceleration of cross-local interactions gradually made for much more complex systems of alignments, some of them *between* localities, and others *across* and *within* localities.

The early waves of countermobilization often threatened the territorial unity of the nation, the federation, or the empire. The mobilization of the peasantry in Norway and in Sweden made it gradually impossible to keep up the union; the mobilization of the subject peoples of the Habsburg territories broke up the empire; the mobilization of the Irish Catholics led to civil war and secession. The current strains of nation-building in the new states of Africa and Asia reflect similar conflicts between dominant and subject cultures; the recent histories of the Congo, India, Indonesia, Malaysia, Nigeria, and the Sudan can all be written in such terms. In some cases the early waves of mobilization may not have brought the territorial system to the brink of disruption but left an intractable heritage of territorial-cultural conflict: the Catalan–Basque–Castilian oppositions in Spain, the conflict between Flemings and Walloons in Belgium, and the English–French cleavages in Canada. The conditions for the softening or hardening of such cleavage lines in fully mobilized polities have been poorly studied. The multiple ethnic-religious cleavages of Switzerland and the language conflicts in Finland and Norway have proved much more manageable than the recently aggravated conflict between *Nederlands*-speakers and *francophones* in Belgium and between Quebec and the English-speaking provinces of Canada.

To account for such variations we clearly cannot proceed

cleavage by cleavage but must analyse *constellations* of conflict lines within each polity.

To account for the variations in such constellations we have found it illuminating to distinguish *four critical lines of cleavage* [see Fig. 9.2]. Two of these cleavages are direct products of what we might call the *National* Revolution: the conflict between *the central nation-building culture* and the increasing resistance of the ethnically, linguistically, or religiously distinct *subject populations* in the provinces and the peripheries (1 in Fig. 9.2): the conflict between the centralizing, standardizing, and mobilizing *Nation-State* and the historically established corporate privileges of the *Church* (2).

Two of them are products of the *Industrial* Revolution: the conflict between the *landed interests* and the rising class of *industrial entrepreneurs* (3): the conflict between *owners and employers* on the one side and *tenants, labourers, and workers* on the other (4).

Much of the history of Europe since the beginning of the nineteenth century can be described in terms of the interaction between these two processes of revolutionary change: the one triggered in France and the other originating in Britain. Both had consequences for the cleavage structure of each nation, but

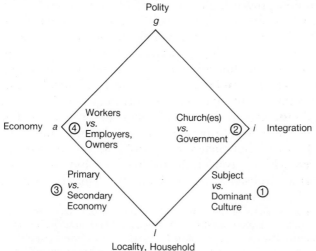

FIG. 9.2. Suggested Locations of Four Critical Cleavages in the *a–g–i–l* Paradigm

the French Revolution produced the deepest and the bitterest oppositions. The decisive battle came to stand between *the aspirations of the mobilizing nation-state and the corporate claims of the churches*. This was far more than a matter of economics. It is true that the status of church properties and the financing of religious activities were the subjects of violent controversy, but the fundamental issue was one of morals, of the control of community norms. This found reflection in fights over such matters as the solemnization of marriage and the granting of divorces, the organization of charities and the handling of deviants, the functions of medical versus religious officers, and the arrangements for funerals. However, the fundamental issue between Church and State focused on the *control of education*.

The Church, whether Roman Catholic, Lutheran, or Reformed, had for centuries claimed the right to represent man's 'spiritual estate' and to control the education of children in the right faith. In the Lutheran countries, steps were taken as early as in the seventeenth century to enforce elementary education in the vernacular for all children. The established national churches simply became agents of the state and had no reason to oppose such measures. In the religiously mixed countries and in purely Catholic ones, however, the ideas of the French Revolution proved highly divisive. The development of compulsory education under centralized secular control for all children of the nation came into direct conflict with the established rights of the religious *pouvoirs intermédiaires* and triggered waves of mass mobilization into nationwide parties of protest. To the radicals and liberals inspired by the French Revolution, the introduction of compulsory education was only one among several measures in a systematic effort to create direct links of influence and control between the nation-state and the individual citizen, but their attempt to penetrate directly to the children without consulting the parents and their spiritual authorities aroused widespread opposition and bitter fights.[7]

[7] For an analysis of the steps in the extension of citizenship rights and duties to all accountable adults, see S. Rokkan, 'Mass Suffrage, Secret Voting and Political Participation', *Archives Européennes de Sociologie*, 2 (1961), 132–52, and the chapter by R. Bendix and S. Rokkan, 'The Extension of Citizenship to the Lower Classes', in R. Bendix, *Nation-Building and Citizenship* (New York: Wiley, 1964).

The parties of religious defence generated through this process grew into broad mass movements after the introduction of manhood suffrage and were able to claim the loyalties of remarkably high proportions of the church-goers in the working class. These proportions increased even more, of course, as the franchise was extended to women on a par with men. Through a process very similar to the one to be described for the Socialist parties, these church movements tended to isolate their supporters from outside influence through the development of a wide variety of parallel organizations and agencies: they not only built up schools and youth movements of their own, but also developed confessionally distinct trade unions, sports clubs, leisure associations, publishing houses, magazines, newspapers, in one or two cases even radio and television stations.

Perhaps the best example of institutionalized segmentation is found in the Netherlands; in fact, the Dutch word *Verzuiling* has recently become a standard term for tendencies to develop vertical networks (*zuilen*, columns or pillars) of associations and institutions to ensure maximum loyalty to each church and to protect the supporters from cross-cutting communications and pressures. Dutch society has for close to a century been divided into three distinct subcultures: the national-liberal-secular, frequently referred to as the *algemene*, the 'general' sector; the orthodox Protestant column; and the Roman Catholic column.

The symmetric representation of the four basic cleavage lines in Fig. 9.2 refers to *average tendencies* only and does not exclude wide variations in location along the *a–i* axis. Conflicts over the civic integration of recalcitrant regional cultures (1) or religious organizations (2) need not always lead to *Verzuiling*. An analysis of the contrasts between Switzerland and the Netherlands would tell us a great deal about differences in the conditions for the development of pluralist insulation. Conflicts between primary producers and the urban-industrial interests have *normally* tended towards the *a* pole of the axis, but there are many examples of highly ideologized peasant oppositions to officials and burghers. Conflicts between workers and employers have always contained elements of economic bargaining, but there have also often been strong elements of cultural opposition and ideological insulation. Working-class parties in opposition and without power have tended to be more *verzuild*, more wrapped up in their own distinct mythology, more insulated against the rest of the society. By contrast the victorious Labour parties have tended to become *ontzuild*, domesticated, more open to influence from all segments within the national society.

Similar variations will occur at a wide range of points on the *territorial* axis of our schema. In our initial discussion of the *l* pole we gave examples of *cultural* and *religious* resistances to the domination of the central national élite, but such oppositions are not always *purely* territorial. The movements may be completely dominant in their provincial strongholds but may also find allies in the central areas and thus contribute to the development of *cross-local* and *cross-regional* fronts.

The opposition of the Old Left in Norway was essentially of this character. It was from the outset a movement of territorial protest against the dominance of the central élite of officials and patricians but gradually broadened into a mass movement of cultural opposition to the dominant urban strata. As the suffrage was extended and the mobilization efforts proceeded it was also able to entrench itself in the central cities and even gain control in some of them. This very broadening of the movement made the Old Left increasingly vulnerable to fragmentation. One wing moved toward the *a* pole and set itself up as an *Agrarian* party (3 in Fig. 9.2); another wing moved toward the *i* pole and after a long history of strains within the mother party established itself as the *Christian People's party* (1 in Fig. 9.2). The Scandinavian countries have seen the formation of several such moralist-evangelist parties opposed to the tolerant pragmatism of the Established Lutheran Church. They differ from the Christian parties on the Continent: they have not opposed national education as such and have not built up extensive networks of functional organizations around their followers; they have been primarily concerned to defend the traditions of orthodox evangelism against the onslaught of urban secularism and to use the legislative and the executive machinery of the state to protect the young against the evils of modern life. In their rejection of the lukewarm latitudinarianism of the national Mother Church they resemble the Nonconformists in Great Britain and the Anti-Revolutionaries in the Netherlands, but the contexts of their efforts have been very different. In the British case the religious activists could work *within* the Liberal party (later, of course, also within Labour) and found it possible to advance their views without establishing a party of their own. In the Dutch case, the orthodox dissidents not only set up their own party but built up a strong column of vertical organizations around it.

The National Revolution forced ever-widening circles of the territorial population to chose sides in conflicts over *values* and *cultural identities*. The Industrial Revolution also triggered a variety of cultural countermovements, but in the longer run tended to cut across the value communities within the nation and to force the enfranchised citizenry to choose sides in terms of their *economic interests*, their shares in the increased wealth generated through the spread of the new technologies and the widening markets.

In our *a–g–i–l* paradigm we have distinguished two types of such interest cleavages: cleavages between rural and urban interests (3) and cleavages between worker and employer interests (4).

The spectacular growth of world trade and industrial production generated increasing strains between the primary producers in the countryside and the merchants and the entrepreneurs in the towns and the cities. On the Continent, the conflicting interests of the rural and the urban areas had been recognized since the Middle Ages in the separate representation of the estates: the nobility and, in exceptional cases, the freehold peasants spoke for the land, and the burghers spoke for the cities. The Industrial Revolution deepened these conflicts and in country after country produced distinct rural-urban alignments in the national legislatures. Often the old divisions between estates were simply carried over into the unified parliaments and found expression in oppositions between Conservative-Agrarian and Liberal-Radical parties. The conflicts between rural and urban interests had been much less marked in Great Britain than on the Continent. The House of Commons was not an assembly of the burgher estate but a body of legislators representing the constituent localities of the realm, the counties and the boroughs. Yet even there the Industrial Revolution produced deep and bitter cleavages between the landed interests and the urban; in England, if not in Wales and Scotland, the opposition between Conservatives and Liberals fed largely on these strains until the 1880s.

There was a hard core of economic conflict in these oppositions, but what made them so deep and bitter was the struggle for the maintenance of acquired status and the recognition of achievement. In England, the landed élite ruled the country, and the rising class of industrial entrepreneurs, many of them religiously at odds with the Established Church, for decades aligned themselves in opposition both to defend their economic interests and to assert their claims to status. It would be a misunderstanding, says the historian George Kitson Clark,[8] to think of agriculture 'as an industry organized like any other industry—primarily for the purposes of efficient production. *It was . . . rather organized to ensure the survival intact of a caste.* The proprietors of the great estates were not just very rich men whose capital happened to be invested in land, they were rather the life tenants of very considerable positions which it was their duty to leave intact to their successors. In a way it was the estate that mattered and not the holder of the estate. . . .' The conflict between Conservatives and Liberals reflected an opposition between two value orientations: the recognition of status through *ascription and kin connections* versus the claims for status through *achievement and enterprise*.

These are typical strains in all transitional societies; they tend to be most intensive in the early phases of industrialization and to soften as the rising élite establishes itself in the community. In England, this process of reconciliation proceeded quite rapidly. In a society open to extensive mobility and intermarriage, urban and industrial wealth could gradually be translated into full recognition within the traditional hierarchy of the landed families. More and more mergers took place between the agricultural and the business interests, and this consolidation of the national élite soon changed the character of the Conservative–Liberal conflict. As James Cornford has shown through his detailed ecological studies, the movement of the business owners into the countryside and the suburbs

---

[8] G. K. Clark, *The Making of Victorian England* (London: Methuen, 1962), 218 (our italics).

divorced them from their workers and brought them into close relations with the landed gentry. The result was a softening of the rural–urban conflict in the system and a rapidly increasing class polarization of the widened electorate.[9]

A similar *rapprochement* took place between the east Elbian agricultural interests and the western business bourgeoisie in Germany, but there, significantly, the bulk of the Liberals sided with the Conservatives and did not try to rally the working-class electorate on their side in the way the British party did during the period up to World War I. The result was a deepening of the chasm between burghers and workers and a variety of desperate attempts to bridge it through appeals to national and military values.

In other countries of the European continent the rural–urban cleavage continued to assert itself in national politics far into the twentieth century, but the political expressions of the cleavage varied widely. Much depended on the concentrations of wealth and political control in the cities and on the ownership structure in the rural economy. In the Low Countries, France, Italy, and Spain, rural–urban cleavages rarely found direct expression in the development of party oppositions. Other cleavages, particularly between the state and the churches and between owners and tenants, had greater impact on the alignments of the electorates. By contrast, in the five Nordic countries the cities had traditionally dominated national political life, and the struggle for democracy and parliamentary rule was triggered off through a broad process of mobilization within the peasantry. This was essentially an expression of protest against the central élite of officials and patricians (a cleavage on the *l–g* axis in our model), but there were also elements of economic opposition in the movement: the peasants felt exploited in their dealings with city folk and wanted to shift the tax burdens to the expanding urban economies. These economic cleavages became more and more pronounced as the primary-producing communities entered into the national money and market economy. The result was the formation of a broad front of interest organizations and co-operatives and the

[9] J. Cornford, 'The Transformation of Conservatism in the Late 19th Century', *Victorian Studies*, 7 (1963), 35–66.

development of distinctive Agrarian parties. Even after the rise of the working-class parties to national dominance, these Agrarian parties did not find it possible to establish common fronts with the Conservative defenders of the business community. The cultural contrasts between the countryside and the cities were still strong, and the strict market controls favoured by the Agrarians could not easily be reconciled with the philosophy of free competition espoused by many Conservatives.

The conflict between landed and urban interests was centred in the *commodity* market. The peasants wanted to sell their wares at the best possible prices and to buy what they needed from the industrial and urban producers at low cost. Such conflicts did not invariably prove party-forming. They could be dealt with within broad party fronts or could be channelled through interest organizations into narrower arenas of functional representation and bargaining. Distinctly agrarian parties have only emerged where strong cultural oppositions have deepened and embittered the strictly economic conflicts.

Conflicts in the *labour* market proved much more uniformly divisive. Working-class parties emerged in every country of Europe in the wake of the early waves of industrialization. The rising masses of wage-earners, whether in large-scale farming, in forestry, or in industry, resented their conditions of work and the insecurity of their contracts, and many of them felt socially and culturally alienated from the owners and the employers. The result was the formation of a variety of labour unions and the development of nationwide Socialist parties. The success of such movements depended on a variety of factors: the strength of the paternalist traditions of ascriptive recognition of the worker status, the size of the work unit and the local ties of the workers, the level of prosperity and the stability of employment in the given industry, and the chances of improvements and promotion through loyal devotion or through education and achievement.

A crucial factor in the development of distinct working-class movements was the *openness* of the given society: Was the worker status a lifetime predicament or were there openings for advancement? How easy was it to get an education qualifying for a change in status? What prospects were there for striking out on one's own, for establishing independent work units? The contrasts between American and European developments must clearly be analysed in these terms; the American workers were not only given the vote much earlier than their comrades in Europe; but they also found their way into the national system so much more easily because of the greater stress on equality and achievement, because of the many openings to better education, and, last but not least, because the established workers could advance to better positions as new waves of immigrants took over the lower-status jobs. A similar process is currently under way in the advanced countries of Western Europe. The immigrant proletariats from the Mediterranean countries and from the West Indies allow the children of the established national working class to move into the middle class, and these new waves of mobility tend to drain off traditional sources of resentment.

In nineteenth- and early twentieth-century Europe the status barriers were markedly higher. The traditions from the estate-divided society kept the workers in their place, and the narrowness of the educational channels of mobility also made it difficult for sons and daughters to rise above their fathers. There were, however, important variations among the countries of Europe in the attitudes of the established and the rising élites to the claims of the workers, and these differences clearly affected the development of the unions and the Socialist parties. In Britain and the Scandinavian countries the attitudes of the élites tended to be open and pragmatic. As in all other countries there was active resistance to the claims of the workers, but little or no direct repression. These are today the countries with the largest and the most domesticated Labour parties in Europe. In Germany and Austria, France, Italy, and Spain the cleavages went much deeper. A number of attempts were made to repress the unions and the Socialists, and the working-class organizations consequently tended to isolate themselves from the national culture and to develop *soziale Ghettoparteien*,[10]

---

[10] This is the phrase used by Ernest Fraenkel, 'Parlament und oeffentliche Meinung', in *Zur Geschichte und Problematik der Demokratie: Festgabe fuer H. Herzfeld* (Berlin: Duncker & Humblot, 1958), 178. For further details on German developments see the recent study by Guenther Roth, *The Social Democrats in Imperial Germany* (Totowa: Bedminster Press, 1963), chs. 7–10.

strongly ideological movements seeking to isolate their members and their supporters from influences from the encom-
passing social environments. In terms of our paradigm, these
parties were just as close to the *i* pole as their opponents in the
religious camp. This 'anti-system' orientation of large sections
of the European working class was brought to a climax in the
aftermath of the Russian Revolution. The Communist movement did not just speak for an alienated stratum of the territorial community but came to be seen as an external conspiracy
against the nation. These developments brought a number of
European countries to the point of civil war in the twenties and
the thirties. The greater the numbers of citizens caught in such
direct 'friend–foe' oppositions to each other the greater the
danger of total disruption of the body politic.

Developments since World War II have pointed towards a
reduction of such pitched oppositions and some softening of
ideological tensions: a movement from the *i* toward the *a* pole in
our paradigm.[11] A variety of factors contributed to this development: the experience of national co-operation during the
war, the improvements in the standard of living in the fifties,
the rapid growth of a 'new middle class' bridging the gaps
between the traditional working class and the bourgeoisie. But
the most important factor was possibly the *entrenchment of the
working-class parties in local and national governmental structures* and
their consequent 'domestication' within the established system. The developments in Austria offer a particularly revealing
example. The extreme opposition between Socialists and
Catholics had ended in civil war in 1934, but after the experience of National Socialist domination, war, and occupation, the
two parties settled down to share government responsibilities
under a *Proporz* system, a settlement still based on mutual
distrust between the two camps but at least one that recognized
the necessity for coexistence. Comparisons of the positions
taken by the two leading Communist parties in Western Europe,

---

[11] One of the first political analysts to call attention to these developments
was Herbert Tingsten, then editor-in-chief of the leading Swedish newspaper
Dagens Nyheter. See his autobiography, *Mitt Liv: Tidningen* (Stockholm: Nor-
stedts, 1963). For further details see S. M. Lipset, 'The Changing Class
Structure and Contemporary European Politics', *Daedalus*, 93 (1964), 271–
303.

the Italian and the French, also point to the importance of entrenchments in the national system of government. The French party has been much less involved in the running of local communities and has remained much more isolated within the national system, while the Italian party has responded much more dynamically to the exigencies of community decision-making. Erick Allardt has implicitly demonstrated the importance of similar factors in a comparison of levels of class polarization in the Nordic countries. He points out that while the percentage of working-class voters siding with the Left (Communists and Social Democrats) is roughly the same in Finland as in Norway and Sweden, the percentage of middle-class leftists used to be much lower in Finland than in the two other countries. This difference appears to be related to a contrast in the chances of upward mobility from the working class: very low in Finland, markedly higher in the other countries.[12] The continued isolation of the Finnish working-class parties may reflect a lower level of participation in responsible decision-making in the local communities and in the nation. This has not yet been investigated in detail, but studies of working-class mobility and political changes carried out in Norway suggest that the principal channels of advancement were in the public sector and that the decisive wave of 'bourgeoisification' came in the wake of the accession of the Labour party to a position of dominance in the system. In Finland the protracted period of underground Communism until 1944 and the deep split in the working-class movement during the next decades tended to keep the two parties from decisive influence on the public sector and maintained the old barriers against mobility; in the other Scandinavian countries the victories of the Social Democrat Labour parties had opened up new channels of mobility and helped to break down the isolation of the working class.

[12] Erik Allardt, 'Patterns of Class Conflict and Working Class Consciousness in Finnish Politics', in E. Allardt and Y. Littunen (eds.), *Cleavages, Ideologies and Party Systems* (Helsinki: Westermarck Society, 1964), 97–131.

THE TRANSFORMATION OF CLEAVAGE STRUCTURES
INTO PARTY SYSTEMS

Conditions for the Channelling of Opposition

Thus far, we have focused on the emergence of *one cleavage at a time* and only incidentally concerned ourselves with the growth of *cleavage systems* and their translations into *constellations of political parties*. But cleavages do not translate themselves into party oppositions as a matter of course: there are considerations of organizational and electoral strategy; there is the weighing of pay-offs of alliances against losses through split-offs; and there is the successive narrowing of the 'mobilization market' through the time sequences of organizational efforts. Here we enter into an area of crucial concern in current theorizing and research, an area of great fascination crying out for detailed co-operative research. Very much needs to be done in reanalysing the evidence for each national party system and even more in exploring the possibilities of fitting such findings into a wider framework of developmental theory. We cannot hope to deal exhaustively with such possibilities of comparison in this volume and shall limit ourselves to a discussion of a few characteristic developments and suggest a rough typology.

How does a socio-cultural conflict get translated into an opposition between parties? To approach an understanding of the variations in such processes of translation we have to sift out a great deal of information about the *conditions for the expression of protest and the representation of interests* in each society.

First, we must know about the *traditions of decision-making* in the polity: the prevalence of conciliar versus autocratic procedures of central government, the rules established for the handling of grievances and protests, the measures taken to control or to protect political associations, the freedom of communication, and the organization of demonstrations.[13]

[13] In a recent review of West European developments Hans Daalder has argued this point with great force. It is impossible to understand the development, structure, and operation of party systems without a study of the extent of élite competition *before* the industrial and the democratic revolutions. He singles out Britain, the Low Countries, Switzerland, and Sweden as the countries with the strongest traditions of conciliar pluralism and points

Second, we must know about the *channels for the expression and mobilization of protest*: Was there a system of representation and if so how accessible were the representatives, who had a right to choose them, and how were they chosen? Was the conflict primarily expressed through direct demonstrations, through strikes, sabotage, or open violence, or could it be channelled through regular elections and through pressures on legitimately established representatives?

Third, we need information about *the opportunities, the pay-offs, and the costs of alliances* in the system: How ready or reluctant were the old movements to broaden their bases of support and how easy or difficult was it for new movements to gain representation on their own?

Fourth and finally, we must know about *the possibilities, the implications, and the limitations of majority rule* in the system: What alliances would be most likely to bring about majority control of the organs of representation and how much influence could such majorities in fact exert on the basic structuring of the institutions and the allocations within the system?

The Four Thresholds

These series of questions suggest a *sequence of thresholds* in the path of any movement pressing forward new sets of demands within a political system.

First, the threshold of *legitimation*: Are all protests rejected as conspiratorial, or is there some recognition of the right of petition, criticism, and opposition?

Second, the threshold of *incorporation*: Are all or most of the supporters of the movement denied status as participants in the choice of representatives or are they given political citizenship rights on a par with their opponents?

---

to the consequences of these preconditions for the development of integrated party systems. See H. Daalder, 'Parties, Elites, and Political Developments in Western Europe', in J. LaPalombara and M. Weiner (eds.), *Political Parties and Political Development* (Princeton: Princeton University Press, 1966). For a fuller discussion of the contrasts in the character of the nation-building process, see S. P. Huntington, 'Political Modernization: America vs. Europe', *World Politics*, 18 (1966), 378–414.

Third, the threshold of *representation*: Must the new move-ment join larger and older movements to ensure access to representative organs or can it gain representation on its own?

Fourth, the threshold of *majority power*: Are there built-in checks and counterforces against numerical majority rule in the system or will a victory at the polls give a party or an alliance power to bring about major structural changes in the national system?

The early comparative literature on the growth of parties and party systems focused on the consequences of the lowering of the two first thresholds: the emergence of parliamentary opposition and a free press and the extension of the franchise. Tocqueville and Ostrogorski, Weber and Michels, all in their various ways, sought to gain insight into that central institution of the modern polity, the competitive mass party.[14] The later literature, particularly since the 1920s, changed its focus to the third and the fourth threshold: the consequences of the electoral system and the structure of the decision-making arena for the formation and the functioning of party systems. The fierce debates over the pros and cons of electoral systems stimulated a great variety of efforts at comparative analysis, but the heavy emotional commitments on the one or the other side often led to questionable interpretations of the data and to overhasty generalizations from meagre evidence. Few of the writers could content themselves with comparisons of sequences of change in different countries. They wanted to influence the future course of events, and they tended to be highly optimistic about the possibilities of bringing about changes in established party systems through electoral engineering. What they tended to forget was that parties once established develop their own internal structure and build up long-term commitments among core supporters. The electoral arrangements may prevent or delay the formation of a party, but once it has been established and entrenched, it will prove difficult to change its character simply through variations in the conditions of electoral

---

[14] For a review of this literature, see S. M. Lipset, 'Introduction: Ostro-gorski and the Analytical Approach to the Comparative Study of Political Parties', in M. I. Ostrogorski, *Democracy and the Organization of Political Parties* (abridged edn.; New York: Doubleday, 1964), pp. ix–lxv.

aggregation. In fact, in most cases it makes little sense to treat electoral systems as independent variables and party systems as dependent. The party strategists will generally have decisive influence on electoral legislation and opt for the systems of aggregation most likely to consolidate their position, whether through increases in their representation, through the strengthening of the preferred alliances, or through safeguards against splinter movements. In abstract theoretical terms it may well make sense to hypothesize that simple majority systems will produce two-party oppositions within the culturally more homogeneous areas of a polity and only generate further parties through territorial cleavages, but the only convincing evidence of such a generalization comes from countries with a continuous history of simple majority aggregations from the beginnings of democratic mass politics. There is little hard evidence and much uncertainty about the effects of *later changes* in election laws on the national party system: one simple reason is that the parties already entrenched in the polity will exert a great deal of influence on the extent and the direction of any such changes and at least prove reluctant to see themselves voted out of existence.

Any attempt at systematic analysis of variations in the conditions and the strategies of party competition must start out from such differentiations of developmental phases. We cannot, in this context, proceed to detailed country-by-country comparisons but have to limit ourselves to a review of evidence for two distinct sequences of change: the rise of *lower-class* movements and parties and the decline of *régime censitaire* parties.

The Rules of the Electoral Game

The early electoral systems all set a high threshold for rising parties. It was everywhere very difficult for working-class movements to gain representation on their own, but there were significant variations in the openness of the systems to pressures from the new strata. The second ballot systems so well known from the Wilhelmine Reich and from the Third and the Fifth French Republics set the highest possible barrier, absolute majority, but at the same time made possible a variety of local alliances among the opponents of the Socialists: the system kept the new entrants underrepresented, yet did not force the old parties to merge or to ally themselves nationally. The blatant injustices of the electoral system added further to the alienation of the working classes from the national institutions and generated what Giovanni Sartori has described as systems of 'centrifugal pluralism':[15] one major movement *outside* the established political arena and several opposed parties *within* it.

Simple-majority systems of the British-American type also set high barriers against rising movements of new entrants into the political arena; however, the initial level is not standardized at 50 per cent of the votes cast in each constituency but *varies from the outset with the strategies adopted by the established parties*. If they join together in defence of their common interests, the threshold is high; if each competes on its own, it is low. In the early phases of working-class mobilization, these systems have encouraged alliances of the 'Lib-Lab' type. The new entrants into the electorate have seen their only chances of representation as lying in joint candidatures with the more reformist of the established parties. In later phases distinctly Socialist parties were able to gain representation on their own in areas of high industrial concentration and high class segregation, but this did not invariably bring about counteralliances of the older parties. In Britain, the decisive lower-class breakthrough came in the elections of 1918 and 1922. Before World War I the Labour party had presented its own candidates in a few constituencies only and had not won more than 42 out of 670 seats; in 1918 they suddenly brought forth candidates in 388 constituencies and won 63 of them and then in 1922 advanced to 411 constituencies and 142 seats. The simple-majority system did not force an immediate restructuring of the party system, however. The Liberals continued to fight on their own and did not give way to the Conservatives until the emergency election of 1931. The inveterate hostilities between the two established parties helped to keep the average threshold for the newcomers tolerably low, but the very ease of this process of

[15] G. Sartori, 'European Political Parties: The Case of Polarized Pluralism', in LaPalombara and Weiner (eds.), *Political Parties*.

incorporation produced a split within the ranks of Labour. The currency crisis forced the leaders to opt between their loyalty to the historical nation and their solidarity with the finally mobilized working class.

This brings us to a crucial point in our discussion of the translation of cleavage structure into party systems: *the costs and the pay-offs of mergers, alliances, and coalitions*. The height of the representation threshold and the rules of central decision-making may increase or decrease the net returns of joint action, but the intensity of inherited hostilities and the openness of communications across the cleavage lines will decide whether mergers or alliances are actually workable. There must be some minimum of trust among the leaders, and there must be some justification for expecting that the channels to the decision-makers will be kept open whoever wins the election. The British electoral system can only be understood against the background of the long-established traditions of territorial representation; the MP represents *all* his constituents, not just those who voted him in. But this system makes heavy demands on the loyalty of the constituents: in two-party contests up to 49 per cent of them may have to abide by the decisions of a representative they did not want; in three-cornered fights, as much as 66 per cent.

Such demands are bound to produce strains in ethnically, culturally, or religiously divided communities: the deeper the cleavages the less the likelihood of loyal acceptance of decisions by representatives of the other side. It was no accident that the earliest moves towards Proportional Representation came in the ethnically most heterogeneous of the European countries, Denmark (to accommodate Schleswig-Holstein), as early as 1855, the Swiss cantons from 1891 onward, Belgium from 1899, Moravia from 1905, and Finland from 1906.[16] The great

---

[16] The basic reference work on the history of PR in Europe is still Karl Braunias, *Das parlamentarische Wahlrecht* (Berlin: de Gruyter, 1932), Vols. 1–2. See S. Rokkan, 'Electoral Systems' [in *International Encyclopaedia of the Social Sciences* (New York: Collier and Macmillan, 1968), v. 6–21. More recent relevant titles include: Andrew McLaren Carstairs, *A Short History of Electoral Systems in Western Europe* (London: Allen & Unwin, 1980); and Giovanni Sartori, 'The Influence of Electoral Laws: Faulty Laws or Faulty Method?', in B. Grofman and A. Lijphart (eds.), *Electoral Laws and their Political Consequences* (New York: Agathon Press, 1986), 43–68, *PM*].

historian of electoral systems, Karl Braunias, distinguishes two phases in the spread of PR: the 'minority protection' phase before World War I and the 'anti-socialist' phase in the years immediately after the armistice.[17] In linguistically and religiously divided societies majority elections could clearly threaten the continued existence of the political system. The introduction of some element of minority representation came to be seen as an essential step in a strategy of territorial consolidation.

As the pressures mounted for extensions of the suffrage, demands for proportionality were also heard in the culturally more homogeneous nation-states. In most cases the victory of the new principle of representation came about through a convergence of pressures from below and from above. The rising working class wanted to lower the threshold of representation to gain access to the legislatures, and the most threatened of the old-established parties demanded PR to protect their positions against the new waves of mobilized voters under universal suffrage. In Belgium the introduction of graduated manhood suffrage in 1893 brought about an increasing polarization between Labour and Catholics and threatened the continued existence of the Liberals; the introduction of PR restored some equilibrium to the system. The history of the struggles over electoral procedures in Sweden and in Norway tells us a great deal about the consequences of the lowering of one threshold for the bargaining over the level of the next. In Sweden, the Liberals and the Social Democrats fought a long fight for universal and equal suffrage and at first also advocated PR to ensure easier access to the legislature. The remarkable success of their mobilization efforts made them change their strategy, however. From 1904 onward they advocated majority elections in single-member constituencies. This aroused fears among the farmers and the urban Conservatives, and to protect their interests they made the introduction of PR a condition for their acceptance of manhood suffrage. As a result the two barriers fell together: it became easier to enter the electorate and easier to gain representation. In Norway there was a much longer lag between the waves of mobilization. The franchise

[17] Braunias, *Wahlrecht*, ii. 201–4.

was much wider from the outset, and the first wave of peasant mobilization brought down the old regime as early as in 1884. As a result the suffrage was extended well before the final mobilization of the rural proletariat and the industrial workers under the impact of rapid economic change. The victorious radical-agrarian 'Left' felt no need to lower the threshold of representation and in fact helped to increase it through the introduction of a two-ballot system of the French type in 1906. There is little doubt that this contributed heavily to the radical- ization and the alienation of the Norwegian Labour party. By 1915 it had gained 32 per cent of all the votes cast but was given barely 15 per cent of the seats. The 'Left' did not give in until 1921. The decisive motive was clearly not just a sense of equalitarian justice but the fear of rapid decline with further advances of the Labour party across the majority threshold.

In all these cases high thresholds might have been kept up if the parties of the property-owning classes had been able to make common cause against the rising working-class move- ments. But the inheritance of hostility and distrust was too strong. The Belgian Liberals could not face the possibility of a merger with the Catholics, and the cleavages between the rural and the urban interests went too deep in the Nordic countries to make it possible to build up any joint antisocialist front. By contrast, the higher level of industrialization and the progress- ive merger of rural and urban interests in Britain made it possible to withstand the demand for a change in the system of representation. Labour was seriously underrepresented only during a brief initial period, and the Conservatives were able to establish broad enough alliances in the counties and the suburbs to keep their votes well above the critical point.

A MODEL FOR THE GENERATION OF THE EUROPEAN PARTY SYSTEM

Four Decisive Dimensions of Opposition

This review of the conditions for the translation of socio- cultural cleavages into political oppositions suggests three conclusions.

First, the constitutive contrasts in the national system of party constellations generally tended to manifest themselves *before* any lowering of the threshold of representation. The decisive sequences of party formation took place at the early stage of competitive politics, in some cases well before the extension of the franchise, in other cases on the very eve of the rush to mobilize the finally enfranchised masses.

Second, the high thresholds of representation during the phase of mass politicization set severe tests for the rising political organizations. The surviving formations tended to be firmly entrenched in the inherited social structure and could not easily be dislodged through changes in the rules of the electoral game.

Third, the decisive moves to lower the threshold of representation reflected divisions among the established *régime censitaire* parties rather than pressures from the new mass movements. The introduction of PR added a few additional splinters but essentially served to ensure the separate survival of parties unable to come together in common defence against the rising contenders of majority power.

What happened at the decisive party-forming phase in each national society? Which of the many contrasts and conflicts were translated into party oppositions, and how were these oppositions built into stable systems?

This is not the place to enter into detailed comparisons of developmental sequences nation by nation. Our task is to suggest a framework for the explanation of variations in cleavage bases and party constellations.

In the abstract schema set out in Fig. 9.2 we distinguished four decisive dimensions of opposition in Western politics:

two of them were products of what we called the *National* Revolution (1 and 2);

and two of them were generated through the *Industrial* Revolution (3 and 4).

In their basic characteristics the party systems that emerged in the Western European politics during the early phase of competition and mobilization can be interpreted as products of *sequential interactions between these two fundamental processes of change*.

Differences in the timing and character of the *National* Revolution set the stage for striking divergencies in the European party system. In the Protestant countries the conflicts between the claims of the State and the Church had been temporarily settled by royal fiats at the time of the Reformation, and the processes of centralization and standardization triggered off after 1789 did not immediately bring about a conflict between the two. The temporal and the spiritual establishments were at one in the defence of the central nation-building culture but came increasingly under attack by the leaders and ideologists of countermovements in the provinces, in the peripheries, and within the underprivileged strata of peasants, craftsmen, and workers. The other countries of Western Europe were all split to the core in the wake of the secularizing French Revolution and without exception developed strong parties for the defence of the Church, either explicitly as in Germany, the Low Countries, Switzerland, Austria, Italy, and Spain or implicitly as in the case of the Right in France.

Differences in the timing and character of the *Industrial* Revolution also made for contrasts among the national party system in Europe.

Conflicts in the *commodity* market tended to produce highly divergent party alliances in Europe. In some countries the majority of the market farmers found it possible to join with the owner interests in the secondary sector of the economy; in others the two remained in opposition to each other and developed parties of their own. Conflicts in the *labour* market, by contrast, proved much more uniformly divisive: all countries of Western Europe developed lower-class mass parties at some point or other before World War I. These were rarely unified into one single working-class party. In Latin Europe the lower-class movements were sharply divided among revolutionary anarchist, anarcho-syndicalist, and Marxist factions on the one hand and revisionist socialists on the other. The Russian Revolution of 1917 split the working-class organizations throughout Europe. Today we find in practically all countries of the West divisions between Communists, left Socialist splinters, and revisionist Social Democrat parties.

Our task, however, is not just to account for the emergence of single parties but to analyse the processes of alliance formation that led to the development of stable *systems* of political organizations in country after country. To approach some understanding of these alliance formations, we have to study the *interactions* between the two revolutionary processes to change in each polity: How far had the National Revolution proceeded at the point of the industrial 'take-off' and how did the two processes of mobilization, the cultural and the economic, affect each other, positively by producing common fronts or negatively by maintaining divisions?

The decisive contrasts among the Western party systems clearly reflect differences in the *national histories of conflict and compromise across the first three of the four cleavage lines* distinguished in our analytical schema: the 'centre–periphery', the State-Church, and the land–industry cleavages generated national developments in *divergent* directions, while the owner–worker cleavage tended to bring the party systems *closer to each other* in their basic structure. The crucial differences among the party systems emerged in the early phases of competitive politics, before the final phase of mass mobilization. They reflected basic contrasts in the conditions and sequences of nation-building and in the structure of the economy at the point of take-off towards sustained growth. This, to be sure, does not mean that the systems vary exclusively on the 'Right' and at the centre, but are much more alike on the 'Left' of the political spectrum. There are working-class movements throughout the West, but they differ conspicuously in size, in cohesion, in ideological orientation, and in the extent of their integration into, or alienation from, the historically given national policy. Our point is simply that the factors generating these differences on the left are *secondary*. The decisive contrasts among the systems had emerged before the entry of the working-class parties into the political arena, and the character of these mass parties was heavily influenced by the constellations of ideologies, movements, and organizations they had to confront in that arena.

A Model in Three Steps

To understand the differences among the Western party systems we have to start out from an analysis of the *situation of the active nation-building élite on the eve of the breakthrough to democratiza-*

tion and mass mobilization: What had they achieved and where had they met most resistance? What were their resources, who were their nearest allies, and where could they hope to find further support? Who were their enemies, what were their resources, and where could they recruit allies and rally reinforcement?

Any attempt at comparative analysis across so many divergent national histories is fraught with grave risks. It is easy to get lost in the wealth of fascinating detail, and it is equally easy to succumb to facile generalities and irresponsible abstractions. Scholarly prudence prompts us to proceed case by case, but intellectual impatience urges us to go beyond the analysis of concrete contrasts and try out alternative schemes of systematization across the known cases.

To clarify the logic of our approach to the comparative analysis of party systems, we have developed a *model of alternative alliances and oppositions*. We have posited several sets of actors, have set up a series of rules of alliance and opposition among these, and have tested the resultant typology of potential party systems against a range of empirically known cases.

Our model seeks to reduce the bewildering variety of empirical party systems *to a set of ordered consequences of decisions and developments at three crucial junctures in the history of each nation*:

first, during the *Reformation*—the struggle for the control of the ecclesiastical organizations within the national territory;

second, in the wake of the '*Democratic Revolution*' after 1789—the conflict over the control of the vast machineries of mass education to be built up by the mobilizing nation-states;

finally, during the early phases of the *Industrial Revolution* —the opposition between landed interests and the claims of the rising commercial and industrial leadership in cities and towns.

Our eight types of alliance-opposition structure are in fact the simple combinatorial products of three successive dichotomies [see Fig. 9.3]. The model spells out the consequences of the fateful division of Europe brought about through Reformation and the Counter-Reformation. The outcomes of the early struggles between State and Church determined the structure of national politics in the era of democratization and mass mobilization three hundred years later. In Southern and Central Europe the Counter-Reformation had consolidated the

FIRST DICHOTOMY: THE REFORMATION

I–IV	V–VIII
State Controls	State Allied to
National Church	Roman Catholic Church

SECOND DICHOTOMY: THE 'DEMOCRATIC REVOLUTION'

I–II	III–IV	V–VI	VII–VIII
National Church	Strong Roman	Secularizing	State Allied to
Dominant	Minority	Revolution	Roman Church

THIRD DICHOTOMY: THE INDUSTRIAL REVOLUTION

	Commitment		Commitment		Commitment		Commitment	
	to		to		to		to	
	Landed	Urban	Landed	Urban	Landed	Urban	Landed	Urban
	Interests		Interests		Interests		Interests	
Type:	I	II	III	IV	V	VI	VII	VIII

FIG. 9.3.

position of the Church and tied its fate to the privileged bodies of the *ancien régime*. The result was a polarization of politics between a national-radical-secular movement and a Catholic-traditionalists one. In North-West Europe, in Britain, and in Scandinavia, the settlement of the sixteenth century gave a very different structure to the cleavages of the nineteenth. The Established Churches did not stand in opposition to the nation-builders in the way the Roman Catholic Church did on the Continent, and the 'Left' movements opposed to the religious establishment found most of their support among newly en-franchised Dissenters, Nonconformists, and Fundamentalists in the peripheries and within the rising urban strata. In Southern and Central Europe the bourgeois opposition to the *ancien régime* tended to be indifferent if not hostile to the teachings of the Church: the cultural integration of the nation came first and the Church had to find whatever place it could within the new political order. In North-West Europe the op-position to the *ancien régime* was far from indifferent to religious values. The broad 'Left' coalitions against the established powers recruited decisive support among orthodox Protestants in a variety of sectarian movements outside and inside the national churches.

The distinction between these two types of 'Left' alliances against the inherited political structure is fundamental for an understanding of European political developments in the age of mass elections. It is of particular importance in the analysis of the religiously most divided of the European polities: types III and IV in our $2 \times 2 \times 2$ schema. The religious frontiers of Europe went straight through the territories of the Low Countries, the old German Reich, and Switzerland; in each of these the clash between the nation-builders and the strong Roman Catholic minorities produced lasting divisions of the bodies politic and determined the structure of their party systems. The Dutch system came closest to a direct merger of the Southern-Central type (VI–VIII) and the North-Western: on the one hand a nation-building party of increasingly secularized Liberals, on the other hand a Protestant 'Left' recruited from orthodox milieus of the same type as those behind the old opposition parties in England and Scandinavia.

The difference between England and the Netherlands is indeed instructive. Both countries had their strong peripheral concentrations of Catholics opposed to central authority: the English in Ireland, the Dutch in the south. In Ireland, the cumulation of ethnic, social, and religious conflicts could not be resolved within the old system; the result was a history of intermittent violence and finally territorial separation. In the Netherlands the secession of the Belgians still left a sizeable Catholic minority, but the inherited tradition of corporate pluralism helped to ease them into the system. The Catholics established their own broad column of associations and a strong political party and gradually found acceptance within a markedly segmented but still cohesive national polity.

A comparison of the Dutch and the Swiss cases would add further depth to this analysis of the conditions for the differentiation of parties within national systems. Both countries come close to our type IV: Protestant national leadership, strong Catholic minorities, predominance of the cities in the national economy. In setting the assumption of our model we predicted a split in the peripheral opposition to the nation-builders: one orthodox Protestant opposition and one Roman Catholic. This clearly fits the Dutch case but not so well the Swiss. How is this to be accounted for? Contrasts of this type open up fascinating possibilities of comparative historical analysis; all we can do here is to suggest a simple hypothesis. Our model not only simplifies complex historical developments through its strict selection of conditioning variables, it also reduces empirical continuities to crude dichotomies. The difference between the Dutch and the Swiss cases can possibly be accounted for through further differentiation in the centre-periphery axis. The drive for national centralization was stronger in the Netherlands and had been slowed down in Switzerland through the experiences of the war between the Protestant cantons and the Catholic *Sonderbund*. In the Netherlands the Liberal drive for centralization produced resistance both among the Protestants and the Catholics. In Switzerland the Radicals had few difficulties on the Protestant side and needed support in their opposition to the Catholics. The result was a party system of essentially the same structure as in the typical Southern-Central cases [types VI–VII].

In our model we have placed France with Italy as an example of an alliance-opposition system of type VI: Catholic dominance through the Counter-Reformation, secularization and religious conflict during the next phase of nation-building in the nineteenth century, clear predominance of the cities in national politics. But this is an analytical juxtaposition of polities with diametrically opposed histories of development and consolidation—France one of the oldest and most centralized nation-states in Europe, Italy a territory unified long after the French revolutions had paved the way for the 'participant nation', the integrated political structure committing the entire territorial population to the same historical destiny. To us this is not a weakness in our model, however. The party systems of the countries *are* curiously similar, and any scheme of comparative analysis must somehow or other bring this out. The point is that our distinction between 'nation-builder' alliances and 'periphery' alliances must take on very different meanings in the two contexts. In France the distinction between 'centre' and 'periphery' was far more than a matter of geography; it reflected long-standing historical commitments for or against the Revolution. As spelt out in detail in Siegfried's classic *Tableau*, the *Droite* had its strongholds in the districts which had most stubbornly resisted the revolutionary drive for centralization and equalization, but it was far more than a movement of peripheral protest—it was a broad alliance of alienated élite groups, of frustrated nation-builders who felt that their rightful powers had been usurped by men without faith and without roots. In Italy there was no basis for such a broad alliance against the secular nation-builders, since the established local élites offered little resistance to the lures of *trasformismo*, and the Church kept its faithful followers out of national politics for nearly two generations.

These contrasts during the initial phases of mass mobilization had far-reaching consequences for each party system. With the broadening of the electorates and the strengthening of the working-class parties, the Church felt impelled to defend its position through its own resources. In France, the result was an attempt to divorce the defence of the Catholic schools from the defence of the established rural hierarchy. This trend had first found expression through the establishment of Christian trade unions and in 1944 finally led to the formation of the MRP. The burden of historic commitments was too strong, however; the young party was unable to establish itself as a broad mass party defending the principles of Christian democracy. By contrast, in Italy, history had left the Church with only insignificant rivals to the right of the working-class parties. The result was the formation of a broad alliance of a variety of interests and movements, frequently at loggerheads with each other, but united in their defence of the rights of the central institution of the fragmented *ancien régime*, the Roman Catholic Church. In both cases there was a clear-cut tendency towards religious polarization, but differences in the histories of nation-building made for differences in the resultant systems of party alliances and oppositions.

We could go into further detail in every one of the eight types distinguished in our model, but this would take us too far into single-country histories. We are less concerned with the specifics of the degrees of fit in each national case than with the overall structure of the model. There is clearly nothing final about any such scheme; it simply sets a series of themes for detailed comparisons and suggests ways of organizing the results within a manageable conceptual framework. The model is a tool and its utility can be tested only through continuous development: through the addition of further variables to account for observed differences as well as through refinements in the definition and grading of the variables already included.

The Fourth Step: Variations in the Strength and Structure of the Working-Class Movements

Our three-step model stops short at a point before the decisive thrust towards universal suffrage. It pinpoints sources of variations in the systems of division within the 'independent' strata of the European national electorates, among the owners of property and the holders of professional or educational privileges qualifying them for the vote during the *régime censitaire*.

But this is hardly more than half the story. The extension of the suffrage to the lower classes changed the character of each national political system, generated new cleavages, and brought about a restructuring of the old alignments.

Why did we not bring these important developments into our model of European party systems? Clearly not because the three first cleavage lines were more important than the fourth in the explanation of *any one national party system*. On the contrary, in sheer statistical terms the fourth cleavage lines will in at least half of the cases under consideration explain much more of the variance in the distributions of full-suffrage votes than any one of the others. We focused on the three first cleavage lines because these were the ones that appear to account for most of the variance *among systems*: the interactions of the 'centre–periphery', State–Church, and land–industry cleavages tended to produce much more marked, and apparently much more stubborn, differences among the national party systems than any of the cleavages brought about through the rise of the working-class movements.

We could of course have gone on to present a four-step model immediately (in fact, we did in an earlier draft), but this proved very cumbersome and produced a variety of uncomfortable redundancies. Clearly what had to be explained was not the emergence of a distinctive working-class movement at some point or other before or after the extension of the suffrage but the *strength and solidarity* of any such movement, its capacity to mobilize the underprivileged classes for action and its ability to maintain unity in the face of the many forces making for division and fragmentation. All the European polities developed some sort of working-class movement at some point between the first extensions of the suffrage and the various 'post-democratic' attempts at the repression of partisan pluralism. To predict the *presence* of such movements was simple; to predict which ones would be strong and which ones weak, which ones unified and which ones split down the middle, required much more knowledge of national conditions and developments and a much more elaborate model of the historical interaction process. Our three-step model does not go this far for *any* party; it predicts the presence of such-and-such parties in polities characterized by such-and-such cleavages, but it does not give any formula for accounting for the strength or the cohesion of any one party. This *could* be built into the model through the introduction of various population parameters (per cent speaking each language or dialect, per cent committed to each of the churches or dissenting bodies, ratios of concentrations of wealth and dependent labour in industry versus landed estates), and possibly of some indicators of the cleavage 'distance' (differences in the chances of interaction across the cleavage line, whether physically determined or normatively regulated), but any attempt in this direction would take us much too far in this all-too-long introductory essay. At this point we limit ourselves to an elementary discussion of the between-system variations which would have to be explained through such an extension of our model. We shall suggest a 'fourth step' and point to a possible scheme for the explanation of differences in the formation of national party systems under the impact of universal suffrage.

Our initial scheme of analysis posited four decisive dimensions of cleavage in Western polities. Our model for the generation of party systems pin-pointed three crucial junctures in national history corresponding to the first three of these dimensions [see Fig. 9.4]. It is tempting to add to this a fourth dimension and a fourth juncture:

There is an intriguing cyclical movement in this scheme. The process gets under way with the breakdown of one supranational order and the establishment of strong territorial bureaucracies legitimizing themselves through the standardizing

Cleavage	Critical juncture	Issues
Centre–Periphery	Reformation–Counter-Reformation: 16th–17th centuries	National vs. supranational religion National language vs. Latin
State–Church	National Revolution: 1789 and after	Secular vs. religious control of mass education
Land–Industry	Industrial Revolution: 19th century	Tariff levels for agricultural products: control vs. freedom for industrial enterprise

Cleavage	Critical juncture	Issues
Owner–Worker	The Russian Revolution: 1917 and after	Integration into national polity vs. commitment to international revolutionary movement

FIG. 9.4.

of nationally distinct religions and languages, and it ends with a conflict over national versus international loyalties within the last of the strata to be formally integrated into the nation-state, the rural and the industrial workers.

The conditions for the development of distinctive working-class parties varied markedly from country to country within Europe. These differences emerged well before World War I. The Russian Revolution did not generate new cleavages but simply accentuated long-established lines of division within the working-class élite.

Our three-step model does not produce clear-cut predictions of these developments. True enough, the most unified and the most 'domesticable' working-class movements emerged in the Protestant-dominated countries with the smoothest histories of nation-building: Britain, Denmark, and Sweden (types I and II in our model). Equally true, the Catholic-dominated countries with difficult or very recent histories of nation-building also produced deeply divided, largely alienated working-class movements—France, Italy, Spain (types V and VI). But other variables clearly have to be brought into account for variations in the intermediary zone between the Protestant North-West and the Latin South (types III and IV, VII and VIII). Both the Austrian and the German working-class movements developed their distinctive counter-cultures against the dominant national élites. The Austrian Socialist *Lager*, heavily concentrated as it was in Vienna, was able to maintain its unity in the face of the clerical-conservatives and the pan-German nationalists after the dissolution of the Habsburg Empire. By contrast, the German working-class movement was deeply divided after the defeat in 1918. Sharply contrasted conceptions of the rules of the political game stood opposed to each other and were to prove fatal in the fight against the wave of mass nationalism of the early thirties. In Switzerland and the Netherlands (both type IV in our scheme), the Russian and the German revolutions produced a few disturbances, but the leftward split-offs from the main working class by parties were of little significance. The marked cultural and religious cleavages reduced the potentials for the Socialist parties, but the traditions of pluralism were gradually to help their entry into national politics.

Of all the intermediary countries Belgium (type VIII in our model) presents perhaps the most interesting case. By our overall rule, the Belgian working class should be deeply divided: a thoroughly Catholic country with a particularly difficult history of nation-building across two distinct language communities. In this case the smallness and the international dependence of the nation may well have created restraints on the internal forces of division and fragmentation. Val Lorwin has pointed to such factors in his analysis of Belgian–French contrasts:

The reconciliation of the Belgian working class to the political and social order, divided though the workers are by language and religion and the Flemish-Walloon question, makes a vivid contrast with the experience of France. The differences did not arise from the material fruits of economic growth, for both long were rather low-wage countries, and Belgian wages were the lower. In some ways the two countries had similar economic development. But Belgium's industrialization began earlier; it was more dependent on international commerce, both for markets and for its transit trade; it had a faster growing population; and it became much more urbanized than

France. The small new nation, 'the cockpit of Europe', could not permit itself social and political conflict to the breaking point. Perhaps France could not either, but it was harder for the bigger nation to realize it.[18]

The contrast between France, Italy, and Spain on the one hand and Austria and Belgium on the other suggests a possible generalization: the working-class movement tended to be much more divided in the countries where the 'nation-builders' and the Church were openly or latently opposed to each other during the crucial phases of educational development and mass mobilization (types V and VI) than in the countries where the Church had, at least initially, sided with the nation-builders against some common enemy outside (an alliance against Protestant Prussia and the dependent Habsburg peoples in the case of Austria; against the Calvinist Dutch in the case of Belgium). This fits the Irish case as well. The Catholic Church was no less hostile to the English than the secular nationalists, and the union of the two forces not only reduced the possibilities of a polarization of Irish politics on class lines but made the likelihood of a Communist splinter of any importance very small indeed.

It is tempting to apply a similar generalization to the Protestant North: the greater the internal division during the struggle for nationhood, the greater the impact of the Russian Revolution on the divisions within the working class. We have already pointed to the profound split within the German working class. The German Reich was a late-comer among European nations, and none of the territorial and religious conflicts within the nation was anywhere near settlement by the time the working-class parties entered the political arena. Among the northern countries the two oldest nations, Denmark and Sweden, were least affected by the Communist–Socialist division. The three countries emerging from colonial status were much more directly affected: Norway (domestically independent from 1814, a sovereign state from 1905) for only a brief period in the early 1920s; Finland (independent in 1917) and Iceland (domestically independent in 1916 and a sovereign

[18] V. Lorwin, 'Working Class Politics and Economic Development in Western Europe', *American Historical Review*, 63 (1958), 338–51.

state from 1944) for a much longer period. These differences among the northern countries have been frequently commented on in the literature of comparative politics. The radicalization of the Norwegian Labour party has been interpreted within several alternative models, one emphasizing the alliance options of the party leaders, another the grass-roots reactions to sudden industrialization in the peripheral countryside, and a third the openness of the party structure and the possibilities of quick feedback from the mobilized voters. There is no doubt that the early mobilization of the peasantry and the quick victory over the old regime of the officials had left the emerging Norwegian working-class party much more isolated, much less important as a coalition partner, than its Danish and Swedish counterparts. There is also a great deal of evidence to support the old [Eduard] Bull hypothesis of the radicalizing effects of sudden industrialization, but recent research suggests that this was only one element in a broad process of political change. The Labour party recruited many more of its voters in the established cities and in the forestry and the fisheries districts, but the openness of the party structure allowed the radicals to establish themselves very quickly and to take over the majority wing of the party during the crucial years just after the Russian Revolution. This very openness to rank-and-file influences made the alliance with Moscow very short-lived; the Communists split off in 1924 and the old majority party 'joined the nation' step by step until it took power in 1935.

Only two of the Scandinavian countries retained strong Communist parties after World War II—Finland and Iceland. Superficially these countries have two features in common: prolonged struggles for cultural and political independence, and late industrialization. In fact the two countries went through very different processes of political change from the initial phase of nationalist mobilization to the final formation of the full-suffrage party system. One obvious source of variation was the distance from Russia. The sudden upsurge of the Socialist party in Finland in 1906 (the party gained 37 per cent of the votes cast at the first election under universal suffrage) was part of a general wave of mobilization against the Tsarist regime. The Russian Revolution of 1917 split Finland down the middle; the working-class voters were torn between their loyalty to their national culture and its social hierarchy and their solidarity with their class and its revolutionary defenders. The victory of the 'Whites' and the subsequent suppression of the Communist party (1919–21, 1923–5, 1930–44) left deep scars; the upsurge of the leftist SKDL after the Soviet victory in 1945 reflected deep-seated resentments not only against the 'lords' and the employers of labour but generally against the up-holders of the central national culture. The split in the Ice-landic labour movement was much less dramatic; in the oldest and smallest of the European democracies there was little basis for mass conflicts, and the oppositions between Com-munist sympathizers and Socialists appeared to reflect essentially personal antagonisms among groups of activists.

IMPLICATIONS FOR COMPARATIVE POLITICAL SOCIOLOGY

We have pushed our attempt at a systematization of the comparative history of partisan oppositions in European pol-ities up to some point in the 1920s, to the freezing of the major party alternatives in the wake of the extension of the suffrage and the mobilization of major sections of the new reservoirs of potential supporters. Why stop there? Why not pursue this exercise in comparative cleavage analysis right up to the 1960s? The reason is deceptively simple: *the party systems of the 1960s reflect, with few but significant exceptions, the cleavage structures of the 1920s.* This is a crucial characteristic of Western competitive politics in the age of 'high mass consumption': *the party alterna-tives, and in remarkably many cases the party organizations, are older than the majorities of the national electorates.* To most of the citizens of the West the currently active parties have been part of the political landscape since their childhood or at least since they were first faced with the choice between alternative 'packages' on election day.

This continuity is often taken as a matter of course; in fact it poses an intriguing set of problems for comparative sociological research. An amazing number of the parties which had estab-lished themselves by the end of World War I survived not only the onslaughts of Fascism and National Socialism but also another world war and a series of profound changes in the social and cultural structure of the polities they were part of. How was this possible? How were these parties able to survive so many changes in the political, social, and economic conditions of their operation? How could they keep such large bodies of citizens identifying with them over such long periods of time, and how could they renew their core clienteles from generation to generation?

There is no straightforward answer to any of these questions. We know much less about the internal management and the organizational functioning of political parties than we do about their socio-cultural base and their external history of participation in public decision-making.

To get closer to an answer we would clearly have to start out from a comparative analysis of the 'old' and the 'new' parties: the early mass parties formed during the final phase of suffrage extension, and the later attempts to launch new parties during the first decades of universal suffrage. It is difficult to see any significant exceptions to the rule that the parties which were able to establish mass organizations and entrench themselves in the local government structures *before* the final drive towards maximal mobilization have proved the most viable. The narrowing of the 'support market' brought about through the growth of mass parties during this final thrust towards full-suffrage democracy clearly left very few openings for new movements. Where the challenge of the emerging working-class parties had been met by concerted efforts of countermobilization through nationwide mass organizations on the liberal and the conservative fronts, the leeway for new party formations was particularly small; this was the case whether the threshold of representation was low, as in Scandinavia, or quite high, as in Britain. Correspondingly the 'post-democratic' party systems proved markedly more fragile and open to newcomers in the countries where the privileged strata had relied on their local power resources rather than on nationwide mass organizations in their efforts of mobilization.

France was one of the first countries to bring a maximal electorate into the political arena, but the mobilization efforts of the established strata tended to be local and personal. A mass organization corresponding to the Conservative party in Britain was never developed. There was very little 'narrowing of the support market' to the right of the PCF and the SFIO and consequently a great deal of leeway for innovation in the party system even in the later phases of democratization.

There was a similar asymmetry in Germany: strong mass organizations on the left but marked fragmentation on the right. The contrast between Germany and Britain has been rubbed in at several points in our analysis of cleavage structures. The contrast with Austria is equally revealing; there the three-*Lager* constellation established itself very early in the mobilization process, and the party system changed astoundingly little from the Empire to the First Republic, and from the First to the Second. The consolidation of conservative support around the mass organizations of the Catholic Church clearly soaked up a great deal of the mobilization potential for new parties. In Wilhelmine and Weimar Germany the only genuine mass organization to the right of the Social Democrats was the Catholic *Zentrum*; this still left a great deal of leeway for 'post-democratic' party formations on the Protestant right. Ironically, it was the defeat of the National Socialist regime and the loss of the Protestant East which opened up an opportunity for some stabilization of the German party system. With the establishment of the regionally divided CDU/CSU the Germans were for the first time able to approximate a broad conservative party of the British type. It was not able to establish as solid a membership organization but proved, at least until the debacle of 1966, amazingly effective in aggregating interests across a wide range of strata and sectors of the federal community.

Two other countries of the West have experienced spectacular changes in their party systems since the introduction of universal suffrage and deserve some comment in this context —Italy and Spain. The *Italian* case comes close to the *German*: both went through a painful process of belated unification; both were deeply divided within their privileged strata between 'nation-builders' (Prussians, Piedmontese) and Catholics; both had been slow to recognize the rights of the working-class organizations. The essential difference lay in the *timing* of the party developments. In the Reich a differentiated party structure had been allowed to develop during the initial mobilization phase and had been given another fifteen years of functioning during the Weimar Republic. In Italy, by contrast, the State–Church split was so profound that a structurally responsive party system did not see the light before 1919—three years before the March on Rome. There had simply been no time for the 'freezing' of any party system before the post-democratic revolution, and there was very little in the way of a traditional party system to fall back on after the defeat of the Fascist regime in 1944. True, the Socialists and the *Popolari* had had their brief spell of experience of electoral mobilization, and this certainly counted when the PCI and the DC established themselves in the wake of the war. But the other political forces had never been organized for concerted electoral politics and left a great deal of leeway for irregularities in the mobilization market. The *Spanish* case has a great deal in common with the *French*: early unification but deep resentments against central power in some of the provinces and early universalization of the suffrage but weak and divided party organizations. The Spanish system of sham parliamentarianism and *caciquismo* had not produced electoral mass parties of any importance by the time the double threat of secessionist mobilization and working-class militancy triggered off nationalist counter-revolutions, first under Primo de Rivera in 1923, then with the Civil War in 1936.

These four spectacular cases of disruptions in the development of national party systems do not in themselves invalidate our initial formulation. The most important of the party alternatives got set for each national citizenry during the phases of mobilization just before or just after the final extension of the suffrage and have remained roughly the same through decades of subsequent changes in the structural conditions of partisan choice. Even in the three cases of France, Germany, and Italy the continuities in the alternatives are as striking as the disruptions in their organizational expressions. On this score the French case is in many ways the most intriguing. There was no period of internally generated disruption of electoral politics (the Petain–Laval phase would clearly not have occurred if the Germans had not won in 1940), but there have been a number of violent oscillations between plebiscitarian and representative models of democracy and marked organizational fragmentation both at the level of interest articulation and at the level of parties. In spite of these frequent upheavals no analyst of French politics is in much doubt about the underlying continuities of sentiment and identification on the right no less than on the left of the political spectrum. The voter does not just react to immediate issues but is caught in an historically given constellation of diffuse options for the system as a whole.

10

TOWARDS A GENERALIZED CONCEPT OF *VERZUILING*

STEIN ROKKAN

My early work on cleavage structures and mass politics in Western Europe focused on the formation of *the full-suffrage party systems* as they emerged during the first quarter of the twentieth century: I tried to develop a parsimonious model for the explanation of variations in the structure of the *electoral alternatives* presented to the citizenry during the final stages of formal democratization.[1] I emphasized again and again that this was a deliberate simplification of a set of complex historical processes: I was fully aware that there were other manifestations of mass politics equally worthy of systematic analysis. In fact in one of my early articles on Norwegian developments I called for detailed analysis of the parallels and the interactions between two sets of organization-building efforts: the structuring of alternatives in what I called the *'numerical democracy'* channel and the building of effective units of action in the *corporate* bargaining channel.[2] Robert Alford and Roger Friedland have recently taken me to task for my failure to bring these two components of mass politics into a unified model:[3] in fact they use my 'two-tier' analysis of the Norwegian regime as a springboard for a critique of my model for the explanation of

Stein Rokkan, excerpted from *Political Studies*, 25/4 (1977), 563–70. Reprinted by permission of Basil Blackwell Limited.

[1] See especially S. Rokkan, *Citizens, Elections, Parties* (Oslo: Universitetsforlaget; and New York: McKay, 1970), ch. 3.

[2] S. Rokkan, 'Norway: Numerical Democracy and Corporate Pluralism', in R. A. Dahl (ed.), *Political Oppositions in Western Democracies* (New Haven: Yale University Press, 1966).

[3] R. Alford and R. Friedland, 'Nations, Parties, and Participation: A Critique of Political Sociology', *Theory and Society*, 1 (1974), 307–28.

variations in the formation of party systems. I accept their basic argument. I can only plead in defence that models have to be built up and tested step by step: it proved easiest to start off with comparisons of party systems but that was clearly only a beginning. A full-fledged model would have to generate hypotheses not only about the emergence of alternatives in the electoral channel but also about the structuring of mass organizations in the corporate channels and about types of interlinkages between the units in the two arenas. This is a demanding set of tasks [but in] . . . this brief note I shall set out some elements of a possible model. I shall first suggest a scheme for the analysis of steps in the translation of cleavages into organizational structures in the two channels and shall then discuss a possible recasting of the earlier party system model for comparisons of interlinkages between developments in the two channels.

Theoretically we can conceive of a number of possible paths from some phase of cleavage accentuation to the later phases of organizational structuring. In our current work on the spread of mass organizations and political parties from central to peripheral communities in Norway we have found it useful to distinguish six steps in this translation process:

first, the initial *generation of cleavage lines* through such macro-processes as monetization and urbanization, industrialization and secularization;

secondly, the *crystallization of cleavage lines in conflicts over public policy*;

thirdly, the emergence of *alliances of political entrepreneurs* actively engaged in the mobilization of support for one set of policies against another;

fourthly, the *choices of mobilization strategies made by such entrepreneurs*: actions through pre-established community networks versus action through the development of distinctive membership organizations

fifthly, the *choice of arenas for the confrontation of mobilized resources*: the aggregation of votes in the territorial channel versus the mobilization of commitment to direct action (demonstrations, boycotts, strikes, sabotage) in the corporate channel

and finally, the *actual pay-offs of such concerted efforts*, whether in the form of legislation or in other forms of corporate agreements about the distribution of rights and obligations.

At each of these steps it is possible to distinguish a number of possible outcomes: the developments or decisions at one step set conditions or constraints for the next. The combinatorics of step-by-step outcomes and/or decisions constitute so many possible *paths of translation*. The full combinatorics have not been worked out: there are obvious redundancies in the scheme and there is no point in freezing a typology of paths without testing against data for at least two structurally different systems. In our work on the Norwegian data we have combined four dimensions to generate a fivefold typology of organizational responses to cleavage crystallization [see Table 10.1].

Type I describes mobilization processes in communities at a low level of differentiation: support for electoral alternatives is generated through alliances among local notables, kinship networks, long-established structures such as churches, sects, or ethnic community agencies. The thrust of the mobilization drive is *territorial*: the enfranchised citizenry is brought out of its traditional apathy to defend established local interests against outside agencies and there is no need to develop additional structures to create incentives for collective action. This was the dominant type of response during the early phases of mobilization wherever the suffrage was extended before the decisive waves of urbanization and industrialization. In Norway we find a number of communes following this path in the early phases of mobilization from the 1870s to the 1890s. In the Northern periphery we even find this type predominant well into the

TABLE 10.1

| | Mobilization base: | | |
Type	Electoral channel	Corporate channel	Level of cross-linkage
I	*Diffuse* network	None	None
II	*Specific* organization	None	None
III	*Diffuse* network	*Specific* organization	*Contingent*
IV	*Specific* organization	*Specific* organization	*Contingent*
V	*Specific* organization	*Specific* organization	*Interlocking*

1950s. Henry Valen and I have shown that in a number of peripheral communes the Labour party could mobilize large numbers of votes without building any distinctive membership organization: the party could count on the support of widespread networks of fishermen, smallholders, and seasonal labourers but their opposition to the powers of the private economy was territorial in character, not easily brought into a cross-local organizational structure.

Type II describes the transition described in so many classical studies of party development: the emergence of local registration societies, electioneering organizations, membership structures. Such organizations may of course often not reflect much more than short-term alliances across well-established networks but nevertheless represent first steps towards the formalization of membership rules and the standardization of decision procedures. Organizations of this type rarely mobilize support on one single cleavage line: they aggregate support through a variety of alliances but none of these is given visible expression in cleavage-specific organizations allied to the party.

Type III represents a first step towards two-level linkage: cleavage-specific mobilization efforts are contingently linked up with cross-cleavage aggregations within electoral fronts. But in this case the development of the corporate mobilization unit *precedes* the formalization of the political organization. This is clearly a transitional situation: we find such cases in our Norwegian data but are not sure whether this phase is long enough to deserve separate analysis.

Types IV and V represent steps towards higher levels of organizational *verzuiling*: I choose to use this well-established Dutch term rather than any fancy neologism to represent the *degree of interlocking between cleavage-specific organizations active in the corporate channel and party organizations mobilizing for electoral action.*

This is a crucial dimension in any model of the structuring of mass politics in pluralist systems: how good a fit is there between the sets of organizational alternatives open in the two channels, how far can it be predicted from the underlying cleavage structure? In any effort of generalized model-building across the two channels we clearly have to 'stretch' this dimension of organizational *verzuiling* to cover the total range of possible organization-to-organization linkage levels. Thus far the literature on cross-channel linkage has concentrated heavily on the systems at the highest levels of *verzuiling*: Benelux, Austria, Switzerland, Northern Ireland. If we are to get anywhere in our efforts to develop a general model we have to distinguish a number of levels of organizational linkage.

At the one end of the continuum there is *no* one-to-one fit between organizations in the corporate channel and organization in the electoral channel: no linkage at the leadership level, no bargaining for support, no segmentation of the mobilized populations on similar cleavage lines. At a further level of *verzuiling* the fit is erratic and instable: there is some overlap in leadership and some segmentation of support, but the bargains struck are temporary and contingent. In our work on the early phases of urbanization in Norway we find a variety of examples of such weak one-to-one linkages across the channels: the cleavage-specific organization developed independently of the parties but entered into a variety of bargains with them for support of candidacies and policies. The links between the religious mass movements and the great opposition party *Venstre* was typically at this level of linkage: the religious groups supported *Venstre* candidates as long as they were able to deliver the goods they promised in the legislature but were always ready to withdraw support if the party did not perform on the promises. The teetotalist movements developed a similar strategy: they were particularly active in the electoral channel and set clear-cut conditions for the mobilization of their membership base for particular slates of candidacies. A large aggregative party will obviously develop a variety of such links with cleavage-specific organization in the corporate channel: the successions of splits and mergers characteristic of so many party histories cannot be studied without detailed analysis of the variations in strength of such alliances.

The greater the strength and the stability of such alliances the closer we come to organizational *verzuiling* in the strict sense: an interlocking network of agencies covering a wide range of sectors of collective activity. Such interlocking can clearly be studied at several levels: the leadership, the recruitment of active members, the mass-level support base. In developing a general model for the explanation of variations in the structuring of mass politics it will clearly be essential to distinguish several *types of sequences* leading to high levels of interlocking: which agencies took the lead in building up such networks? what was the cleavage basis for these efforts, and how did the consequent concentration of organization around one central focus of identity affect the overall system of alliances and oppositions in the polity?

Theoretically we could posit three basic patterns:

first, a sequence initiated by *cultural agencies* such as churches, sects, or ethnic-linguistic communities;

secondly, a sequence initiated by a *diffuse electoral network* or an *organized party* in an effort to stabilize its population base;

thirdly, a sequence initiated by *agencies in the economy*, such as farmers' organizations and unions.

In practice it is often difficult to disentangle the processes at work in each case. In Catholic Europe, the Church clearly offered the best basis for network-building but the incentives and the costs varied very much from system to system. In the Netherlands, the Catholic Church does not seem to have taken the decisive initiative in network-building: I take it to be the thrust of Hans Daalder's argument that the party—and the competition among the parties for the votes of the newly enfranchised—counted as heavily in the process. In Protestant Europe we have a number of examples of network-building of this type from a cultural base: religious parties grew out of lay movements opposing the established State Churches, the few ethnically based parties were simply extensions of organizations already set up outside the electoral channel. The same was the case with agrarian and social democratic parties: they tended to be electoral extensions of organizations already active in the corporate channel.

None of this can be sorted out systematically without detailed analyses of the actual cleavage bases of the movements: we have to look at the sequences of cleavage crystallization and we must find how far the first mobilizing agencies were able to exploit the electoral and the membership markets before the next set of agencies emerged. I tried to construct a model of cleavage crystallizations in my early work on party systems but will clearly have to recast the scheme if it is to be useful in the

ECONOMY-BASED RESPONSES		TERRITORY-BASED RESPONSES			CULTURE-BASED RESPONSES	
ECONOMY-BASED *VERZUILING*: Multiplication of *cultural* organizations around economy-oriented identities	ECONOMIC SEGMENTATION: accentuation of economic cleavages *within* local population	ECONOMICALLY ORIENTED TERRITORIAL DEFENCE: accentuation of economic distinctiveness of localities/regions	UNDIFFERENTIATED TERRITORIAL DEFENCE	CULTURALLY ORIENTED TERRITORIAL DEFENCE: accentuation of cultural distinctiveness of localities/regions	CULTURAL SEGMENTATION: accentuation of cultural cleavages *within* local population	CULTURE-BASED *VERZUILING*: multiplication of *economic* organizations around cultural identities

FIG 10.1. A Typology of Organizational Response Forms

study of levels and dimensions of mass political *verzuiling*. I shall conclude this note with a brief presentation of the scheme I have tried to work out on the basis of our analyses of the emergence of the early counter-cultural movements in Norway.

The scheme posits two axes of differentiation. The first I call a *centre-periphery* dimension, essentially measuring the extent of *exposure to cleavage-crystallizing changes*: urbanization and industrialization on the economic side, standardization and secularization on the other. The second I call the *organizational response* dimension: this classifies conflict alignments from one extreme of *cultural* segmentation to another of *economic* segmentation. The second dimension differs from the first in its metric structure: the two poles have important features in common and stand in clear contrast to the mid-point of pure territoriality.

The basic structure of the dimension is set out in a seven-point array in Figure 10.1. The combinatorics of the two dimensions give the basic model set out in Figure 10.2: the cell entries indicate the location of the major mass-political movements in Norway. To reduce complexity the response types have been regrouped into four: two economic, two cultural.

The model was developed in an effort to generate hypotheses about the sources of differentiation among the three major counter-cultural response types in Norway: the orthodox Lutheran movement against the established State Church, the teetotalist organizations, the campaign for the rural counter-language. To produce precise hypotheses about local contexts likely to increase the receptivity to the one rather than the other of these counter-cultural appeals, the model will clearly have to be 'dynamicized': rates of movement from one type of locality to another, from one sector of the economy to the other, will have to be built in and an effort will also be made to trace the *diffusion* of organizational response types both through studies of the interaction among entrepreneurs and through analyses of migration flows. Research on these lines is particularly important for an understanding of the differences in the conditions for the success of *linguistic* versus *religious/moralist* movements. In the crude model set out in Figure 10.2 the language movement is identified as a *territorial-cultural response*: it mobilizes to defend the distinctiveness of the culture of particular peripheries. By contrast the religious and the teetotalist movements represent efforts of *cultural segmentation*: they emphasize oppositions *within* local populations, they accentuate social boundaries.

Obviously this contrast between territorial and segmental responses must be studied against information about migration flows. The language movement was at first an intellectual response of peasant-born students to the standards of the metropolis but it quickly established dominance in a number of rural peripheries: in these localities the movement represented a territorial response since the standards it stood for found

| | ECONOMY | | CULTURE | |
	Segmental response	Territorial response	Territorial response	Segmental response
CENTRE	Accentuation of class contrasts in secondary/ tertiary economy: workers vs. owners	Accentuation of economic boundaries towards other systems: state interests vs. capital interests	Accentuation of cultural boundaries towards other systems: cultural conservatism vs. cultural radicalism	Accentuation of class/ origin contrasts in life style and/or religious identity: lay religious groups, teetotalists vs. bourgeoisie
PERIPHERY	Accentuation of class contrasts in primary economy: rural proletariat vs. owners/ creditors	Accentuation of distinctiveness of rural economy: agrarian vs. urban interests	Accentuation of distinctiveness of rural culture: rural language movement vs. central standards	

FIG. 10.2. A Three-dimensional Model for the Analysis of the Structuring of Cleavages and the Emergence of Response Forms in Norway.

general acceptance and did not build up marked counter-movements. The situation was obviously different in the urbanizing and the central areas: there the language movement also engaged in segmental mobilization among the immigrants from the peripheries but from all accounts found it much more difficult to establish a mass base comparable to those built up by the religious and the teetotalist movements. These movements were essentially responses to the *anomie* and the *déracinement* produced by urbanization and secularization: in the model these movements are given a floating location between centre and periphery to indicate that their spread is essentially a function of migration.

Clearly to get closer to an understanding of these differences among counter-cultural movements we have to inquire further into the processes of identity-building and the mechanisms of identity-maintenance. There is a fundamental difference between language and religion as identity-defining stigmata: you cannot easily exit from your linguistic commitments once they have been established through childhood socialization, but you will not find it very costly, at least in differentiated urban environments, to exit from your religious commitments by dropping out of the habits of church-going and other rituals. You cannot function in a territorial community without a language: there may be variations in standards within the language and there may be a variety of class stigmata attached to such variations but there is still a much closer tie-in between language and territory than there is between religion and territory.

This sets very different tasks for mobilizing entrepreneurs. You do not need to build up a network of organizations to defend a peripheral language in its core areas: the physical distance from the centre of the dominant language constitutes enough of a barrier. You do need to build organizational barriers once enough of the peripheral population has moved into direct physical day-to-day contact with the dominant culture: *verzuiling* increases *social* distance where the *physical* distance can no longer guarantee cultural distinctiveness. To maintain *religious* identities you need distinctive organizations even in the peripheries: the Church does not only offer sites for the affirmation of ritual commitments, it also develops a variety of mechanisms to maintain the loyalty of the next generation. Where one Church remains unchallenged in a territory, there is rarely any need for additional mobilization to protect identities: an example would be the position of the Roman Catholics in Limburg and Noord-Brabant in the early phase of mass politics in the Netherlands. The push towards *verzuiling* is generated through urbanization and secularization: again there is the need to build up social boundaries where the physical barriers have crumbled.   .

The interpretation of the teetotalist movements is much more difficult. These are clearly boundary-building movements designed to protect the young from the evil of alternative standards: they create a distinctive culture by setting clear limits to communication with others. There are many ways of defining the contents of this distinctive culture: secularized Puritanism, *innerweltliche Askese*. But the essence of the culture is probably best described as the *negation of the diffuse conviviality which had helped to maintain class hierarchies* even in a period of rapid change and extensive mobility: in this sense teetotalism stood for a refusal of diffuse communication across class barriers, an insistence on specific, work-related communication only. In this sense teetotalism can be interpreted as a defence against downward mobility in situations of anomie and social uncertainty: once other agencies such as unions and state bureaucracies had reduced the chances of rapid proletarianization the incentives to maintain such distinctive cultures seem to have been reduced.

To account for the ups and downs in these boundary-building movements we clearly have to 'dynamicize' the model by distinguishing sequences of phases and by differentiating developments by locality as a function of population flows. Only when this has been done at some level of precision will it be possible to move towards the final step: the development of a unified model for the study of the linkages between the cleavage-specific movements in the corporate channel and the successive party-forming alliances in the electoral channel.

I I

THE SOCIOLOGY OF PARTIES:
A CRITICAL REVIEW

GIOVANNI SARTORI

I. DO PARTIES REPRESENT CLASSES?

It is useful to draw at the outset a distinction between *sociology of politics* and *political sociology*. The former is a sub-field of sociology, whereas the latter points to a real interdisciplinary approach, to a balanced cross-fertilization among sociologists and political scientists.[1] My purpose is to show that the transformation of the sociology of politics into political sociology still lies ahead of us, and that the difference between the two remains very substantial.

A major stream of the *sociology of politics* investigates the imprint of social classes and stratification upon mass political behaviour—at various levels, thereby including the political party level. While the political scientist is inclined to explore to what extent parties and party systems intervene in the political process as independent variables, the sociologist tends to perceive parties and party systems as dependent variables. This is

Giovanni Sartori, from *Party Systems, Party Organisations, and the Politics of New Masses*, Otto Stammer (ed.) (Berlin: Institute for Political Science, Free University at Berlin, 1968), pp. 1–25. Used with permission.

[1] It should be clear that I do not have in mind the Duverger-type political sociology. In his recent volume, *Sociologie Politique* (Paris: Presses Universitaires: 2nd edn., 1967), Duverger maintains the view that 'in a general way, the two labels (political sociology and political science) are synonymous' (p. 24). This view is very convenient, for it enables Duverger to publish the same book (with small variations) under two different titles, *Methodes de la Science Politique* in 1954, and *Methodes des Sciences Sociales* in 1959. In actuality, however, Duverger muddles the two approaches weirdly, for his laws concerning the influence of electoral systems—indeed the most manipulative instrument of politics—are presented as an instance of 'sociological laws'.

quite right, I mean, the distinctive contribution of the sociologist to the study of parties *is* to investigate to what extent parties and party systems are a response to, and a reflection of, social stratification, the solidarity structure of the society, its socio-economic and socio-cultural cleavages, its degree of heterogeneity and of integration, its level of economic growth, and the like.[2]

A classic formulation of the sociological approach is in Lipset's *Political Man*: 'In every democracy conflict among different groups is expressed through political parties which basically represent a "democratic translation of the class struggle". Even though many parties renounce the principle of class conflict or loyalty, an analysis of their *appeals* and their *support* suggests that they do *represent the interests* of different classes.'[3]

To be sure, Lipset makes the point that 'there have been important exceptions to these generalizations . . . and class is only one of the structural divisions in society which is related to party support'. Nevertheless it is clear that Lipset's thread is, in *Political Man*, the class thread. 'More than anything else', he goes on to say, 'the party struggle is a conflict among classes, and the most impressive single fact about political party support is that in virtually every economically developed country the lower-income groups vote mainly for parties of the left, while the higher-income groups vote mainly for parties of the right.'[4]

It is unnecessary to stress that these views display a familiar Marxist ring. In their 1957 perceptive review of the state of the art Bendix and Lipset themselves acknowledge that the chief impetus in the voting behaviour studies 'stems from an "interest theory" of political behaviour and goes back ultimately to the Marxian theory of class consciousness'.[5] Given the fact that the sociology of parties relies heavily on correlations with

[2] This is not to say that the sociologist does not have other concerns, but to sort out the most distinctive concern.

[3] S. M. Lipset, *Political Man* (Garden City, NY: Doubleday, 1960), 220 (italics mine). These are the opening lines of ch. 7.

[4] Ibid. 221, 223–4. But see the very different emphasis in *The First New Nation*, ch. 9 (n. 46 below).

[5] 'Political Sociology: An Essay and Bibliography', in *Current Sociology*, 6 (1957), 80. But see n. 36 below.

voting behaviour, the statement is equally true for the party topic: also the chief impetus of the sociology of parties goes back, ultimately, to Marxist assumptions.

A comment should be added, however, with reference to the interest theory of politics; and I would rather say the 'interest terminology' inspired by, and derived from Arthur Bentley. The interest terminology is a convenient dilution of Marxism, but hardly offers a substantial alternative. In the Bentleian school, 'interest' is a synonym for 'activity', and when Bentley says that there can be no activity without interest he says merely that there can be no activity without motivation. Nothing could be more patently true, but to use 'interest' in this sense is both superfluous and equivocal. It follows that the interest terminology either leads to fuzzy theorizing, or acquires its substance from the more or less covert assumption that 'interest' generally is 'economic interest'. It is not surprising, therefore, that the refinement of the interest theory has made much less headway than the refinement of Marxist theory. This is also to suggest that the Bentleian side of the coin may be safely set aside.

Reverting to the point, Lipset rightly sorts out three aspects: (i) a class-type *appeal*, (ii) a *support* based on class loyalties, (iii) the actual *representation* of class interests. It is superfluous to warn that these features may, or may not, hang together. It is more interesting to illustrate, on these premises, four possible ways of arguing the case.

(a) The class appeal is played down to a point of invisibility precisely because the support of class loyalties is firm (e.g. when the appeal is directed to cross-class floating voters).

(b) Conversely the class appeal is very visible and explicit, precisely because class support is low (or class loyalty dwindles).

Since the foregoing suggests that class *appeal* is an equivocal indicator, we are left with the indicator provided by a class support, and the rest of the argument can be developed according to the following two possibilities:

(c) Class support is beyond question, and yet class interests are misrepresented: in actuality the party betrays class interests.

(d) No class support is apparent, and yet the party is an inter-class disguise for representing and serving class interests.

The first three arguments suggest, then, that neither a class appeal, nor a class support, can show that class interests are actually represented. And the fourth argument shows that there is no way of pinning down a true believer: under any and all circumstances he can maintain that politics is class politics. This is tantamount to saying that the theory winds up a formulation that escapes empirical verification. When we come to the notion of 'representation of class interests' we are deferred to a conjecture that is beyond proof and cannot be falsified.

The thorny point, is, then, the *representation of class interests*. Lipset is very cautious on this matter, but one finds only too often, in the literature, the assertion that 'parties act as representatives of different class interests'; that 'political parties have developed largely as instruments of various class interests', and 'historically have come to represent specific coalitions of class interests'.[6] Given the fact that statements of the sort are delivered by many sociologists as if they were self-evident, let me present the view that I find them obscure, historically incorrect, and scientifically unacceptable.

The first question is: which is the assumption? Surely we are deferred, more or less implicitly, to a *general theory of politics*, according to which politics is, ultimately, a struggle between classes pursuing their class interests. However, this reply does not suffice to clarify the assumption. The interest of a class can either conflict or coincide with the interest of other classes. More technically put, inter-class relations may be zero-sum but may also be positive-sum. And, clearly, a zero-sum class theory is radically different from a positive-sum class theory. Yet sociologists are seemingly unaware of the distinction. As a

[6] R. R. Alford, in S. M. Lipset and S. Rokkan (eds.), *Party Systems and Voter Alignments* (New York: Free Press, 1967), 69. I am not discussing, however, a particular author; the quotations are for the sake of illustration.

result, we are left to wonder what the theory of class interest and conflict is supposed to mean, and what each author is actually trying to say.

If the general assumption remains obscure, the same conclusion applies to a second, more specific question, namely, what is 'class interest'?

Assuming (*pace* Bentley) that interest means economic interest, an economic minded orientation may be imputed to an actor without being consciously held by the actor himself, or pursued by the actor according to his perception of self-interest. In the first case both the interest and the class are 'reconstructed': we are saying only that all the people to whom the observer attributes the same economic interest can be placed in a same categorical class. And the fantastic distance between these 'reconstructions' and the real world of politics hardly needs underpinning. It is only in the second case, then, that economic interests may lead to class voting, class parties, and so called class politics. If so the thesis applies to *some*, not *all* parties; and can be applied only, historically, to the post-enfranchisement developments of party systems.

The third, and even more crucial question, is: what do we mean by 'representation'? Once more, we are confronted with an astonishing lack of sophistication, for it appears that representation is conceived as a pure and simple *projection*. The argument seems to run as follows: since individuals have a 'class position' which is reflected in their 'class behaviour', it follows that millions of such individuals will be represented by thousands of other individuals on account of similar social origins. If one is reminded, however, that not even *individual* representative behaviour can be safely inferred from class origin and position, one is bound to be dazzled by the transplantation of such a naïve projective logic at the level of entire *collectivities*.

The fantastic irreality of the argument that an entire 'class' is being 'represented' (in some meaningful sense of the term) by such a complex organization as a mass party, has been recently spelled out in a very cogent manner by Mancur Olson. According to this author it is contradictory to assume that individuals are motivated by material self-interest, and that individuals so motivated will seek to achieve their common or group interests.

In other terms, the more individuals pursue their self-interest, and the more numerous these individuals, the less their interests can be represented by large scale organizations—for this reason: 'if the members of a large group rationally seek to maximise their personal welfare, they will *not* act to advance their common or group objectives.'[7]

In conclusion, the theoretical status of the 'class sociology' of parties is poor. In the first place, the concept of representation is patently abused. Projectively speaking we are only permitted to say that parties *reflect*, or may reflect, social classes. This means that one may find 'class resemblance' between party voters on the one hand, and the party personnel on the other hand. From this finding one may draw the inference that voters and leaders are linked by a state of socio-psychological *empathy* —but one cannot infer more. The difference between 'empathy' and 'representation' is abysmal, as has been known for over twenty centuries to jurists, constitutional thinkers and, in everyday experience, to anyone involved in representational dealings. Empathy facilitates understanding; representation poses the intricate problem of replacing one or more persons with another person in such a way that the representative acts in the interest of the represented. Hence it is entirely gratuitous to assert that parties 'represent' classes. In fact we can only verify, on sociological grounds, whether parties 'reflect' classes.[8] It would be much to the advantage of clarity, therefore, to drop the notion of representation altogether, both with reference to 'class' and to 'interest'.

The theoretical status of our subject-matter is equally unsatisfactory with regard to the notion of conflict. In this respect the problem is how classes relate to one another. Most of us seem to abide by a 'conflict model'. However, the class theory of conflict is radically different from the pluralistic theory of conflict. In his philosophical writings Marx is unquestionably

---

[7] Mancur Olson, jun., *The Logic of Collective Action: Public Goods and the Theory of Groups* (Cambridge, Mass.: Harvard University Press, 1965), 2 and *passim*. The italics are in the original.

[8] For a summary overview of the technical complexity of the concept, see e.g. my article 'Representational Systems' in the *International Encyclopedia of the Social Sciences* [xiii. 465–74].

Manichaean.[9] Therefore conflict—i.e. the class struggle—is only a temporary necessity, and is necessary only in so far as it is conducive to the victory of the (good) slave over the (bad) master. This is clearly shown by the fact that his end-state—the classless society—is imagined as a conflictless monochromatic society. Contrarywise, in the pluralistic approach conflict—i.e. antagonisms, contestation, and dissent—is positively valued not only because all parties may stand to gain, but especially because conflict results from variety, and variety is *per se* seminal.

Clearly, therefore, Marxists and pluralists are not speaking of a same conflict: the word has a very different descriptive and evaluative meaning in the two approaches. Instead much of the current sociology of politics muddles a class conflict with a pluralistic conflict. This is not only to say that the notion of conflict remains hopelessly cross-contaminated, but also to suggest that by testing whether social conflicts are zero-sum or positive-sum, we would also be in a position to decide which of our conflict models applies—the Marxist or the pluralistic.

Finally, the theoretical poverty of the class sociology of parties (and of politics) is particularly striking with regard to the very notion of 'class', which is hopelessly cross-contaminated—as we shall suggest later—with the notion of 'status'. Meanwhile let the caution simply be—in the words of Raymond Aron—that we are 'at the same time obsessed by the notion of class and incapable of defining it'.[10]

2. CLASS VOTING

Whatever the theoretical failings, which are the empirical findings? Research has been heavily concentrated on 'class voting', under the assumption that class voting reveals to what extent party systems reflect socio-economic cleavages, and

---

[9] The specification is necessary because in his more circumstantial writings—especially historical essays or occasional pamphlets, such as *The Eighteenth Brumaire of Louis Bonaparte*—Marx is more concerned with realistic details. But the *Weltanschauung* of Marx refers us to his historical materialism, or his dialectical materialism, which is outlined in his philosophical writings.

[10] R. Aron, *La Lutte de Classes* (Paris: Gallimard, 1964), 87.

particularly the class structure of the society. Alford's comparative survey of the Anglo-American democracies can be taken as an illustration of the standard approach, that is, of the statistical method of correlating occupation and class position with voting behaviour.[11]

The overall finding of Alford's *Party and Society* is that England, and to a lesser degree Australia, are class-polarized polities, while the United States and Canada belong to the less class-polarized systems. More precisely, Alford's index of class voting shows, for the period 1952–62, a mean of 40 in Great Britain, 33 in Australia, 16 in the United States, and 6 in Canada. These and other findings are of great interest precisely because they replace commonplaces with figures. However, when one reads Alford's conclusion that 'Great Britain . . . has a relatively "pure" class politics'[12] one cannot help wondering how this conclusion relates to the figures.

According to what standard are we to assess a situation of a *relatively pure* class *politics*? Apparently Alford had decided that this was the case with England long before assembling his evidence. For the figures warrant only the conclusion that England displays *relatively more* class *voting* than the other three countries—which is indeed a very different conclusion. The difference between relatively 'pure' and relatively 'more' is highlighted by the estimate of R. T. McKenzie and Allan Silver 'that at most elections (from 1884) the Conservatives have won about one-third of the working class vote, and that this working class element has constituted about one-half of the party's total electoral support'.[13]

Likewise, the difference between class *voting* and class *politics* can be highlighted by noting that over the last seventy years, i.e. from 1896 to 1966, the English 'labour party has obtained only twice a sufficient governing majority, and that since 1922 . . . it has been in power for 15 years only'.[14] If class voting

[11] See, *passim*, Robert R. Alford, *Party and Society: The Anglo-American Democracies* (Chicago: Rand McNally, 1963). [12] Ibid. 289–90.
[13] In *Party Systems and Voter Alignments*, p. 117. Cf. R. T. McKenzie, A. Silver, *Angels in Marble* (London: Heinemann, 1968).
[14] Richard Rose, 'Classes Sociales et Partis Politiques en Grande-Bretagne dans une Perspective Historique', in *Revue Française de Sociologie*, Special Number (1966), 643.

was the same as class politics the paradox would be that Britain has been generally governed by a party that allegedly represents a small 'class minority'. It seems more sensible to argue, therefore, that the English Conservatives are a cross-class party that manages to win a governing majority precisely because it does not practise 'class politics', i.e. a governmental policy inspired by class interests and criteria. Therefore one may hold that class 'voting' represents the major support of the English Labour party, but one can hardly pass on to assert that Britain represents a significant instance of class 'politics'.

If one inspects, furthermore, the comparative evidence, nothing supports the contention that class is the major single determinant of voting behaviour. Indeed, a reviewer could well subtitle Alford's book as bearing on *non-class voting* in the Anglo-American democracies. The argument is developed by Alford as if religious, regional, and ethnic factors were intervening variables. None the less, his actual data indicate that this is contrary to fact in two out of four cases.

Let it be added that a comparative assessment also weakens the significance of the English case. The reason that class appears prominent in Britain may well be, in fact, that all the other dimensions of cleavage have withered away. If so, one may well argue that even under the most favourable conditions (the absence of countervailing cleavages) the class imprint is very poorly—indeed impurely—reflected in the English voting behaviour. In short, England represents a fiasco.

However that may be, the overall evidence offered by Alford warrants only the following hypothesis: class is the major determinant of voting behaviour *only* if no other cleavage happens to be salient. Thus the correct formulation of the problem is: given a multiplicity of cleavages, can it be shown that there is a hierarchy of cleavages according to which the class cleavage tends to prevail?

As a matter of fact, the thesis that parties reflect, roughly, social classes is buttressed by continental Europe far better than by the English-speaking world. Mattei Dogan has compared the voting behaviour of the industrial workers in ten European countries, and according to his estimates class voting in Europe finds its peak in Finland, where 80 per cent of the industrial workers are supposed to vote either Communist (45 per cent) or Socialist (35 per cent). Finland is followed by Norway (75 per cent), Sweden, Denmark, Italy, France, and, *seventh*, England.[15]

This evidence is prima facie rather impressive, but we should not lose sight, to begin with, of the fact that the foregoing percentages leave aside half or more than half of the total voting population. Sweden, Norway, England, and Finland are the countries in which the Socialist and/or Communist left gains roughly half of the total returns; in Italy and France the working-class parties are at a 40 per cent level; and in Holland and Western Germany the proportion is still lower. Now, if half and often more than half of the total vote is given to parties which in terms of class politics should be largely outnumbered, how can this discrepancy be explained? Surely the proportion between the well-to-do and the have-less is nowhere even, no matter how these categories are apportioned.

Even if we restrict the problem to the class voting of the working class, the evidence appears far less impressive when we come to the breakdowns. For one thing, the data aggregate the Socialist and Communist turnout, an easy thing to do in statistics, but a more difficult thing to understand in politics. If the assumption is that voting behaviour basically follows class patterns, then the problem presented by the evidence of Finland, Italy, and France is not class voting, but class splitting. From the point of view of the sociology of politics the question is: can class splitting, and the choice between a Socialist and a Communist allegiance, be explained by socio-economic factors? As for the countries with no significant class splitting, the puzzling evidence is that three of the four countries having the highest proportion of the working class in the adult population (England, Belgium, and Western Germany) are at the same time the countries in which the workers are less likely to vote Socialist, i.e. to follow class loyalties. Of course the cases of England, Belgium, and Western

---

[15] '*Il Voto Operaio in Europa Occidentale*', in *Il Mulino*, no. 94, pp. 250–75; also in *Revue Française de Sociologie*, 1 (1960). The percentages are purely indicative and should be accepted with caution, for in a number of cases—especially in Italy and Germany—a large portion of the respondents refuse to divulge the party affiliation.

Germany can be explained, but hardly in terms of a theory of class politics.[16]

The problem can be attacked, then, from two sides. One is to explain why most workers *do* vote for 'their party'. The other is to explain *class splitting* and/or *class deviants*. I submit that the first approach leaves the issue at a trivial stage of explanation.

Whether or not a party should be considered a class party is usually decided by ascertaining which parties do obtain a class support on the basis of a class appeal. The class appeal says: vote for the party that will augment your wages, diminish your working load, and shift the balance of power from your class enemies to yourself. In short, vote for the party that discriminates in your favour. This is like having a bank that offers to pay an interest of 15 per cent, while the other banks offer only 3 per cent. To be sure, an observer may be terribly interested in discovering why a majority of depositors does switch to the 15 per cent bank; but my guess is that economists would want to explain why a substantial portion of depositors does not switch.

According to the analogy, the non-trivial problem is posed by the 'working class tories',[17] by the fact that a substantial portion of workers fail to respond to the class appeal. As Dogan puts it, the problem is why so many workers do *not* vote left.[18]

[16] The closest explanation in line with the class assumption is that the three countries in question have a high vertical mobility which favours cross-class coalitions. However, this argument shifts the emphasis from social cleavages to social mobility, and is not entirely convincing either. As we shall see in section 3 below, religion explains far more, at least in the French case; whereas in the Belgium case the major factor is ethnicity and language. As for England, I have suggested above that it represents a fiasco.

[17] This is the title of the book of Eric A. Nordlinger published by MacGibbon and Kee (London, 1967).

[18] This is not only the thread of the article cited above, but also a persistent theme of all the writings of Dogan, which emphasize over and over again the 'feeble relationship' between the size of the working class and the electoral turnout of the working-class parties. Among the more recent writings see: 'Le Vote Ouvrier en France: Analyse Ecologique des Elections de 1962', and 'Comportement Politique et Condition Sociale en Italie', both in *Revue Française de Sociologie*, 6 (1965), 435–71, and 7 (1966), 700–34; and esp. Dogan's chapter (in the cited Lipset, Rokkan volume) 'Political Change and Social Stratification in France and Italy', pp. 129–95. With regard to the problems discussed in this paper it is important to note that the growing sophistication of ecological analysis—i.e. the Dogan-type analysis—undermines the Alford-type 'correlation method'.

Both in England and in France one-third of the working-class vote is not given to working-class parties; in Western Germany until 1957 almost one worker out of two had voted the Christian-Democratic party; in Italy almost 20 per cent of the working-class vote is retained by parties which are neither Communist nor Socialist; and even in the countries which are led by social-democratic majorities—Sweden, Norway, and Denmark—one-fourth of the working class still votes for the bourgeois parties. Why so?

In addition to class deviants and class splitting, a third difficulty is posed by *non-class voting*, I mean, by those countries in which no class parties can be said to exist. Some, if not all these difficulties are apparently overcome if we merely speak of *left*—as when we assert that workers tend to vote left, or that the world goes left, and the like. But what does 'left' mean? The usual way of getting around the problem is to say that 'left' *includes* Communist, Socialist, and Labour parties, plus whatever exists more-on-the-left than on-the-right wherever such parties do not exist. This is hardly a reply, however. The question is precisely according to which criterion, or criteria, these parties are included, and other parties are excluded, from the 'left' categorization.

One criterion is clear enough: property rights. According to this criterion the left opposes private property, or advocates collective property, while the right opposes collective property and defends private property. But the criterion has two short-comings. One is that it leaves out a number of countries in which the left does not believe in collective property and is not particularly obsessed by the problem of private property (e.g. the United States). The second, and major, shortcoming is that to explain the *economic* meaning of left does not explain the *political* meaning of left. Hence the critical question is: what is 'left' in political matters? Aside from the decisions affecting private property or the distribution of wealth and income, how is one to behave 'leftwards' in all the other areas of decision?

Here we are at a loss, at least if one is to judge by the extravagance or the fuzziness of a number of proposed definitions.[19]

---

[19] Both qualities are combined, for example, in the following clarification: 'Left is structural criticism and reportage and theories of society which at

162   GIOVANNI SARTORI

I would still adhere, among the sensible interpretations, to the suggestion of Goguel: left means, politically, 'more change', the attitude of moving ahead faster and of opposing the status quo.[20] This yardstick is, however, too loose and somewhat too relativistic. Obviously enough, the politics of the left is to oppose the status quo of the non-left; in victory, however, the left opposes the changes proposed by its opponents and upholds its own status quo. Accordingly the Soviet Communist party should be reclassified by now as a conservative force, and it would be hard to explain in what sense the British trade unions remain a progressive force.

It is not sufficient to say, then, that left is 'more change'; we are required to qualify the statement by adding: change in favour of the underprivileged. Even so we are still in trouble. For it is hard to understand why, according to this criterion, Fascism, Nazism, Peronism and the like should be excluded from 'left'. These movements advocated change (and eventually did produce change). Surely they had large working-class support, and possibly took as much care of the underprivileged as many Communist parties in power have done so far. On the other hand, it would not do to say that 'left' cannot be a dictatorship: Communist regimes surely are dictatorships.

It would seem, therefore, that 'left' is actually defined—no matter how unawares—by the following three stipulations: first, that Marxist parties and voters are left by definition; second, that if no such parties exist we may have recourse to a supplementary criterion, i.e., discrimination in favour of the underprivileged; third, that the second criterion does not apply to the parties which propound an anti-Marxist philosophy, even if they advocate change and express a protest of the lower strata. If so, the 'left lumping' is little more than a weird ideological aggregate. Whatever its ideological validity, its scientific validity is highly dubious. Granted that 'left' may be used as a convenient shorthand, it does not follow that such an aggregate helps our understanding.

some point are focused politically as demands and programs . . . To be left means to connect up cultural with political criticism.' (C. Wright Mills, *Power, Politics and People* (New York: Oxford University Press 1962), 26.)

[20] His distinction actually is between 'movement' and 'established order'. See F. Goguel, *Geographie des Elections Françaises 1870–1951* (Paris:Colin, 1951),9.

Why is it that the worker's allegiance largely goes, in some countries, to Communist parties, in other countries to Socialist parties, in some other countries to both, and still in other countries to neither? Conversely (at least according to the convention that Fascism is, by definition, a 'right'), under what conditions does, or can, the protest of the underprivileged be expressed on the right? Finally, why it is that in some countries—not necessarily the wealthy ones—no real 'left' has yet materialized? These are the problems that need investigation—and these are precisely the problems beheaded a priori by the 'left lumping'.

To sum up, class voting studies cannot warrant a class theory of politics—nor a class theory of parties—unless these studies lead to the formulation of a 'law' of class voting which incorporates and explains non-class voting (or cross-class voting). This is how political scientists are required to demonstrate the effects of electoral systems on electoral behaviour; and the same requirements apply to any demonstration of the effects of class on electoral behaviour. Why should 'sociological laws' be exempt from the test required of 'politological laws'?

Meanwhile one is entitled to conclude that the average performance of the statistical line of inquiry has been largely trivial. Given the fact that one can always find socio-economic data, the field has largely developed as a by-product, as an outgrowth of the data. If one is reminded, however, that 'data is empirical information processed and refined so as to measure theoretical concepts',[21] the point remains that the data in question is seldom 'theory relevant'.

These conclusions are hardly surprising in the light of the theoretical misgivings spelled out in the previous paragraph. I take it, in fact, that if the conceptual framework is poor, the findings will follow suit. And we still have to discuss the central concept. So far I have reviewed the sociology of voting as if at least the meaning of 'class' was clear. But I am afraid that also much of the evidence collected under the class rubric is hopelessly confused and confusing.

[21] H. A. Alker, jun., 'The Comparison of Aggregate Political and Social Data', in S. Rokkan (ed.), *Comparative Social Science Research* [The Hague: Mouton, 1968].

3. THE HYPOTHESIS REVERSED

It is generally acknowledged that there is a difference between 'subjective' and 'objective' class. Only prima facie, however, does this distinction clarify the problem: because 'subjective class' takes on two very different meanings, and even the notion of 'objective class' is far from being unequivocal.

When we speak of subjective class it is seldom clear whether we mean *status self-perception* or *class consciousness* or both. In any case, more often than not the distinction is inadequately underpinned.[22]

Status applies to a problem of ranking, i.e. to the fact that individuals are able to locate themselves along a stratification scale. We thus obtain a set of 'prestige levels' and a prestige hierarchy. Does status awareness correspond to some kind of 'class awareness'? This inference is, at best, permissible only if we make clear that the slices of a stratification system do not correspond to the slices of a class system, neither in number nor in kind.[23] Furthermore, it should be equally clear that 'class awareness'—the fact that class is perceived—is by no means the same as 'class consciousness', which is a far more serious matter bearing on the belief system.

Class consciousness meant to Marx, and still means to much of the European reality and literature, a sense of *belonging* to a socio-economic class. That is to say that the notion of class

[22] In his article on 'Political Sociology' for the *International Encyclopedia of the Social Sciences* Morris Janowitz observes that the studies on the social basis of political cleavage and consensus 'are mainly derived from a social stratification theory of politics (derived in turn from Marx) and have been characterized by a progressive refinement of categories of analysis from broad concerns with class and occupation to much more refined measures of social status' [xii. 300]. Since this is a fair representation of the general development of the discipline, my point can be reformulated by noting, first, that Marx has been misread, and, second, that 'measures of social status' do not belong to the same dimension, or continuum, as 'class'.

[23] This distinction is forcibly stated by Ralf Dahrendorf, *Class and Class Conflict in Industrial Society* (London: Routledge and Kegan Paul, 1959). Whether or not one agrees with Dahrendorf's subsequent treatment of the relationship between status and class, he is surely right *vis à vis* the 'class-status mélange' accepted by Janowitz and by much of the American sociology of politics.

consciousness points to class minded individuals, to class devotees who actually live a 'class ideology'. The first implication is that 'stratification' is irrelevant to a 'class identifier'. He neither perceives nor follows the whole line from soldier to general; he simply dichotomizes between 'we' and 'they', the class enemies or the class exploiters. Another implication is that class consciousness confronts us with a 'living reality', that is, with a subjective class which is also, in some sense, an objective reality. In Aron's wording, this class exists as a 'collective reality', as a 'real totality'.[24]

If properly underpinned, then, status awareness on the one hand, and class consciousness on the other, are not even at shouting distance. To perceive one's position along a stratification scale is one thing, to be class minded is quite another thing. At most status sensitivity may lead to 'status polarization';[25] but even a situation of status polarization is hardly conducive to a class-type conflict. Every society is a 'stratarchy'; but relatively few societies are 'class polarized'. In particular, a system of status *stratification* is far removed from class *action*.

As for the objective notion of class we need not get entangled in the controversy about the 'reality' of collective nouns. Whether class consciousness and action are also an objective reality is immaterial for the present discussion, since both Marxists and non-Marxists agree to the effect that the objective starting-point is provided by class conditions. It will be sufficient, therefore, to retain the notion of 'class conditions', with the understanding that we are deferred to an index of objective measures. The notion is surely objective but merely denotes a categorical class.

Bearing these distinctions in mind, let us take a fresh look into the matter. Given the fact that the various class approaches tend to argue the case with reference to class voting, the preliminary query is: what does class voting indicate?

---

[24] *La Lutte de Classes*, pp. 67–9.

[25] The 'status polarization' conceptualization represents a distinctive contribution of the Michigan Survey Center group, and correctly implies that a status-polarized society is not a class-polarized society. See, e.g., Angus Campbell and associates, *The American Voter* (New York: Wiley, 1960).

Most people would reply that class voting is an indicator of class consciousness. But we have seen that this is by no means sure. In some countries so-called class voting may simply reflect status polarization; in other countries it may reflect a combination of both, status sensitivity as well as class consciousness. Moreover, as I shall suggest shortly, class voting may well be an indicator of something else. The trouble is that the discriminating power of the indicator 'class voting' is almost nil. For one thing, voting is more an act than an action, I mean, voting reflects a very discontinuous and superficial layer of behaviour. This is also to say that class voting does not suffice to detect 'class action'—unless we are satisfied with the tautology that class action merely signifies class voting. But I would rather say that class action and class voting point to very different stages or levels of *activation*. Hence class action comprises class voting, but the vice versa is not true. In the second place, and especially, class voting does not suffice to detect 'class consciousness'—unless we are satisfied, once again, with the tautology that class consciousness merely signifies class voting.

Whether or not class voting flows from class consciousness, from adherence to a class ideology, can be ascertained only via interviewing. But here we pay the price for the theoretical poverty of the category. For the information supplied by the interviews is generally indicative of status self-perception (or of status estimation, if one uses the reputational method); but often inadequate for the purpose of identifying class consciousness. Granted that it is easier to elicit responses about status than about ideology, yet a research can be so designed as to capture both kinds of information in their distinctiveness. However, if status and class are conceptually muddled, the research design and the research findings will be equally muddled. If so, we are left to wonder if so-called class voting is *real* class voting, i.e. whether we are dealing with class consciousness or not.

We are thus left to confront directly the crucial issue, namely, how do we pass from class conditions to class consciousness and action. As Max Weber already pointed out, 'no differentiation of life opportunities, no matter how deep, produces by itself "class action", that is, a common (collective) action of those

I class conditions	II status awareness
III class consciousness	IV class action

FIG. 11.1.   Breakdowns of 'class'

belonging to the class'.[26] This is unquestionably the crux of the matter. Yet, and surprisingly enough, the issue is generally dismissed. Let us try to understand why with the help of the four breakdowns recapitulated in Figure 11.1. If the problem is formulated by asking 'how does objective class relate to subjective class?' we may either envisage the passage from quadrant I to quadrant II, or the passage from quadrant I to quadrant III. Hence, if the notion of 'subjective class' remains unfolded, it is only too easy to confuse the step from I to II with the step from II to III. And precisely this quid pro quo goes a long way towards explaining why the crucial point has been side-stepped.

We have discovered, in fact, that an index of class measures tends to correspond fairly well with status self-perception. But this is hardly surprising, given the fact that our respondents have been taught to rate their status precisely on the basis of education, occupation, and income. As is only to be expected, therefore, quadrants I and II are likely to vary, across Western nations, along a semantic more than any other dimension, i.e. depending on whether 'worker' or 'middle-class' are good or bad words. Thus the European polling data reveals an inflation of 'workers' whereas the American interview data reveals an inflation of 'middle-class'.

So far, so good. But the interchangeability between I and II—between objective occupational level and self-rated status —does not imply in the least that I or II are equally interchangeable with III. As a matter of fact, the problem of how class conditions relate to class consciousness has not even been touched upon. And we have already seen that status awareness

---

[26] Max Weber, *Economia e Società* (Milan: Comunità, 1961), ii. 231 (*Wirtschaft und Gesellschaft*, viii, sect. 6).

168 GIOVANNI SARTORI

has little, if anything, to do with class consciousness. Hence the question is once again: how do we pass from quadrant I to quadrant III, and ultimately to quadrant IV? In substance, how do we know that class conditions are *the cause* of class consciousness and action?

The reply is, very simply, that we do *not* know. This is the same as saying that between class conditions on the one hand, and class action on the other hand, there is a wide gap, a major missing link. Presumably, therefore, we must search for an *intervening variable*.

In the course of his argument Alford notes in passing that 'it seems probable that the relative strength of labour unionism is both a cause and a consequence of class politics'.[27] Admittedly Alford is justified in leaving the argument at its bifurcation, for correlations cannot warrant a causal relation. For instance, a positive correlation between conservative voting and bald-headed males would not prove that the loss of hair is the cause of conservatism.[28] But further probing has revealed that while the English class vote is highly correlated with trade union affiliation, no class vote can be said to exist for the non-union members of the working class, who actually split their vote between the Labour and the Conservative parties.[29]

Now, suppose that a country by country probe confirmed that class voting correlates significantly with trade union affiliation (not with non-union members). Suppose, further-more, that the research design included an *organizational variable* —a systematic mapping of 'networks' implemented by indexes of organizational coverage and pressure—and that the findings

[27] *Party and Society*, p. 292.

[28] Mattei Dogan provides a pertinent illustration of how misleading statistical 'coincidences' can be. In analysing the 1962 referendum and general election he notes that 'in France the proportion of workers is about 40 p.c.; the proportion of NO's (against de Gaulle in the referendum) is very close: 38.8 p.c. and also quite close to the communist-socialist turnout: 38.8 p.c.'. Yet the probing reveals that 'the coefficient of correlation among these variables is not significant' (*Revue Française de Sociologie*, 6 (1965), 471).

[29] According to a 1964 Gallup poll the proportion of union workers voting for the Labour party is 4 to 1. See also Martin Harrison, *Trade Unions and the Labour Party since 1945* (London: Allen and Unwin, 1960); and Jean Blondel, *Voters Parties and Leaders: The Social Fabric of British Politics* (Harmondsworth: Penguin Books, 1963) (with reference to the 1958 general elections).

did support the hypothesis that a thoroughgoing organizational network is a necessary condition of class consciousness and behaviour, for the latter varies with, and follows the destiny of, the organization.[30] More specifically, suppose that the countries in which the Communist parties outweigh the Socialist parties are found to be the countries in which the Communists were the first to establish the 'apparatus mass party'; or the first to seize at the downfall of a regime the pre-existing strategic networks and control positions;[31] and suppose, therefore, that the lasting success of Communism was found to coincide systematically with the occupancy of an organizational void, rather than with objective conditions of deprivation.

If these conjectures were adequately tested and buttressed, the conclusion would be that what we are really observing, via class behaviour, is the impact of an organizational variable: *the influence of party and trade union control*. Far from being the 'efficient cause', class conditions are only a 'facilitating condition'.[32] To put it bluntly, it is not the 'objective' class (class conditions) that creates the party, but the party that creates the 'subjective' class (class consciousness). More carefully put, whenever parties reflect social classes, this signifies *more* about the party end than about the class end of the interaction. The party is not a 'consequence' of the class. Rather, and before, it is the class that receives its identity from the party. Hence, class behaviour presupposes a party that not only feeds, incessantly, the 'class

---

[30] What happened for instance to the class consciousness of the Italian workers during Fascism? Or to the class consciousness of the German worker under Hitler, in spite of a long tradition of class action?

[31] This was definitely the case in the aftermath of World War Two in Italy; to a lesser extent in France; and (for different reasons) in Finland; while exactly the opposite happened in West Germany. As far as the Italian case is concerned, it is a fact that the Communist apparat managed to take over from the Allied Military Government an exceedingly high number of control positions as soon as they were returned to civilian rule. Had the Socialists or the Catholics been equally organized it is my conjecture that Italy would not display currently the strongest Communist party of Western Europe.

[32] This is not to deny the relevance of other factors, but to affirm that the explanatory power of the 'organizational hypothesis' is greater (especially in communication and cybernetic terms) than the explanatory power of any other single factor.

image', but also a party that provides the structural cement of 'class reality'.[33]

The point can be restated from the angle of my former assertion that class is an ideology. Classes materialize in the real world in close correspondence with belief systems in which 'class' becomes the central idea-element; and it is the ideology of class that obtains 'class action'. If so the question becomes how ideologies take hold. And to this effect I would subscribe to the statement that 'no idea has ever made much headway without an organization behind it . . . Wherever ideologies seem to be important in politics they have a firm organizational basis.'[34] In summary, large collectivities become class structured only if they are *class persuaded*. The most likely and apt persuader is the party (or the union) playing on the class appeal resource. In any case, ideological persuasion requires a powerfully organized network of communications.[35]

To be sure, and once again, these are only conjectures. However, if the assumption that 'class conditions' are the prime mover had been seriously probed, there would be no room for such conjectures—they would have long been disproven. Hence the fact that alternative hypotheses have hardly been put to the test goes to show to what extent the causal explanation of the sociologist has been taken for granted not only much too readily, but in uncritical fashion.

It is interesting to wonder, therefore, why the naïve class explanation of the sociologist finds audiences of predisposed believers with so much ease. I am not satisfied by the reply that the sociologist tends to be a more or less subconscious Marxist, in the sense that Marxism implicitly privileges a science of society. For the question turns on the lasting success—in scientific quarters—of a nineteenth-century derivation of Hegelian philosophy; and to this question I would reply that precisely in scientific quarters we are the victims of a naïve

---

[33] This conclusion has a familiar Leninist ring. Even Marx, though less consistently and explicitly, grasped the point better than many Marxist-inspired scholars.

[34] Samuel H. Barnes, 'Ideology and the Organization of Conflict', *Journal of Politics*, 28 (1966), 522.

[35] The foregoing applies to 'class', not to 'status'. This points again to the importance of the distinction.

quest for ultimate objectivity. It is this *crude objectivism*—which belongs to our inferiority complexes *vis à vis* the physical sciences—that helps to explain, in turn, the lasting popularity not only of Marx but also of social Darwinism, i.e. the idea that man is a creature of his environment.[36]

The reason that we are predisposed to believe in the causal explanation of the sociologist is, then, that we are the victims of an 'objectivist bias'. The underlying argument is something like this: the polity (and politics) is an 'artifact', whereas in the society we find the 'facts'. The argument might also be that the political scientist deals with short range predictions, whereas socio-economic indicators detect long range trends. But also in this form the argument reflects an 'objectivist superstition'. For the long range validity attributed to socio-economic forecasts (in political matters) represents another instance—of belief accepted without evidence.

An objectivist bias also explains the unequal treatment given, respectively, to 'religion' and 'class'. Why is it, in fact, that religion is seldom presented as a prime mover, but far more often is presented as an intervening (and disturbing) variable?

If one inspects the evidence with an innocent mind, the striking fact is precisely the extent to which religion remains important in spite of the pace of secularization. Indeed, wherever one finds different religions one finds that denominational cleavages relate to political behaviour just as much, or even more, than class cleavages. This is the case, for example, with the Netherlands and the United States. And the case may not be very different with all-Catholic countries such as France, Austria, and Italy. In France, for instance, it is the Catholic influence that explains—according to Dogan—'the absence of

---

[36] On the impact of social Darwinism see, e.g., David C. McClelland, *The Achieving Society* (Princeton: Van Nostrand, 1961), 391. This is also to concur with Lipset's view that 'some of those who uphold the single attribute position are far from being Marxists. They do not believe that position in the economic structure determines all other aspects of status; rather, they would suggest that statistical analysis suggests the presence of a basic common factor' (*Revolution and Counterrevolution* (New York: Basic Books, 1968), 149). My point equally applies, however, to statistical analysis, for an underlying objectivist bias not only privileges the statistical evidence, but also facilitates our acceptance of appallingly crude data.

a relationship between the importance of the working class and the electoral strength of the parties which call upon such class'.[37] In a similar vein Converse notes that 'even in current France one can predict with greater accuracy whether a citizen will be a partisan of the "left" or of the "right" by knowing his position on the clerical question than by knowing his position on the more central issues typically associated with the left–right distinction'.[38]

Let us note first this difference: Converse is merely suggesting that the clerical question is a parsimonious predictor and, as such, a good indicator—he is not committing himself to the view that religion motivates political behaviour. There is a striking difference, then, between our caution in handling the religious factor, as against the lack of caution with which we accept the assumption that class motivates political behaviour.

Why so? In my interpretation, the religious factor is 'weighed less'—no matter how unwittingly—on two counts: (i) because we can forget that class is subjective, but hardly that religion is subjective, and (ii) because the hold of religion is patently related to Church, i.e. to an organizational backing which is, in turn, a 'superstructure'. The discrimination is apparent: religion is 'too subjective' to be a prime mover—hence we have to fall back on class.[39]

Let there be no misunderstanding about my argument. I do not deny that—in politics—class may be, or become, more important than religion. I am saying, instead, that the causal factors involved are, in both cases, the same: the relative strength of the *organizational support* of each belief system. Whenever the class appeal outweighs the religious appeal, this is not because class is an 'objective reality'; rather, this is because the ideology of class wins the 'belief battle', in conjunc-

---

[37] 'Le Vote Ouvrier en France', p. 466.

[38] Philip E. Converse, 'The Nature of Belief Systems in Mass Publics', in D. Apter (ed.), *Ideology and Discontent* (New York: Free Press of Glencoe, 1964), 248. The findings are in Converse and Dupeux, 'Politicization of the Electorate in France and the United States', *Public Opinion Quarterly*, 26/1 (1962).

[39] Note that the causal factor 'race' would do just as well, or even better. But race raises unpleasant associations, while class points to a positively valued ideology.

tion with the prevalence of a new organizer, the mass party, over the former organizer, the Church.

4. FROM SOCIOLOGY OF POLITICS TO POLITICAL SOCIOLOGY

Thus far I have reviewed a major stream of the sociology of politics properly called.[40] It is with exclusive reference, then, to the *sociology* of politics that I have noted an impressive disproportion between assumptions and accomplishments. But it would be unfair to conclude the review at this point.

In fact, a fundamental and most promising reorientation of the discipline is under way, as is shown by the Lipset and Rokkan introductory chapter of *Party Systems and Voter Alignments: Cross-National Perspectives*,[41] which represents, in my view, a landmark. In the Lipset–Rokkan approach the question which *is* conducive to causal explanations and does grapple with the real problems is: how are conflicts and cleavages translated into a party system?

The first advantage of this approach is that it gives equal attention to *any kind* of conflict and cleavage. Race and ethnicity, region and locality, culture and tradition, religion and ideology, point to dimensions of cleavage which may be as important as its class dimension. Conflicts are not only economic and related to the class structure, but also regional, ethnic, linguistic, religious, and ideological. To assume that these latter sources of conflict are destined, in the long run, to give way to 'objective' economic factors amounts to a naïve view of the complexity of human nature, at least in politics. The

[40] One may say that I have reviewed the more traditional line of inquiry, while neglecting the technical development of the discipline along the line of 'multiple regression analysis', for example. Even so, no technical sophistication can obviate theoretical false starts.

[41] Pp. 1–64 (n. 6 above). As the editors of the volume indicate, their introductory chapter 'was undertaken *after* most of the articles were completed' (p. xii). Therefore, in spite of other excellent chapters (e.g. the two chapters of Juan Linz, or the one of Allardt and Pesonen on Finland) the introduction stands alone. The assertion that 'the introduction represents an effort to synthesize the knowledge . . . presented by the chapter authors' (ibid.) understates the Lipset–Rokkan accomplishment.

second advantage is that the inquiry is not correctly focused on the real problem—*translation*. This is indeed the crucial consideration, as a couple of reminders will help to underline.

Prima facie, racial cleavages would appear the more irreducible source of conflict. However, they are not 'translated', for instance, in the party system of the United States; in other words, they remain below the threshold of the North American political culture. The case of Brazil is perhaps even more interesting, for in this instance the very perception of a racial border appears to be missing. On the other hand, we are often confronted with conflicts and cleavages which appear, at least prima facie, far less deep-rooted, and yet prove to be irreducible. The Irish question was settled only by secession; the French-speaking Canadians are currently more bitter than they were in the past; the cleavage between Flemish and Walloons in Belgium has grown deeper and the conflict is more acute in the sixties than it has ever been. Now, surely these conflicts could be managed better if we knew more about them, and particularly if political sociology explained how they become, and why they may not become, 'translated' into a party system.

So far we have been content with saying that when cleavages are cross-cutting, or overlapping, they are likely to neutralize one another, whereas they otherwise tend to be cumulative and hence to reinforce one another. However, as Dahl rightly points out, the assumption that cross-cutting cleavages encourage conciliation does not hold 'if all the cleavages are felt with equal intensity'; it holds only under the condition that 'some cleavages are less significant than others'.[42] Moreover, if the notion of translation is taken seriously—as it should be—it points to an additional important question: whether cleavages are deviated and domesticated, or instead intensified and exasperated, precisely by *translation handling*. And here enters politics.

This is another novelty that equally deserves to be highlighted. To most sociologists, politics is little more than a *projection*. To be sure, Lipset and a number of other sociologists have always refused to reduce politics to an epiphenomenon.

---

[42] In R. A. Dahl (ed.), *Political Oppositions in Western Democracies* (New Haven: Yale University Press, 1966), 378.

Yet if one compares the earlier with the current Lipset, it is apparent that the 'weight of politics' is no longer the same. In the 1957 Lipset–Bendix 'Essay and Bibliography' what cannot be explained by social and economic status merely is 'the competing strategies of the political struggle': the peculiar essence of politics is reduced to the 'strategy' of conflict management.[43]

It is only on account of this element that politics is weighed on its own right. In the 1967 Lipset–Rokkan 'Introduction', however, politics emerges as a major independent variable. No small part of the inquiry is focused, in fact, on the following variables: (i) traditions and rules of decision-making (e.g. conciliar or autocratic); (ii) channels for expression and mobilization of protest; (iii) opportunities, pay-offs, and costs of alliances; (iv) limitations and safeguards against direct majority power.[44]

The foregoing may well appear an analytical breakdown of what Lipset had previously in mind when speaking of 'strategies'. But now a mere chapter heading has been followed up, now it stands as a chapter. Furthermore, a source of political alignments is traced back to the *'we' versus 'they' interaction*. And here we reach at the very roots of alignment-making in terms of a strictly political factor of alignments.[45] All in all, then, the Lipset–Rokkan approach represents a momentous rebalancing of the discipline.[46] In my terminology, Lipset and Rokkan definitely surpass the old-style sociology of politics and unquestionably inaugurate the new political sociology.

---

[43] *Current Sociology*, 6 (1957), 85, 83.

[44] See *Party Systems and Voter Alignments*, esp. pp. 26–33.

[45] Ibid. 3. The authors draw the inference that 'parties themselves might . . . produce their own alignments independently'. The suggestion is not really followed up, however.

[46] With Lipset this evolution is already very evident if one compares *Political Man* with *The First New Nation* (New York: Basic Books, 1963; Garden City: Anchor Books, Doubleday edn., 1967). In the 1963 volume Lipset writes that 'sociologists tend to see party cleavages as reflections of an underlying structure', thereby putting forward an image of social systems 'at odds with the view of many political scientists . . . [But] an examination of comparative politics suggests that the political scientists are right, in that electoral laws determine the nature of the party system as much as any other structural variable' (pp. 335–6, 1967 edn.).

Politics is no longer a mere projection, and the problem becomes 'translation'.

The turning-point having been turned, let me go on to force the Lipset–Rokkan text, hopefully in accord with their intentions. The problem is not only that 'cleavages do not translate themselves into party oppositions as a matter of course'.[47] The problem is also that some cleavages are *not translated* at all. Furthermore, the importance of the notion of translation lies in the implication that translation calls for *translators*, thereby focusing attention on translation handling and/or mishandling. The old-style sociology of politics took for granted that cleavages are *reflected in*, not *produced by*, the political system itself. As a result, there is very little that we really know concerning the extent to which conflicts and cleavages may either be channelled, deflected, and repressed, or, vice versa, activated and reinforced precisely by the operations and operators of the political system. But now we are required to wonder whether 'translation mishandling' may largely contribute to the cleavage structure that one finds in the polities characterized by low coincidence of opinion.

Another breakthrough of the Lipset–Rokkan 'Introduction' bears on the importance given to the historical dimension. In their own words, 'to understand the current alignments of voters behind each of the parties, we have to map variations in the *sequences of alternatives* set for the . . . citizens . . . In single-nation studies we need not always take this history into account . . . But as soon as we move into comparative analysis we have to add an historical dimension. We simply cannot make sense of variations in current alignments without detailed data on differences in the sequences of party formation . . .'[48] The accomplishment is superb, and the gains in depth and perspective are invaluable. On the other hand, the emphasis is constantly one of historical explanation; and this implies that some inherent limitations should also be noted.

History leads to *genetic* explanation, that is, to the understanding of the origins and of whatever follows from the take-off matrix, to the extent that the explanation can proceed from antecedent to consequence on the basis of a same propellent.

---

[47] *Party Systems and Voter Alignments*, p. 26.   [48] Ibid. 2.

However, at a certain point Lipset and Rokkan are struck and intrigued by the 'freezing' of party systems (and of voter alignments) i.e. by the fact that, in spite of the tremendous rate of socio-economic change, the 'party systems of the 1960s reflect, with few but significant exceptions, the cleavage structures of the 1920s.[49]

In my framework this freezing represents the stage of 'structural consolidation' of a party system. With the freezing the cycle of the origins ends, and another cycle begins: either the propellent is no longer the same, or the original propellent is exhausted. Therefore, in my interpretation the 1920 freezing of party systems and alignments is intriguing only as long as we persist in understanding party systems as dependent variables. It is not intriguing, however, if we realize that a freezed party system is simply a party system that intervenes in the political process as an independent *system of channelment*, propelled and maintained by its own laws of inertia.[50] This is the same as saying that the stage of structural consolidation of party systems confronts us with the point at which historical explanations leave off.[51]

My suggestion is thus that the final establishment of political sociology *proprie dicta* still requires another step. In the Lipset –Rokkan approach, politics enters basically via the historical reconstruction. But politics should enter from another door as well. However, before proposing an agenda for the future let us recapitulate on the route travelled thus far.

(1) Political sociology is often a misnomer, for what goes under the name of political sociology generally is a sociological reduction of politics—in reality, then, a

---

[49] Ibid. 50.

[50] This notion of 'structural consolidation', as well as the focus on party systems qua 'channelling systems', is developed in my volume, *Parties and Party Systems* (Cambridge: Cambridge University Press, [1976]). See also my article 'Political Development and Political Engineering', in *Public Policy*, 17 (1968).

[51] It seems to me, therefore, that Lipset and Rokkan evade the problem when they conclude the discussion on the 'freezing of political alternatives' by saying that 'to understand the current alignments . . . it is not enough to analyse . . . the contemporary sociocultural structure; it is even more important to go back to the initial formation of party alternatives . . .' (p. 54). I agree, but this conclusion misses the limits of historical explanations.

sociology of politics that merely pushes aside political science. Instead, political *sociology* is only born when sociologists and political scientists converge half-way. A real political sociology is, then, a discipline that contains what is *sociological* in politics together with what is *political* in sociology.[52]

(2) The encounter that gives rise to a real political sociology is hindered by two major obstacles: an objectivist superstition, and poor causal reasoning. With regard to the first fallacy, the sociologist should take stock of the fact that he deals with artifacts just as much as the political scientist does. With regard to the second fallacy, the sociologist should realize that he cannot cover all the way from the society to the polity by extrapolation, i.e. with crude projective techniques. A fundamental condition of causal inference is that the effect must be contiguous, or contiguous enough, to the cause. Hence *distal effects* cannot be demonstrated as if they were *proximal effects*.

(3) With specific reference to our topic, a real political sociology calls for a simultaneous exploration of how parties are conditioned by the society *and* the society is conditioned by the party system. To say that a party system is a response to a given socio-economic environment is to present half of the picture as if it were all. The complete picture requires, instead, a joint effort to assess to what extent parties are dependent variables reflecting social stratification and cleavages and, vice versa, to what extent these cleavages reflect the channelling imprint of a structured party system.

These points flatly run counter to the Bendix–Lipset agenda of ten years ago, namely, that in the long run we should look

---

[52] In his already cited *Encyclopedia* article Janowitz holds that along with the stratification approach there has always been an 'institutional approach' to political sociology stemming from the influence of Max Weber, in which 'political institutions emerge as . . . independent sources of societal change'. Without denying the influence of Weber, I would rather say that it counteracts on a more sophisticated level the influence of Marx, hardly that the 'institutional approach' belongs to the inner logic of development of the sociological focus.

forward to establishing 'a theoretical framework for political sociology as an integral part of sociology *sans phrase*'.[53] In my opinion it is fortunate that the reorientation of the discipline has disregarded the advice. However—as I was saying—a final step remains on our future agenda: the full recognition of the *programming of the managers*.

The sociology of politics deals with the consumer and ignores the producer. According to the analogy, this is like explaining an economic system as a system of buyers without sellers. Political sociology is required, instead, to account for the producer's no less than for the consumer's end. In the perspective of political sociology a party system is not only a response to the consumer's demand, but is equally a feedback of producer's options. There can be no customers without political entrepreneurs, just like there cannot be political entrepreneurs without customers.

To be sure, in terms of reconstructed explanations a sociology of politics can recount the whole story without accounting for the initiative of the managers. But this does not even begin to prove that the *reconstruction* accounts for the *actual construction*. There are almost infinite ways of regressing *ex post* from consequences to causes. When the outcome is given, nothing is easier than to adjust the alleged cause to its (known) effect. And my contention is that the reconstructed explanation of the sociologist (the pure sociologist) does not account for the actual construction.[54]

Taking a step back, the question is: do we have a way of probing whether or not an *ex post* reconstruction remains true to the actual construction? In my opinion reconstructed explanations can be tested, and should be warranted, on the basis of their predictive potentiality. The question turns, then, on how the sociology of politics performs on predictive grounds. And I

[53] *Current Sociology*, 6 (1957), 87.
[54] In principle one could say that the theories that require first development of the substantive substructure, and then assume that politics will be a reflection, 'reverse the actual sequence of events. In virtually every historical instance, substantive change in economy, society, culture, or elsewhere was brought about by political action'. (Herbert J. Spiro, *Africa, The Primacy of Politics* (New York: Random House, 1966), 152.)

would argue that the sociology of politics predictably fails to pass the test.

Take the cleavage thread, the assumption that party systems reflect socio-economic cleavages. Under this premiss it is fairly obvious, in the first place, that we shall detect past, not emerging cleavages. It is fairly obvious, that is, that we shall obtain not only a static, but also an eminently retrospective picture. In the second place if we start from societal cleavages it is equally clear that we shall miss all the conflicts which have a non-cleavage origin. These are not only the issue-conflicts —e.g. a crisis of legitimacy and the issue about the regime itself—but also the *within-élite* conflicts which remain important even if they largely escape visibility. In the third place, the sociology of politics is likely to miss the fact that 'objective cleavages' can be largely manipulated, that is, used as *resources*, and thereby over or underplayed according to alignment and coalition strategies.

If we turn to the class thread, its predictive implausibility can be highlighted on similar grounds. With reference to the United States Converse makes the point that 'if we take as a goal the explanation of political *changes* . . . as opposed to questions of more static political structure, then the explanatory utility of the social-class thread is almost nil'.[55] Now, 'explanation of change' is surely a central aspect of what I call predictive potentiality. And there are good reasons for assuming that the conclusion of Converse equally applies to most countries.

If the class thread is actually supplied by an index of class conditions, we are confronted with this dilemma: if we construct a 'hard index' it will not register emerging variations, and hence will predict perpetuation rather than change; whereas if we construct a more sensitive 'soft index' it will account for variations which may not affect in the least the political system. In any case the trouble is that we are confronted with *distal causation*, that is, with distal effects that cannot be predicted, almost by definition, with any useful degree of accuracy. Hence, objective class conditions may change, and the polity may not—or may react rather than reflect.

The sociologist may concede on the foregoing points and yet

[55] In *Ideology and Discontent*, p. 260 n. 44.

argue that his socio-economic indicators are more powerful, in the long run, than the more subjective indicators utilized by political scientists. But the 'long run' argument is a convenient alibi for anyone, for the political scientist no less than for the sociologist. In long run terms there is always an ulterior future—beyond the future that has already deceived us—to which the verification of our predictions can be deferred. Therefore, either we indicate 'how long' the run is supposed to be, or we enter an entirely futile debate. For the sake of the argument let it be assumed that we agree to a deadline of fifty years. If so, I find no convincing evidence in favour of the contention that the sociologist detects 'long range' trends, while the political scientist is confined by his subjectivism to 'short range' predictions. Surely the sociological forecast is more complicated than the forecast demanded of the demographer. Yet even the record of demographic predictions is a record of persistent miscalculations—and this before the advent of birth control techniques.

I would thus rejoin my earlier point that the widely spread belief that socio-economic indicators have a higher predictive potentiality than any other indicator actually represents another instance of the 'objectivist superstition'. I take it, instead, that socio-economic indicators are advantaged by the fact that they are quantifiable; but are handicapped (let alone their reliability and crudity) by their 'distal' nature. On the other hand, indicators such as structural variables, organizational factors, belief systems, and the like, are handicapped by their non-measurability, but are at advantage on account of their 'proximal' nature. On balance, we need a *real* political sociology in which distal and proximal factors are combined.

A final comment by way of conclusion. We live in an ever more politicized world. This does not merely mean that political participation and/or political mobilization are becoming world-wide phenomena. This means that the *power of power* is growing at a tremendous pace—almost with the pace of technology—both with reference to the expansion of state intervention in largely extra-political areas, and with regard to the manipulative and coercive capability of political power. Now the greater the range of politics, the smaller the role of 'objective factors'. All our *objective certainties* are increasingly exposed to, and conditioned by, *political uncertainty*. If so, it is an extraordinary paradox that the social sciences should be ever more prompted to explain politics by going *beyond* politics. This essay is predicated upon the opposite assumption, namely, that the sociologist should catch up with the 'uncertainties' of politics.

PART III

THE TRANSFORMATION OF
PARTY SYSTEMS

12

PERSISTENCE AND CHANGE IN WESTERN PARTY SYSTEMS, 1945–1969

RICHARD ROSE AND DEREK W. URWIN

The literature of politics is full of statements about the dynamic properties of parties and party systems. Sometimes it is suggested that there are irreversible *evolutionary* trends: a party of a certain type will be strong at one point in time and lose support to another type of party at a later point. A modified version posits reversible *secular* trends: one type of party will govern under a given set of circumstances, another gain office when circumstances change. The pendulum theory of party politics posits a *static equilibrium*: support for parties is expected to fluctuate continuously around a central balance point. Logically, it is also possible to conceive of a party system in which no change occurs and party strength is *constant* from election to election and generation to generation.

The theories advanced to explain different varieties of change are drawn from several of the social sciences. Evolutionary theories usually assume social determinism, including demographic changes in the electorate; the former often has explicit ideological overtones and the latter may suggest almost actuarial precision.[1] In both instances, change in partisan support is the dependent variable and extra-political influences are the independent variables. Theories of secular trends assume that within a system different parties will dominate in

Richard Rose and Derek W. Urwin, excerpted from 'Persistence and Change in Western Party Systems Since 1945', *Political Studies*, 18/3 (1970), 287–319. Reprinted by permission of Basil Blackwell Limited.

[1] Cf. S. M. Lipset, *Political Man* (New York: Doubleday, 1960), and David Butler and Donald Stokes, *Political Change in Britain* (London: Macmillan, 1969).

contrasting political circumstances. For example, the image of one may be that of peace and depression and of the other, prosperity and war. More simply, the governing party may be associated with the goodness or badness of the times. In both instances, the electoral strength of a party will be determined by the reaction of voters to the relation between its image and prevailing social and political conditions.[2] Party leaders too may influence votes by making salient to the electorate those issues that maximize their potential vote.[3] The model of static equilibrium can be explained, as Anthony Downs has shown, by an economic theory of democracy, with parties presented as extremely flexible competitive institutions operating in a market with perfect information.[4] This model suggests that not only do voters shift their preferences but also that parties themselves change through time in a cybernetic process of adjustment. The case for the null hypothesis—party support is constant—has been stated in general terms by S. M. Lipset and Stein Rokkan in their review of the origins of parties and party systems. The analysis, which stops at the end of the First World War, emphasizes the persistence of the same types of parties in the half-century since. The assumption of nil change can also be supported by referring to studies showing the importance of the inter-generational transmission of party identification.[5]

Statements about the changing character of parties and party systems have a number of characteristics in common. First, they are general in nature and thus well suited to comparative analysis; it is ironic that this should be so, since many generalizations are clearly inspired by the circumstances

---

[2] Cf. Angus Campbell *et al.*, *The American Voter* (New York: Wiley, 1960).

[3] Cf. E. E. Schattschneider, *The Semi-Sovereign People* (New York: Holt, 1960).

[4] Anthony Downs, *An Economic Theory of Democracy* (New York: Harpers, 1957).

[5] S. M. Lipset and Stein Rokkan, 'Introduction', to *Party Systems and Voter Alignments* (New York: Free Press, 1967). Survey data—not to mention recent history—in France and Germany raise questions about simple persistence hypotheses. See, e.g., Sidney Verba, 'Germany: The Remaking of a Political Culture', in L. W. Pye and S. Verba (eds.), *Political Culture and Political Development* (Princeton: University Press, 1965) and Philip Converse and G. Dupeux, 'The Politicization of the Electorate in France and the United States', *Public Opinion Quarterly*, 26/1 (1962).

of a single country, normally Britain or America. Secondly, some propositions and hypotheses are mutually exclusive: for example, theories of change attempt to explain patterns the very existence of which is denied by a theory of constancy. Thirdly, because the statements refer to aggregate electoral strength, they are empirically testable and testable for substantial periods of time. The purpose of this paper is first of all to examine the change—or absence of change—that has occurred in Western party systems since 1945. Given this data, one can then test hypotheses concerning causes of change and constancy in individual parties, and the consequences as well as causes of party systems with different kinds of dynamic properties.

The concept of change is here used generically to refer to trends or fluctuations in electoral strength or to some combination of the two. The concept of a trend is straightforward: it occurs when the vote for a party rises, falls, or shows no alteration, taking one election with another, over a period of three elections or more. The concept of fluctuation in electoral strength is more complex. Votes can fluctuate in relation to several different basing points, e.g. from an average vote, from a trend line, from a minimum figure, or in relation to successive pairs of elections. Different indices are required to measure each type of change.

Trends in party strength are appropriately indicated by regression lines, for this statistic provides both an indication of the direction in which the party's strength is changing—up, down, or remaining virtually constant—as well as an indication of the magnitude of any trend. Trends are here expressed in terms of the size of the annual percentage change in a party's vote as a share of the total national vote.[6] The number of national elections in this period varies considerably; there were six elections in five countries, seven in seven countries, eight in two countries, nine in three countries, and ten in two countries, Denmark and Australia. The average in the period is 7.5 elections, higher than the total resulting from fixed quadrennial elections on the American pattern. Calculating changes in

---

[6] In political terms, a proportionally large change—e.g. the doubling of the vote of a party from 1 per cent to 2 per cent—may be less important than a proportionately smaller shift at higher levels of electoral strength.

party strength on a per annum basis is more suitable for testing hypotheses of social change than calculating changes between elections separated by irregular lengths of time. The cumulative change in a party's strength can be derived by multiplying the per annum rate of change by the number of years spanned by the party's election record. Change at the rate of 0.25 per cent of the vote per annum is here regarded as the minimum meriting description as meaningful change. It represents a one per cent gain in voting strength in a four-year period, a 2.5 per cent gain in a decade, and a 6.0 per cent gain in a period of 24 years.[7]

There are thus three possible courses a party could follow: it could show a trend up, a trend down, or nil trend. The general pattern is that of nil trend in the period, for two-thirds of all parties change at a rate of less than 1.0 per cent per four-year period. The stability of parties in the five Scandinavian countries is extraordinary: 80 per cent show nil trend. Notwithstanding the comments made about the alleged instability of 'Continental' political cultures, 66 per cent of parties there registered nil trend, compared to 57 per cent in Anglo-American societies (Table 12.1). Another way to summarize trends during the period is to calculate the total change during the period in which a party has fought post-war elections. This introduces a control for differences in the span of electoral contests and for differences between 'flash' parties and those that have been continuously in the field since 1945. Cumulative trends are also very low. The median Western party has shown a cumulative change of between 3.00 and 3.99 per cent of the vote in the span of a generation, and one-third of all parties have shown a trend of less than 2.0 per cent. Only eight parties have shown a trend of 10.0 per cent or more: they are the Belgian Christian Social party; the French Christian Democrats and Gaullists; the German Christian Democrats and the Social Democrats; Fine Gael and Clann na Poblachta in Ireland; and the Swedish Liberals. The small amount of a change is further emphasized by the fact that the distribution is skewed in the direction of nil trend.

[7] In practice, the trend is measured from the first election contested to the last one fought, even if this did not cover the whole electoral period. Of the ninety-two parties analysed here, nineteen failed to contest every election.

TABLE 12.1.   Summary of Post-War Party Trends per annum

	Up (% .25 or more)	Nil (+.24 to − .24)	Down (− .25 or more	Median*
Anglo-America	2	12	7	0.20
Scandinavia	I	24	5	0.14
Continent	6	27	8	0.15
Totals	9	63	20	0.15
	10%	68%	22%	

* Plus and minus signs ignored.

Fluctuations in a party's electoral strength are not equal to totals of floating voters. When an individual voter floats from one party to another, this results in changes in the aggregate vote of two parties. When the movements of voters in different directions tend to cancel out, then the aggregate fluctuation in vote will be substantially less than the total of floating voters. A variety of indices are necessary and practical to measure different types of fluctuation in party support through time. The vote of a party may be relatively *elastic or inelastic,* i.e. substantial variations in electoral strength are not only hypothetically possible but also exist historically. The elasticity of voting strength is measured by the percentage difference between the largest and the least share of the vote a party obtained at elections in the period. This simple measure, while not allowing for *potential* fluidity, does have an objective empirical basis. The measure of elasticity in Table 12.2 shows that the limited cumulative trends truly reflect little change, for the median party has had its vote range 7.0 per cent. The distribution is normal. The Gaullist party (or parties) shows the greatest range, for candidates fighting in support of the General polled only 1.6 per cent of the vote in November 1946, and 46.1 per cent in 1968. The Canadian Conservatives are second highest with an elasticity of 26.2 per cent. Parties with elasticity ratings of greater than 14 per cent were also found in Ireland, the United States, Germany, and Belgium. Once again, the Scandinavian parties showed the least change, with 23 of the 30 evidencing an elasticity of less than 8 per cent in more than two decades.

TABLE 12.2. The Elasticity of Party Support

	0–1.99%	2.–3.99%	4.–5.99%	6.–7.99%	8.–9.99%	10.–11.99%	12.–13.99%	14% Plus	Median
Anglo-America	0	1	3	5	3	3	1	5	9.0
Scandinavia	1	6	8	8	3	3	1	0	6.0
Continent	3	8	6	6	7	3	4	4	7.2
Totals	4	15	17	19	13	9	6	9	7.0
	4%	16%	18%	21%	14%	10%	7%	10%	

The *steadiness* or *variability* of a party's vote refers to the normal range of fluctuation in its vote, controlling for an extreme result. The standard deviation from the mean vote of a party is the appropriate statistic to measure variability. The steadiness of election results is illustrated by the figures in Table 12.3. The median party had a standard deviation of 2.6 per cent, and the distribution is skewed in the direction of steadiness. Once again, the Scandinavian societies show the steadiest results, and the Anglo-American societies the most fluctuation.

A party that is gaining or losing strength at a steady rate, a condition often hypothesized in evolutionary theories of long-term change, will plot an increasingly variable and elastic course because of its *persisting* pattern of change. The standard error from the trend line provides a straightforward index of the persistence of a party's strength, whether or not changing cumulatively through time. A party that consistently deviated from its trend line would therefore have a much higher standard error. In the United States the absence of any persisting pattern is extreme: the standard error from the projected Democratic party vote is 7.9 per cent, and for the Republican vote 8.1 per cent. In Canada too, there are irregular and wide swings in party strength: the standard error for the Liberals is 5.5 per cent and for the Conservatives 8.4 per cent.

The calculations in Table 12.4 once again emphasize the very limited amount of fluctuation that parties have experienced. The median for 92 parties is a standard error of 2.8 per cent. The Scandinavian parties show the highest degree of persistence, and Anglo-American parties the greatest irregularities.

The fluctuations in a party's electoral strength in a pair of successive elections is yet another facet of its propensity to change. In a period of about seven elections, one would be very surprised if a party polled an exactly identical proportion of the vote each time. One would expect some fluctuations to appear randomly, albeit of limited magnitude. To test the *significance* or *randomness* of observed changes, each successive pair of post-war election results has been subjected to a two-tailed significance test, treating the latter result as if it had been derived from a sample of 100, and the former result as the 'true' figure. It is

TABLE 12.3. The Variability of Party Support

| | Standard Deviation less than | | | | | | | |
	1.0%	2.0%	3.0%	4.0%	5.0%	6.0%	7.0% plus	Medium
Anglo-American	0	5	4	5	2	2	3	3.1
Scandinavia	1	13	11	4	1	0	0	2.0
Continent	4	10	8	10	4	2	3	2.8
Totals	5	28	23	19	7	4	6	2.6
	5%	30%	25%	21%	8%	4%	7%	

TABLE 12.4. The Persistence of Party Support

| | Standard Error less than | | | | | | | |
	1.0%	2.0%	3.0%	4.0%	5.0%	6.0%	7.0%	Median
Anglo-America	0	4	3	6	1	3	3	3.2
Scandinavia	1	10	13	3	3	0	0	2.3
Continent	3	7	10	3	3	3	5	3.1
Totals	4	21	26	20	7	6	8	2.8
	4%	23%	28%	22%	8%	6%	9%	

TABLE 12.5 Summary of the Significance of Inter-Election Changes

	Random (P = .50+)		Non-Chance (P = .49–.05)		Significant (P = below .05)	
	N	%	N	%	N	%
Anglo-America	66	50	55	41	12	9
Scandinavia	122	64	66	35	4	2
Continent	132	60	73	34	17	7
Totals	320	59%	194	35%	33	6%

particularly important to note that the significance test is extremely sensitive to fluctuations of a few per cent. Major thresholds of significance are thus crossed at points that might not be obvious by casual visual inspection of election returns.

Conventionally, in survey work figures are regarded as significant only if there is a probability of 0.05 or less that variations are due to chance. Applying this criterion to post-war election results shows that only 5 per cent of all fluctuations in the electoral strength of parties can be regarded as statistically significant. A weak but still meaningful classification would distinguish between results that are random (i.e. the probability is greater than 0.50 that the fluctuation between elections is due to chance), non-random (i.e. the probability is less than 0.50 and greater than 0.05 that the fluctuation is not due to chance), and significant (i.e. the probability is less than 0.05 that the fluctuation is a chance one). Even this extremely weak measure of meaningful fluctuation shows a pattern of no change (cf. Table 12.5). In Scandinavia 64 per cent of all fluctuations in electoral strength between elections are random changes. Continental parties are also very stable, with 60 per cent of their changes random, and only 7 per cent significant. The United States is pre-eminent among 19 countries in that four-fifths of all fluctuations there are non-random.

Whatever index of change is used—a measure of trends or any of several measures of fluctuations—the picture is the same: the electoral strength of most parties in Western nations since the war had changed very little from election to election, from decade to decade, or within the lifespan of a generation. The consistency of this finding increases confidences in the indicators used. In short, the first priority of social scientists concerned with the development of parties and party systems since 1945 is to explain the *absence* of change in a far from static period in political history.

13

ELECTORAL VOLATILITY IN WESTERN EUROPE, 1948–1977

MOGENS N. PEDERSEN

I. THE PROBLEM

During the 1960s it was a widely held view among political scientists that European party systems were inherently stable structures which—with a few exceptions—reflected the societal cleavage structures of the past.[1] This view was even bolstered with strong empirical evidence pertaining to the party system at the level of the electorate. Thus Rose and Urwin were able to conclude that 'the electoral strength of most parties in Western nations since the war had changed very little from election to election, from decade to decade, or within the lifespan of a generation.'[2]

Recent European political history has produced some rather unexpected events which make it somewhat difficult to reconcile this theoretical view with the political realities. Thus the number of competing parties has increased considerably in some of the Northern European countries over the last few years, and the distribution of electoral strength in several countries has changed in unpredictable ways. The relationship between voters and parties has apparently undergone an alteration, in some countries detectable as a tendency towards

Mogens N. Pedersen, excerpted from 'The Dynamics of European Party Systems: Changing Patterns of Electoral Volatility', *European Journal of Political Research*, 7/1 (1979), 1–26. Copyright 1979. Reprinted with permission of Kluwer Academic Publishers.

[1] S. M. Lipset and Stein Rokkan, 'Cleavage Structures, Party Systems and Voter Alignments: An Introduction', in Lipset and Rokkan (eds.), *Party Systems and Voter Alignments* (New York: Free Press, 1967), 50.

[2] Richard Rose and Derek Urwin, 'Persistence and Change in Western Party Systems since 1945', *Political Studies*, 18/3 (1970), 295.

decreasing party identification; in some as a tendency towards an increased frequency of unconventional political behaviour; and in a few cases as an outright defection of large portions of the electorate from older parties to new parties which are neither classifiable as traditional mass parties, nor as 'catch-all' parties in the sense of the late O. Kirchheimer.[3]

These are developments which are by now clearly visible. They seem to indicate that even if party systems may still reflect the traditional cleavage structure in the society, the significant exceptions that Rokkan and Lipset were talking about are no longer few, but constitute a larger and growing part of all European party systems.

We want to know if these phenomena of change which are visible primarily, but not solely, in the Northern European countries represent fundamental transformations of the party systems, or if they are better interpreted as mere fluctuations, temporary deviations from an otherwise stable pattern? Do they fit into a pattern, or are they just some atypical events with no connection with the past history of these societies or with the development going on in other countries in Europe? Are party systems in Europe converging, becoming more uniform, or are they diverging through the 1970s? Is it possible to speak about distinct periods of stability and change, and, if so, are these periods country-specific, or do they apply to larger parts of the European polities? Are fluctuations randomly distributed across time and countries, or do they make up trends of increasing and decreasing rates of change?

Phrased this way we are dealing with a very broad problem with a great many facets. When we want to map and understand the extent and the direction of party system change in Europe, the first problem we encounter is one of delimitation of the problem, the narrowing down of a broad question to a manageable problem. This delimitation goes as follows.

The concept of *party system change* is not a simple and straightforward one. We may learn that a party system is a 'system of

---

[3] Otto Kirchheimer, 'The Transformation of the Western European Party Systems', in Joseph LaPalombara and Myron Weiner (eds.), *Political Parties and Political Development* (Princeton: Princeton University Press, 1966), 177–200.

interaction resulting from inter-party competition'.[4] But such interaction and competition can be observed at different levels, or—to put it in other terms—this system can itself be interpreted as consisting of various subsystems. A concise mapping of party system change would have to cover the levels of parliament and government, the level of the party as an organization, and the level of the electorate. Party system change can be defined as *the total set of changes in patterns of interaction and competition at these three levels as well as between them.*

It is not possible to encompass all these dimensions at this stage. I have deliberately chosen to concentrate attention on the level of the electorate. This analysis is thus based upon the assumption that 'election results are important to politicians and to political scientists'.[5] One may also say that even if elections are far from always being decisive events, they are still the best available vantage point for a study of change, because change will either be a result of elections, or elections will register any change which may occur in the party system.

At the electoral level, as well as on other levels, the party system may be described in terms of various theoretical concepts. Party systems differ with regard to polarization, fragmentation, institutionalization etc.

As long as a party system can be considered a system of 'parts', we may, however, from time to time find it useful to return to the simplest definition of *party system format*. The format of the electoral party system can be described in terms of the number of parties contesting the elections, and the distribution of electoral strength among these parties.

Given the central role of elections in the process of party system change, it is relevant—and we hope not over-ambitious —to examine the evolving patterns of format change in Europe, i.e. changes in the number of parties, and in the relative distribution of electoral strength among the competing parties.

---

[4] Giovanni Sartori, *Parties and Party Systems: A Framework for Analysis* (Cambridge: Cambridge University Press, 1976), i. 44.

[5] Rose and Urwin, 'Persistence and Change in Western Party Systems since 1945', p. 288.

The phenomenon which we are singling out for analysis is *electoral volatility*, by which will be meant *the net change within the electoral party system resulting from individual vote transfers*.[6]

Even a concept as simple as this is not without its problems. Traditionally political scientists have been very much preoccupied with the number of parties, because this number was considered important for the mechanics of the party system. Since the late 1960s it has become customary to describe the format in terms of number of parties as well as distribution of party strength. Many attempts have been made to provide single number quantitative indices of format which would make it possible to compare party systems and to describe intra-system changes. These measures like Rae's *index of fractionalization*[7] have mostly been locational or static measures for which reason alone they are not optimal for a study of the dynamic properties of party systems.[8]

If we want to concentrate attention on ongoing format change, we therefore have to devise measures of change that will discriminate among systems; which will reflect similarities and differences between diachronic patterns; and which are fairly easy to interpret in a theoretically meaningful way. These requirements can be met by using one or another kind of summary measure of *rate of change* in the party system. Several such measures have been proposed and applied recently.[9] In this paper we will use a measure of electoral volatility which is derived in the following manner.

Let $p_{i,t}$ stand for the percentage of the vote, which was obtained by party i at election t. Then the change in the strength of i since the previous election will be:

[6] W. Ascher and S. Tarrow, 'The Stability of Communist Electorates: Evidence from a Longitudinal Analysis of French and Italian Aggregate Data', *American Journal of Political Science*, 19/3 (1975), 480–1.

[7] Douglas Rae, *The Political Consequences of Electoral Laws* (New Haven: Yale University Press, 1967).

[8] Mogens N. Pedersen, 'La Misurazione del Mutamento nei Sistemi Partitici: Una critica', *Rivista Italiana di Scienza Politica*, 8/2 (1978), 243–61 [English version in *Comparative Political Studies*, 12/4 (1980), 387–403].

[9] Rose and Urwin, 'Persistence and Change in Western Party Systems since 1945'; Adam Przeworski, 'Institutionalization of Voting Patterns, or Is Mobilization the Source of Decay?', *American Political Science Review*, 69/1 (1975), 49–67; Ascher and Tarrow, 'Stability of Communist Electorates'.

$$\Delta p_{i,t} = p_{i,t} - p_{i,t-1}$$

and if we do not consider sign differences we have the following relation for the party system:

$$\text{Total Net Change (TNC}_t) = \sum_{i=1}^{n} |\Delta p_{i,t}|$$

$$0 \leqslant \text{TNC}_t \leqslant 200$$

where n stands for the total number of parties competing in the two elections.

Remembering that the net gains for winning parties numerically are equal to the net losses of the parties that were defeated in the election, one may also wish to use another indicator which is slightly easier to calculate and to interpret, namely:

$$\text{Volatility } (V_t) = 1/2 \times \text{TNC}_t$$

$$0 \leqslant V_t \leqslant 100$$

V_t is simply the cumulated gains for all winning parties in the party system, or—if the symmetrical interpretation is preferred—the numerical value of the cumulated losses for all losing parties. Its range of variation has a straightforward explanation, and it can be expressed in terms of percentage.

A description of the European systems in terms of volatility will at least give a partial answer to the broader questions about change and stability in European party systems. It may thus lead to an identification of what are the typical and what are the deviant patterns of development.

2. NATIONAL PATTERNS OF VOLATILITY

The measure of volatility tells to what extent party strength is being reallocated from one election to the next between losing and winning parties. An examination of national patterns will thus indicate, if the relative positions of parties are fairly constant, or if they fluctuate in ways which may eventually reflect basic electoral realignments. The extent of volatility may differ across countries as well as over time; differences may be of a random character or they may be subject to change according to certain political regularities. A first task for any analysis is to look for such regularities.

If the measure of volatility is applied to data from the thirteen countries, a picture is obtained which in the light of earlier analyses contains expected as well as not so familiar features (see Fig. 13.1).

That France comes out as the country in which average electoral volatility is the highest will probably not surprise many; nor will the fact that the post-war politics of Austria and Switzerland have been characterized by negligible volatility. All those who are familiar with the long-term trend in the German electorate since 1949, will not be surprised to find that the average net gains/losses in the German system amount to approximately 10 per cent per election. On the other hand it was probably not expected by many that the Nordic countries differ widely in this respect, nor that Denmark scores second-highest among the thirteen nations, nor that the European party systems on the whole differ considerably with regard to volatility.

Such observations may conceal a lot. An average may not be typical for the diachronic pattern, but may for instance reflect the occurrence of one or a few highly atypical elections. In order

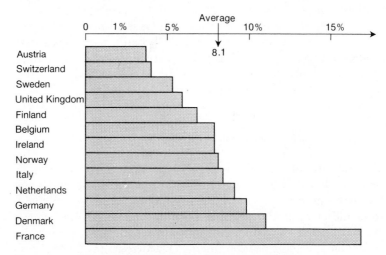

FIG. 13.1   The Volatility of European Party Systems 1948–77: Average Net Gains for Winning Parties in Elections

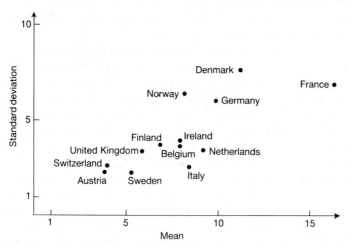

FIG. 13.2   The Relationship between National Mean Volatility and the Dispersion around the Mean

to pass judgements on volatility, we will therefore as a natural next step examine the dispersion of observations around their respective national means. In Fig. 13.2 this has been done by means of a plot of the relationship between means and their corresponding standard deviations. This plot affirms that Austria, Switzerland, and also Sweden are nations in which the relative strength of parties has hardly changed from one election to the next. It further identifies a group of six other nations, United Kingdom, Finland, Belgium, Ireland, Italy, and the Netherlands, with a somewhat higher average volatility and a uniform pattern of dispersion.

One intriguing finding appears in the plot next. The two big nations, Germany and France, and the two smaller nations, Denmark and Norway, apparently come out as fairly alike in their statistical patterns: a relatively high average volatility is combined with a high degree of fluctuation around that mean.

The interpretation of these findings is far from simple. A great many diachronic patterns of volatility might produce such means and standard deviations. But Fig. 13.2 provides a clue for further examination, because it shows in clear statistical terms that at least two 'families' of party systems exist, viz. a group of party systems with a relatively stable distribution of party strength, and a group of systems in which volatility has been changing considerably over time.

In passing it is tempting to mention that these two clusters of party systems do not have any affinity with the way in which students of party systems and democratic political systems traditionally classify European countries. The two clusters transcend the classifications of Almond (immobilist versus working multiparty systems); of Duverger and Neumann (classification according to number of parties); of Lijphart (centrifugal, centripetal, consociational and depoliticized democracy); and of Sartori (moderate versus polarized pluralism etc.). Such a discrepancy may be of no theoretical importance; it may, however, also imply that the usefulness of these classifications is restricted and even decreasing over time.

A step towards further clarification can be taken by introducing the time variable, i.e. by changing the perspective from an examination of the range of fluctuations to an examination of

TABLE 13.1   The Volatility of European Party Systems 1948–77: Average Net Gains Compared Across Time and Countries

Country	Period			National average	No. of election periods
	1948–59	1960–69	1970–77		
Switzerland	1.9%	3.7%	6.4%	4.0%	6
Austria	4.1%	3.9%	3.1%	3.7%	8
United Kingdom	4.4%	5.2%	7.9%	5.9%	8
Finland	4.4%	6.9%	9.1%	6.8%	8
Sweden	4.8%	4.3%	6.6%	5.2%	9
Netherlands	6.3%	7.9%	12.7%	9.1%	8
Belgium	7.9%	10.3%	5.5%	7.9%	9
Italy	10.3%	8.0%	6.8%	8.4%	6
Ireland	10.9%	6.8%	5.0%	7.9%	8
Norway	3.4%	5.2%	17.1%	8.1%	7
Denmark	5.5%	8.9%	18.7%	11.0%	12
Germany	15.2%	9.5%	4.9%	9.8%	7
France	21.8%	11.9%	10.6%	16.8%	7
Period average	7.8%	7.3%	9.2%	8.1%	
No. of election periods	36	34	33		103

the diachronic patterns of volatility. In Table 13.1 the two groups of party systems have been sorted by means of a crude periodization.

At once a clear pattern of change and stability emerges from the data. The group of party systems with a high level of volatility and high standard deviations clearly falls into two distinct subgroups: the German and the French party system, in which volatility has decreased over time considerably, especially at the beginning of the period, and the Norwegian and the Danish party system, in which exactly the opposite trend is visible, i.e. where volatility has tended to increase, especially in the last part of the period. But it is also important to note that the party systems in the other group also tend to fall into two subgroups: in Austria, Belgium, Ireland, and Italy volatility has tended to diminish over time, while it has increased in Switzerland, the United Kingdom, Finland, Sweden, and the Netherlands.

This finding suggests a new way of classifying European party systems according to their trends of volatility: the data apparently falls into three, or maybe even four, fairly distinct groups or 'families' of party systems.

This idea can be pursued further by adding a new dimension to the search for order. If it holds true that the thirteen party systems differ with regard to their secular trends, then an obvious next step in the mapping operation consists in examining the data for trends and for statistical linearity. The question becomes then if volatility tends to increase or decrease in a linear way, or if the apparently orderly picture in Table 13.1 reflects more complicated developmental patterns, e.g. patterns in which decades or other temporal sequences play an ordering role. Table 13.2 gives the answer.

This set of regression equations and correlation coefficients tells a clear story. Party systems in Europe do indeed differ with regard to the level of volatility, and with regard to the direction of change in volatility. The overall tendency towards a relatively stable pattern which comes out if data from all nations are artificially aggregated, disappears and is replaced by an array of widely differing trend lines. The data suggests a classification with three classes, differentiated from each other by means of the rate of change, i.e. the slope of the regression line.

TABLE 13.2 National Trends of Electoral Volatility. Countries
Rank-ordered According to Slope of Regression Line

Country	Regression equation	Pearson's r
Norway	$V_t = -\ 2.08 + 0.60t$	$r =\ \ 0.805$
Denmark	$V_t =\ \ \ 1.92 + 0.57t$	$r =\ \ 0.689$
Netherlands	$V_t =\ \ \ 3.53 + 0.33t$	$r =\ \ 0.832$
Switzerland	$V_t = -\ 1.27 + 0.30t$	$r =\ \ 0.821$
Finland	$V_t =\ \ \ 3.01 + 0.24t$	$r =\ \ 0.570$
United Kingdom	$V_t =\ \ \ 3.48 + 0.15t$	$r =\ \ 0.327$
Sweden	$V_t =\ \ \ 3.56 + 0.10t$	$r =\ \ 0.370$
Austria	$V_t =\ \ \ 4.87 - 0.07t$	$r = -0.244$
Belgium	$V_t =\ \ 10.09 - 0.13t$	$r = -0.340$
Italy	$V_t =\ \ 11.66 - 0.19t$	$r = -0.670$
Ireland	$V_t =\ \ 11.11 - 0.23t$	$r = -0.630$
Germany	$V_t =\ \ 20.22 - 0.62t$	$r = -0.856$
France	$V_t =\ \ 25.87 - 0.70t$	$r = -0.784$
All nations	$V_t =\ \ \ 7.31 + 0.05t$	$r =\ \ 0.070$

Explanatory note: regression equations have been calculated after setting
t = actual election year—1948. The V_t-values can thus be interpreted as the
predicted gains (in %) per year for winning parties.

The two small Scandinavian countries, Norway and Denmark, evidently stand distinctively apart from most other
European countries in terms of volatility patterns, and so do the
two major nations, France and Germany. In both cases the
regression analysis also supports the impression which could be
had from a visual inspection of period averages (Table 13.1),
namely that the trends for these four countries fit very well with
a linear model.

3. A CLASSIFICATION OF EUROPEAN ELECTIONS

From what was said in the previous section it follows that
high-volatility elections as well as low-volatility elections are
not randomly scattered across time and nations. It may be
useful to identify various types of elections across Europe. By
means of such a mapping we get not only a picture of the
occurrence of these events which are often dramatic, but also a

more simple, and yet informative summary of the national patterns.

The 103 elections which were held between 1948 and 1977, are not normally distributed around the European mean of 8.1 per cent volatility. Fig. 13.3 shows that the distribution is highly skewed, with 64 elections below the mean and 39 elections above. A few elections stand out because of their extraordinary degree of volatility. This is true of the 1973 election in Denmark, when the number of parties in the system doubled; of some of the French elections in the 1950s; and of the German election in 1953, when the CDU won its biggest victory in the post-war period.

The very shape of the distribution leads us to draw some distinctions, based upon pure statistical reasoning. Thus the elections in what is approximately the lowest quartile stand somewhat apart from those in the two middle quartiles, and these again form a cluster distinct from that formed by the elections in the highest quartile.

The map of European elections that can be drawn by means of this tripartite classification is presented in Fig. 13.4. This figure recapitulates some of the findings which were reported in

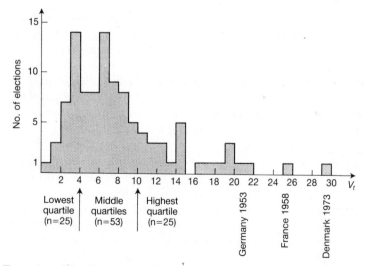

FIG. 13.3. The Frequency Distribution for the Variable Electoral Volatility (V_t)

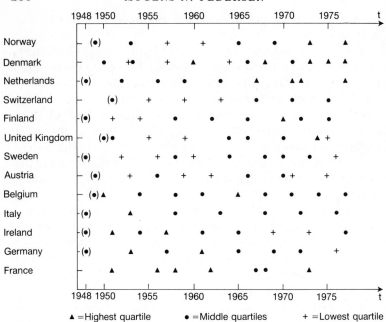

FIG. 13.4. European Elections: Classified According to Extent of Volatility

the previous section, but it also adds some new features. Thus we see, first, that some countries, viz. Switzerland, Sweden, and Austria, have never in the post-war period experienced high-volatility elections. Second, one notes that some countries on the contrary never experienced low-volatility elections. This holds true not only for France, but for Italy, Belgium, and the Netherlands as well. Third, we note that the European countries differ considerably in the sense that in some of them high-volatility elections are to a considerable extent a thing of the past—of the 1950s—while such elections are very much a 1970s phenomenon in some other countries. Finally, a comparison of decades indicates a general European trend towards relatively more high-volatility elections and relatively fewer low-volatility elections, with the 1960s being the decade in which these two types of elections were relatively limited.

As late as 1970 it was possible and also valid to argue that 'the first priority of social scientists concerned with the development of parties and party systems since 1945 is to explain the *absence* of change in a far from static period in political history'.[10] In the light of the preceding pages we are entitled to, and even forced to, qualify this statement. At the end of the 1970s the first priority is to understand why some party systems still appear to be stable while other systems either have been undergoing a transformation or have gone through a period of considerable instability. Even if electoral volatility is only one among several possible indicators of persistence/change, it is a sufficiently important indicator to warrant this statement.

[10] Rose and Urwin, 'Persistence and Change in Western Party Systems since 1945', p. 295; italics in the original.

14

PARAMETERS OF CHANGE

PETER MAIR

The Location of Change

In developing their theory of the structuring of mass politics in
Western Europe, Lipset and Rokkan point out that there exists
'a hierarchy of cleavage bases (which may) tend to undergo
changes from time to time',[1] and stress that it is the '*most*
important of party alternatives . . . (which) have remained
roughly the same through decades of partisan choice'.[2] As such,
any discussion that seeks to assess the continued validity of the
Lipset–Rokkan thesis must first concern itself with the relative
salience of any change that might have taken place. Wolinetz
hints at the importance of this parameter when, in his discussion of the possibility of realignment in European multi-party
systems, he suggests that newly emergent issues that might
force a realignment of a two-party system may affect only one or
two of the parties in a multi-party system, and so the change
may be localized to the extent that the party system as a whole
is unaffected.[3] Schattschneider, in his excellent if now somewhat neglected *Semi-Sovereign People*, indicates a similar possibility when, emphasizing the notion of the 'conflict of conflicts',
he points out that the dominance of one or two particular

Peter Mair, excerpted from 'Adaptation and Control: Towards an Understanding of Party and Party System Change', in Hans Daalder and Peter
Mair (eds.), *Western European Party Systems: Continuity and Change* (Sage Publications, 1983), pp. 405–29. Used by permission.

[1] S. M. Lipset and Stein Rokkan, 'Cleavage Structures, Party Systems and
Voter Alignments: An Introduction', in Lipset and Rokkan (eds.), *Party
Systems and Voter Alignments* (New York: Free Press, 1967), 6.

[2] Ibid. 52; emphasis added.

[3] Steven B. Wolinetz, 'The Transformation of Western European Party
Systems Revisited', *West European Politics*, 2/1 (1979), 3.

cleavages may mask the concurrent existence of a series of subordinate conflicts which may not be mobilized in any serious sense.[4] This subordination may be very evident in a two-party system such as the American one, with which Schatt-schneider was primarily concerned; it can also be presumed to exist in a multi-party system, however, where we may speak of the 'primacy of particular conflicts' as against the possible secondary nature of those mobilized by minor parties on the fringes of the political system. As such, any discussion of party system change must clarify the extent to which this change impinges on the primary conflicts of the system, rather than simply involving the displacement of one secondary conflict by another.

A second point that follows from this concerns the extent to which change involves simply the party alternatives or also affects the actual conflicts that are articulated within the party system, since it is at least conceivable that particular party organizations may rise and fall while the conflict along which they are mobilized continues, i.e., a scenario in which the actors change but the politics remain the same. Such a pattern has already been associated with the French experience, where voters are said to identify with particular conflict positions or even symbols, rather than with formal parties or party groupings per se,[5] and hence evidence of political continuity can be seen to accompany severe organizational fissiparousness. And while the extreme French position may not be fully replicated in other Western European party systems, some elements of the pattern may be present in the form of a widespread identification with a 'tendance' over and above the identification with the particular parties that articulate that 'tendance'.

The contrast between a change in parties on the one hand, and in 'tendances' or political or conflict areas on the other is itself a useful means of assessing the overall change in Western European party systems, providing as it does a rough measure

[4] E. E. Schattschneider, *The Semi-Sovereign People* (New York: Holt Rinehart and Winston, 1960), ch. 4.

[5] David R. Cameron, 'Stability and Change in Patterns of French Parti-sanship', *Public Opinion Quarterly*, 36/1 (1972), 19–30; Philip E. Converse and George Dupeux, 'Politicization of the Electorate in France and the United States', *Public Opinion Quarterly*, 26/1 (1962), 23–45.

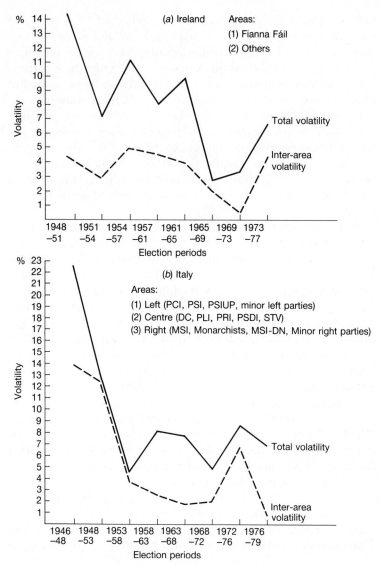

FIG. 14.1. Contrast between Total Volatility and Inter-area Volatility: (*a*) Ireland, (*b*) Italy, (*c*) Norway, and (*d*) Sweden

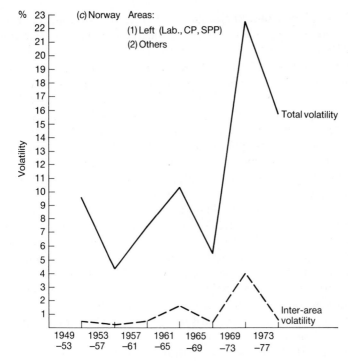

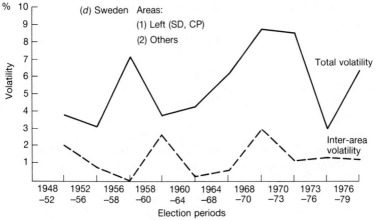

of the salience of that change. Earlier in this volume,[6] Pedersen presented evidence of changing patterns of electoral volatility in Western Europe. Adopting the same measure, Figure 14.1 above contrasts these patterns in Ireland, Italy, Norway, and Sweden with those shown by dividing these party systems into particular conflict areas. As in Pedersen's case, total volatility is defined as the cumulative gains of all winning parties in the system, while inter-area volatility is defined as the cumulative gains of all winning areas in the system. The areas are defined in terms of an approximation to the dominant opposition in each party system: in Ireland, Fianna Fáil v. the rest; in Italy, left v. centre v. right; in Norway, Labour, the Communist party, and the Socialist Peoples' party v. the bourgeois parties; in Sweden, the Social Democrats and the Communist party v. the bourgeois parties. These distinctions are not definitive, and it could be claimed, for instance, that the Communist parties in Norway and Sweden should not be grouped with the Socialists. Nevertheless, rough as the distinctions are, the contrast between the two types of volatility does afford us the opportunity to measure the extent to which political continuity may exist despite substantial aggregate electoral change. It should also be emphasized that at least one area in each system must contain more than one party if the measure is to be meaningful.

As can be seen from Figure 14.1, inter-area volatility is substantially less than total volatility. The contrast is particularly striking in the case of Norway: in Pedersen's analysis this is shown to be one of the most increasingly volatile systems; and yet, when we pit the combined left against the bourgeois parties, we see that inter-area volatility is remarkably low. The contrast in Sweden is also marked, while the differences in Ireland and Italy are less striking. In the Italian case, however, it is interesting to note the different patterns in the crucial elections of 1976 and 1979, in that a major component of the

[6] [See Hans Daalder and Peter Mair (eds.), *Western European Party Systems: Continuity and Change* (London: Sage Publications, 1983). The chapter by Pedersen is entitled 'Changing Patterns of Electoral Volatility in European Party Systems, 1948–1977: Explorations in Explanation', pp. 29–66, and is an expanded version of his earlier article in the *European Journal of Political Research*, 7/1 (1979), 1–26. See also Chapter 13 above.]

1976 change was composed of inter-area volatility, while that of 1979 was almost wholly what we term within-area change.

It seems hardly necessary to emphasize the importance of recognizing such conflict areas in assessments of party system change. To concentrate on political parties *per se* is to emphasize organizational persistence or change. To concentrate on conflict areas, on the other hand, seems more appropriate to an understanding of the persistence or change of the basic political cleavages. Warwick's recent study of the durability of coalition cabinets is an interesting and parallel case in point, in that he found that the substitution of cleavages for parties as the basic unit of analysis added significantly to the explanation of durability.[7]

Returning to our initial parameter, therefore, we can extend the notion of the location of change to include the question of whether the change takes place largely within conflict areas or between conflict areas. Both types of change are clearly relevant to any discussion of developments in Western European parties and party systems, but while within-area change may involve only the possible displacement of one party by another while leaving the primary conflict(s) intact, inter-area change may involve the very dynamics of the party system itself.

This still leaves the question of whether new parties that emerge simply represent a variation within an existing conflict area, or create a wholly new conflict area within the party system. The sudden growth of the Scottish and Welsh nationalist parties in Britain offers an appropriate example of this problem, since, on the face of it, the new nationalist wave represented a major challenge to the established British party system. It is also true, however, that the adoption of a pro-devolutionist stance by the British Labour party in general, and by the Scottish Council of the Labour party (SCLP) in particular, did much to defuse the appeal of the new parties. For a variety of reasons, including the traditional pro-nationalist sentiments in sections of the SCLP and the Labour party in Wales, as well as the association of socialism and separatism through the common language of protest against the status quo,

[7] Paul Warwick, 'The Durability of Coalition Governments in Parliamentary Democracies', *Comparative Political Studies*, 11/4 (1979), 465–98.

Labour proved substantially more capable than the Conservatives of incorporating devolutionist demands into its programme.[8] In this way, much of the nationalist impetus was absorbed into Labour's conflict area, and so was funnelled into the existing pattern of competition. Whether this absorption process will survive is an open question, as is whether that element of nationalism which has remained separately organized will be sufficient to define a new conflict area. Nevertheless, because Labour proved to have a strong adaptive capacity in this case, much of the disruptive threat of the new nationalist wave was avoided.

This in turn raises the question of whether certain parties are more 'adaptable' than others, and indeed whether certain issues or conflicts are more capable of being adapted than others. Further, in so far as the notion of adaptation suggests that the response of parties can help determine whether issues or conflicts will be contained within an existing area rather than emerging to affect inter-area competition, it is then a notion that takes us back to the centrality of party *per se*, as well as to the identification of further parameters.

The Extent of Change

In an ideal world we would not only know the extent of aggregate change in a political system, but would also have a good idea of the extent of individual-level change, data for which can emerge only from sophisticated survey analysis over time. At the aggregate level, there is often difficulty in devising indices to measure the exact degree of change,[9] as well as in deciding what constitutes meaningful change. The selection by Rose and Urwin of 0.25 per cent per annum as representing a meaningful trend is intuitively plausible, but it is also worth noting, had they chosen 0.20 as their cut-off point, they would

[8] Peter Mair and Ian McAllister, 'Territory Versus Class as a Source of Intra-Party Tension? A Working Paper on the Labour Parties of the British Isles Periphery', paper presented to the Workshop on Factionalism in the Political Parties of Western Europe, ECPR Joint Sessions, Florence, 1980.

[9] Mogens N. Pedersen, 'On Measuring Party System Change: A Methodological Critique and a Suggestion', *Comparative Political Studies*, 12/4 (1980), 387–403.

have found that some 40 per cent of the parties had evidenced such a significant trend, as compared with the 32 per cent that they noted at the 0.25 level.[10]

The extent of change is also of course an indication of its relevance, and hence is related to its location, since even if we could agree on what constitutes 'a lot' of change, the significance of that change could still be in dispute. The transition matrices that have been derived from panel data in a number of countries are revealing in this regard. In Denmark, for instance, 40 per cent of 1971 voters changed to different parties in 1973, and there is little doubt that this constitutes large-scale change. Yet among these volatile voters, only 3 per cent shifted between the old, conventional parties. The remainder either shifted within the conventional Socialist or bourgeois blocs (9 per cent), or shifted to new, minor parties (27 per cent).[11] Panel data from Germany also indicate that the shifts between the conventional sides of the major opposition are relatively minor, with only an average of some 25 per cent of those who leave the SPD going to the CDU, and only some 34 per cent of those who leave the CDU shifting to the SPD.[12] And of those few who actually did transfer from the SPD to the CDU or vice versa, an even smaller proportion actually stayed with the alternative party.[13]

Allied to the problem of determining the extent of change and of then trying to assess its significance for the party system as a whole is the further problem of the different perspectives of the observer on the one hand and the participant on the other. It goes without saying that what may seem like one small step to the political science observer may seem like one giant leap to the party or parties directly involved. In so far as we are

[10] Cf. data in Richard Rose and Derek Urwin, 'Persistence and Change in Western Party Systems since 1945', *Political Studies*, 18/3 (1970), 314–19.

[11] Ole Borre, 'Recent Trends in Danish Voting Behaviour', in Karl H. Cerny (ed.), *Scandinavia at the Polls* (Washington, DC: American Enterprise Institute, 1977), 9; see also Borre and Daniel Katz, 'Party Identification and its Motivational Base in a Multiparty System: A Study of the Danish General Election of 1971', *Scandinavian Political Studies*, 8 (1973), 76–8.

[12] Calculated from data in Helmut Norpoth, 'Party Identification in West Germany: Tracing an Elusive Concept', *Comparative Political Studies*, 11/1 (1978), Table 1.

[13] Ibid. 42–3.

concerned with the responses of parties to change, and with their ability to adapt to that change, then it is their perception of the change that becomes of crucial importance. The utility of Pedersen's volatility index must be emphasized here, since it stresses the relative change from one election to the next, and since therefore it is more likely to approximate to the immediate concerns of the parties and the voters themselves.

The Duration of Change

It is also particularly important to know whether any change that occurs is particularly sudden, or manifests itself gradually over time. Denmark's 'protest election' of 1973[14] might be characterized as a relatively recent example of sudden change, as might those changes triggered off in Norway by the EEC issue;[15] while the pattern in their Scandinavian neighbour, Sweden, seems more characteristic of gradual change. Pedersen's index of volatility seems again an appropriate measure in this instance, in that it facilitates the identification of high-volatility elections. The above distinction between within-area change and inter-area change is also relevant here, since a high incidence of the latter gives us some idea of the number of critical elections. However, it is only through more system-specific analysis that we can discover the extent to which a particularly sharp change is lasting, as opposed to cases where, say, the impact of a second high-volatility election simply restores the pre-volatile status quo.

It is probably safe to assume that, the more gradual the change, the more likely it is that the party can adapt. A classic example is that of a party that derives its support from a specific social stratum which, in turn, declines steadily as a proportion of the total voting population. Such might be the case, for instance, of a socialist party confronted with the steady demographic decline of the blue-collar working class or, as in the case of the Swedish Centre party, of an agrarian party which sees the

---

[14] Ole Borre, 'Denmark's Protest Election of December 1973', *Scandinavian Political Studies*, 9 (1974), 197–204.

[15] Henry Valen, 'National Conflict Structure and Foreign Politics: The Impact of the EEC Issue on Perceived Cleavages in Norwegian Politics', *European Journal of Political Research*, 4/1 (1976), 47–82.

gradual erosion of the agricultural sector of the population. Sudden change is presumably less easily adapted to, as for instance would be the case where the abrupt emergence of a new issue rapidly revitalizes a somewhat dormant cleavage (Norway), or where the party system is suddenly confronted with a wave of political protest (Denmark). It should also be noted, however, that in such cases of abrupt change, the parties may tend to try and ride out the resulting turbulence, on the assumption that any phenomenon that emerges so quickly will equally rapidly disappear. As such, any adaptation process may be consciously perfunctory.

15

THE TRANSFORMATION OF WESTERN EUROPEAN PARTY SYSTEMS

STEVEN B. WOLINETZ

I. THE CATCH-ALL THESIS AND CHANGE IN WESTERN EUROPEAN PARTY ALIGNMENTS

Twelve years ago, Otto Kirchheimer argued that a transformation of Western European party systems was under way. According to Kirchheimer, former class and denominational parties of mass integration were transforming themselves into ideologically bland catch-all parties, more interested in winning the next election than the defence of principle or the pursuit of more distant ideological goals. This was occurring, Kirchheimer argued, because the advent of an affluent and consumer-oriented society had loosened the bonds between parties of mass integration and their clienteles. Ideology was no longer an exclusive motive for voting behaviour.

Aware of the change and afraid of diminishing support, political parties were responding by scuttling excess 'ideological baggage', stressing the qualities of their leaders, avoiding controversy, and seeking the support of interest groups. This in turn transforms both the role and function of political parties. Parties de-emphasize their 'expressive functions'—the articulation of demands and grievances—abandon 'attempts at the intellectual and moral *encadrement* of the masses', and operate largely as electoral agencies, bidding for votes wherever they can be found. As a result, the style and mode of political competition are transformed. Because the catch-all party is a

Steven B. Wolinetz, from 'The Transformation of Western European Party Systems Revisited', reprinted from the second issue of *West European Politics* published by Frank Cass & Co. Ltd. Copyright Frank Cass & Co. Ltd.

superior instrument of competition, other parties imitate it, and the central features of party competition cease to be 'the formation of action preferences', advocacy of causes or defence of a *classe gardée*. Instead, we find an opportunistic battle among bland parties trying to achieve the best marketing results.[1]

One aspect of Kirchheimer's scenario lends itself to a simple test. If Kirchheimer's argument is correct—if decreasing loyalties have caused mass parties to adopt catch-all strategies, and if the adoption and success of a catch-all strategy spurs imitation—then we should expect to find substantial changes in the party alignments of countries in which catch-all strategies have been employed. Because catch-all parties are superior instruments of competition, they should win votes from parties which fail to adapt. As a result, party systems should become less fragmented. In addition, because of weakened loyalties and the opportunistic style of party competition, we should expect increased fluctuation in party strengths and greater traffic among political parties.

In the absence of either detailed aggregate analysis or longitudinal survey data, measuring traffic across party lines is difficult. We are forced to fall back on national electoral data. Although this can never give us a fully accurate measure of shifts among parties, it allows us to make rough estimates and form impressions which may be helpful in later research. If we consider electoral trends in Western Europe, the impression which we get depends on the vantage point which we select. If we choose the late 1960s, the dominant impression is one of stability. Writing in 1967, Lipset and Rokkan contended that most West European party alignments had been frozen since the advent of universal suffrage some fifty years earlier.[2] Examining persistence and change in nineteen democracies

---

[1] Otto Kirchheimer, 'The Transformation of the Western European Party Systems', in Joseph LaPalombara and Myron Weiner (eds.), *Political Parties and Political Development* (Princeton: Princeton University Press, 1966), 177–200. See especially pp. 181–95, 198–200.

[2] S. M. Lipset and Stein Rokkan, 'Cleavage Structures, Party Systems and Voter Alignments: An Introduction', in S. M. Lipset and Stein Rokkan (eds.), *Party Systems and Voter Alignments* (New York: Free Press, 1967), 50–4.

from 1945 to 1968, Rose and Urwin came to the same conclusion.[3]

We can affirm this by considering the election outcomes. Except for fluctuations in the immediate post-war elections—usually the result of temporary surges by Communist parties—most party alignments were stable. The principal exceptions were France and West Germany. The former display sharp fluctuations during the Fourth Republic, followed by the emergence of the Gaullists as a dominant party in the Fifth Republic. In West Germany, the Christian Democrats and later the Social Democrats enjoyed sustained growth at the expense of minor parties. The steadiness of party percentages in most systems suggests that there were relatively few switches and that there were few voters available for the growth of catch-all parties.

The picture in the mid-1970s is different. Electorates have become more volatile. However, there is little evidence for the growth or ascendancy of catch-all parties. Instead, several systems have become more fragmented as minor—and often newly created—parties have gained votes at the expense of established parties.

If Kirchheimer's assertions were correct, then we should have discovered decreased fragmentation in a number of party systems. Instead, increased fluctuations in the 1960s and 1970s have been paired with the emergence and success of minor parties. There are two questions which we must answer: first, why have catch-all parties emerged and gained strength in some countries but not in others, and second, why has increased fluidity led to increased fragmentation rather than the growth of catch-all parties?

Neither question lends itself to a simple answer. Kirchheimer argued that decreasing loyalties to mass parties would force parties to adopt catch-all strategies and assumed that parties employing these strategies would be more successful than others. But, although we can find examples of parties moderating their doctrines or adjusting their appeals, outside of France or West Germany we have little evidence for the growth or

---

[3] Richard Rose and Derek Urwin, 'Persistence and Change in Western Party Systems Since 1945,' *Political Studies*, 18/3 (1967), 296–7.

success of catch-all parties. To account for this, we need to know more about the nature of voters' attachments to parties and more about the ways in which these attachments condition changes in party alignments.

In subsequent sections, we will argue that in most systems in the first fifteen or twenty years after World War II, strong and persistent attachments to political parties put a brake on the emergence of catch-all parties, and that large catch-all parties succeeded only in systems in which voters' attachments to parties were weak or non-existent. These were primarily countries which experienced severe disruptions in political development and countries whose common characteristic was neither a decline of ideology nor a disappearance of conflict, but rather crisis and its successful resolution. Elsewhere, few loose votes were available for changes in party systems. In recent years, though, voters' attachments to political parties have weakened. However, because the growth of a floating vote has coincided with the emergence of new concerns and anti-government reactions, these votes have been available not only to potential catch-all parties but also to a host of smaller parties. One reason why this has occurred is that many established parties have indeed undergone the changes in strategy, style, and functions which Kirchheimer indicated. As a result, they are less able to fulfil the expressive functions of political parties.

2.   MASS ATTACHMENTS AND CHANGES IN PARTY ALIGNMENTS

Mass attachments are crucial to the study of changes in party alignments. Party alignments change when there are either significant changes in the number of parties competing or when there are substantial changes in the proportion of the electorate won by different parties. If voters have no links to parties—i.e. if every election is a new and random event—then the likelihood of changes in party alignments is high: the market is wide open and voters are available to all comers. On the other hand, if voters have deep and abiding loyalties to parties, then the number of voters available for either shifts in the party balance or the entry of new parties is necessarily more limited: the stronger and more widespread the attachments, the more structured the electorate and the less the likelihood of change. The weaker the attachments, the more fluid the electorate, and the greater the likelihood of change.

Unfortunately, there is little agreement on the nature of voters' attachments to political parties. The most commonly held view derives from the work of the Survey Research Center: voters develop party identifications which predispose them to vote for the same party in election after election. Recently this has come under attack. Some students of voting behaviour in Western Europe have discovered surprisingly low levels of party identification, while others have found that party identifications change as frequently as voting preferences. The role of party identification in American voting behaviour is seen as an artifact of the number of elected positions: voters are said to need underlying predispositions to simplify the choices confronting them. This is not the case in Western Europe. Elections are less frequent and there are fewer decisions to be made. Parties are more closely tied to social groups, and voting decisions are said to reflect underlying class or group loyalties, ideological preferences, or exposure to the cues and pressures of churches and trade unions, or the influence of segmented social structures.[4]

It is neither necessary nor possible to resolve this dispute here. For the purpose of the present analysis, we will assume that the determinants of voting behaviour vary within and among political systems and examine the ways in which different determinants affect the likelihood of changes in party systems. The impact of party identifications is well known: party identifications are said to intensify with age or length of psychological membership. If these same identifications are passed from parents to children, then party alignments are likely to continue from generation to generation. Change will

[4] See, for example, W. Phillips Shively, 'Party Identification, Party Choice and Voting Stability', *American Political Science Review* 66/4 (1972), 1204–6, 1222–5; or Jacques Thomassen, 'Party Identification as a Cross-National Concept: Its Meaning in the Netherlands', in Ian Budge, Ivor Crewe, and Dennis Farlie (eds.), *Party Identification and Beyond* (London: John Wiley, 1976), 63–80. See also David Butler and Donald Stokes, *Political Change in Britain*, 2nd edn. (London: Macmillan, 1974), 39–47.

occur only if the salience of candidates or issues causes voters to deviate from their underlying predispositions or if new voters enter the electorate with substantially different identifications and loyalties.[5]

The consequences of other types of attachments are not all that different from those of party identifications. If voters decide on the basis of class or group interests, and if there is a clear connection between the class or group and support for a particular party, it is likely that loyalties to parties will develop, be reinforced over time, and be passed down from generation to generation. The same could be said of voters motivated primarily by ideological considerations. However, in this instance, we should expect somewhat greater variation in party choice because these voters will be more likely to measure party performance against their own ideals. Even if voters are not self-motivated, but are mobilized by the pressure and influence of organizational networks, we can still expect a high degree of continuity: voters will remain loyal to their parties as long as the organizational networks and pressures persist and as long as voters remain exposed to them. Should the pressures or cues cease, however, such voters are likely to be available to all comers.

We can now apply these suppositions to Western European party alignments. In most countries, party alignments crystallized in the late nineteenth and early twentieth centuries and reflected the class and religious differences salient at that time. Because substantial proportions of these electorates were mobilized by mass parties and trade unions or by churches or conservative forces competing for the support of newly enfranchised voters, we can assume that party preferences originally derived from the combined effects of organizational pressures, class or group loyalties, and, in some cases, ideological predispositions. To the extent that these pressures and predispositions were consistent—and pointed to a vote for one

[5] See Angus Campbell, Philip Converse, Warren Miller, and Donald Stokes, *The American Voter* (New York: John Wiley, 1960), 120–46, 523–31; and Philip Converse, 'Of Time and Partisan Stability', *Comparative Political Studies* 2/2 (1969), 141–8 ff., 165–7. See also Butler and Stokes, *Political Change*, 48–67.

and not for several parties—we can also assume that voters developed durable commitments to political parties. Repeated in successive elections, these attachments should harden over time and be passed down from generation to generation. If so, then as long as elections continue to be held, and as long as the same choices continue to confront voters, then party alignments should continue with very few changes over time. Change will occur only if voters entering the electorate hold substantially different loyalties than voters dying out, or if voters change their preferences. The latter will depend on the availability of alternatives: if there is more than one party representing a particular group or class or more than one party representing an ideology, then we can probably expect more frequent shifts. Nevertheless, because many voters are likely to be exposed to consistent pressures and influences, we can still expect a high degree of continuity in party alignments.

We can now return to our earlier discussion. In our survey of Western European alignments, we found catch-all parties emerging and gaining strength in only a few countries while party alignments elsewhere remained fairly stable. If the foregoing is correct, then the explanation for the stability of party alignments in most countries in the 1950s and 1960s is fairly simple: if catch-all parties are to succeed, votes must be available for changes in the party alignment. Kirchheimer thought that the advent of an affluent and consumer-oriented society would weaken attachments to parties, but in the short run, attachments already formed should be reinforced rather than eroded.

There are several reasons for this: first of all, although increased prosperity, and changes in income or occupation may alter class structures, this will not happen overnight, not will it have immediate effects on voting behaviour. Voters are likely to retain earlier predispositions and remain exposed to the same organizational pressures and cues. Second, parties which have shared in power should be able to retain followers' loyalties by adjusting their appeals and claiming credit for prosperity and well-being. Even if they are not in power, parties should be able to take a different tack and argue that things would be better if they were. In short, although changes in party style may occur, if existing parties are able to evoke underlying loyalties, then few changes in party alignments will occur because few loose votes will be available. Only in systems in which underlying loyalties to parties never crystallized, or in systems where these loyalties have somehow been eroded, are catch-all strategies likely to succeed or produce changes in party configurations.

Let us look more closely at the countries in which Kirchheimer claimed that the catch-all phenomenon was most advanced. Kirchheimer names four: Britain, France, West Germany, and Italy. All of these countries have broadly based parties, but only three—France, Germany, and Italy—have experienced substantial changes in their party alignments in the post-war years. However, what these three have in common is not a record of widespread affluence or a decline of conflict, but rather common legacies of disrupted political development. In Britain, the decline of the Liberals and the rise of the Labour party was an inter-war phenomenon and one which reflected changes in the composition of the electorate (the completion of suffrage extension) and splits within the Liberal party. The existence of broadly based parties in the post-war period is more a reflection of two-party competition than changes in class structure or post-war affluence. In Italy, substantial changes in the party alignment took place immediately after World War II, but these reflected the Vatican's decision to cast its lot with democracy, accept a secular Italian state, and mobilize within it. The rapid growth of Christian Democracy in the late 1940s was a direct result of this decision. Changes in the party alignment reflected the completion of long delayed electoral mobilization. Since the 1940s, the Italian party alignment has been frozen. Until recently the only real change has been the slow but steady growth of the Communist party as younger voters entered the electorate.

Changes in France and West Germany coincide with rapid economic growth and the rise of consumer-oriented societies. Nevertheless, although prosperity undoubtedly contributed to the growth of the Gaullists in Fifth Republic France, and the Christian Democrats and Social Democrats in West Germany, other factors are more telling. Both countries share a common legacy of crises, disruptions in political development, and changes in the rules of electoral competitions. In France, party attachments in the Fourth Republic were weak and the electorate was extremely volatile.[6] The rise of the UDR reflected not only the prosperity of the Fifth Republic, but also constitutional changes, the political magnetism of de Gaulle, and the boon of political stability. Crises and constitutional changes were especially important. The collapse of the Fourth Republic provided de Gaulle with an opportunity to assert his leadership, while the change from a parliamentary to a presidential regime and the introduction of a directly elected Presidency altered the conditions of competition. The lure of a powerful, indivisible, and directly elected Presidency was sufficient to encourage bloc formation. The coalescence of the Gaullist family in turn encouraged alliances on the left.

In West Germany, the growth of the CDU and the SPD and the consolidation of the party system reflect not only the economic miracle, but also disruptions in political development, the reconstruction of the political system, and changes in the constitution and the electoral law. The party systems of both Imperial Germany and the Weimar Republic were extremely fragmented. The change from a polarized multi-party system to the present three-party configuration took place in the early 1950s in a divided and truncated country. Twelve years of Nazi rule had destroyed much of the old social structure. Though a multi-party system re-emerged in 1949, the 5 per cent threshold successively eliminated smaller parties. The three parties which survived were among the four originally licensed by the occupying powers. Two of these were built on the bases of former mass parties—the pre-war SPD and the Centre party.

The political systems in which catch-all parties have succeeded differ from other Western democracies. France, Germany, and Italy have each experienced major crises which hindered either the formation of the nation state or the transition from oligarchy to liberal democracy. Disruptions in the development or operation of the party system either eroded voters' attachments to parties or prevented their formation in the first place, leaving sizable portions of the electorate avail-

---

[6] Philip Converse and George Dupeux, 'Politicization of the Electorate in the United States and France', in Angus Campbell et al., *Elections and the Political Order* (New York: John Wiley, 1966), pp. 277–283.

able for the growth of catch-all parties. The histories of the Low Countries, Scandinavia, Switzerland, and Britain are different: both the formation of the nation-state and the transition to liberal democracy proceeded more smoothly. As a result, politics has been less marred by the deep cleavages, scars, and recriminations that we find in France, Italy, or pre-war Germany. Because political systems have been more stable, party systems have had greater continuity, and voters have had more chance to develop strong attachments to political parties. Because many parties had blocks of loyal supporters, and because these loyalties could be transferred from generation to generation, there were few votes available for either the growth of catch-all parties or the entry of newer parties. In the last few years, however, electorates have become fluid, but so far, this has led not to the growth of catch-all parties, but rather to increased fragmentation. How can we explain this?

3. PARTY SYSTEMS IN THE 1970S: SOURCES OF FRAGMENTATION

Earlier, we argued that in the short run, economic growth and prosperity should reinforce partisan loyalties. The long run effects are likely to be different. Electorates are constantly renewed by the death of older generations and the entry of younger cohorts. Because younger voters often share parental loyalties, this usually produces only gradual change in party alignments. However, in advanced industrial societies, new generations entering the electorate are likely to be available to a wider range of parties. There are several reasons for this: because of greater physical and social mobility, younger voters are likely to find themselves in different locations in class and occupational structure. They are also less likely to be exposed to the pressures of organizational networks. Shifts into white collar and service sector occupations are likely to reduce the influence of trade unions, and decreasing religiosity weakens the influence of churches. Instead, electronic media are likely to play a greater role in disseminating political information and providing cues for voters. At the same time, voters raised in an affluent and materially secure society are likely to have different values than voters who came of age during the depression, war, or immediate post-war years. Because basic material needs have been assured, such voters are less likely to respond to traditional economic or religious appeals.[7]

Thus far, we have been describing conditions which should facilitate the growth of catch-all parties. However, both the emergence of new cleavages and the very strong possibility of reactions against the politics and policies of post-war welfare states make fluid electorates equally available to minor parties. As we noted earlier, Kirchheimer's scenario is based on the assumption that the principal change in the post-war world has been a decline of ideology. This is not true. Increased consensus on the desirability of a welfare state or a managed economy has not led to a decline of political conflict, but rather a more complex pattern of cleavage. In many countries, the decreased salience of class and religious issues has permitted the emergence of secondary cleavages and new concerns. In some instances, communal issues, based on language or ethnic differences, have come to the fore. Elsewhere, uneven economic development has exacerbated tensions between centre and periphery and generated regional demands. In other cases, changes in party ideologies or changes in party positions have spurred the formation of factions or the organization of new parties: for example, in several countries, either the abandonment of Marx or support for NATO has produced schisms in Social Democratic parties. More recently, issues such as Common Market membership have divided parties in Britain, Denmark, and Norway. Where there were no latent issues, new ones have sometimes been created—e.g. demands in the Netherlands for improvements in the quality of life or quality of democracy. At the same time, other voters continue to respond to more traditional class or religious appeals. The result is an exceedingly complex pattern of cleavage, difficult to aggregate into only two or three political parties.

This has been compounded by growing reactions against the politics and policies of the post-war welfare state. Since

---

[7] Ronald Inglehart, 'The Silent Revolution in Europe: Intergenerational Change in Post-Industrial Societies', *American Political Science Review* 65/4 (1971), 991–3 ff., 1009–017.

World War II, governments in Western Europe have been increasingly responsible for the management of the economy. Providing full employment and ensuring a minimum level of economic security have produced considerable expansion in government activities and placed an increasingly high load on decision-makers. Governments are now held responsible for the well-being of the entire society. Although governments and governing parties can be praised for good times, they can also be blamed for any shortcomings or reversals which occur. The affluence and prosperity of the 1960s generated high expectations—voters began to regard material security, increased prosperity, and continuing improvements in the quality of life as natural and unending. However, the costs of existing programmes have sky-rocketed, and governments find it increasingly difficult to expand or maintain existing programmes without unacceptable increases in taxation. At the same time, the inability of governments to control inflation and maintain full employment has generated additional strains. The combination of high expectations, increased load on governments, and disappointments can lead to sharp reactions against those in power.

The emergence of new concerns and growing reactions against government policies facilitate the entry and growth of minor parties. Kirchheimer assumed that catch-all parties would thrive because they could appeal to a wide range of voters. However, although parties may be able to modify their positions somewhat in order to retain doubtful supporters or win new voters, few parties can stretch their appeals indefinitely. Appeals aimed at one group may alienate others. The emergence of new cleavages and anti-government reactions places established parties at a severe disadvantage *vis-à-vis* minor parties. Although established parties may want to bid for additional support, they are constrained by past habits, and by the need to retain existing supporters and placate factions within the party. They must also defend past policies. As a result, established parties may not be able to react quickly or credibly enough to pick up new demands or mobilize discontent. New or minor parties are neither burdened by the weight of existing organization nor compromised by participation in cabinets or complicity in government policy. Free of the constraints of office, they are better able to articulate new issues and concerns, better able to mobilize discontent, and better able to fulfil the expressive functions of political parties. Lack of organization is no obstacle: the party's message can be spread easily and rapidly via the mass media.

It is this greater ability to fulfil the expressive functions of political parties which accounts for the fragmentation of European party systems in the 1970s. If we survey the political systems which have changed, it should be obvious that the immediate causes of fragmentation vary from system to system. In Belgium, increased fragmentation in the 1960s reflects the increased salience of the language issue and tension between two peripheries. In the Netherlands, changes in the party system in the late 1960s and early 1970s are the product of reactions to consociational practices and the perceived lack of opposition among the five major parties, the emergence of demands for furthergoing democratization of political and social life, and changes in the Dutch Catholic Church and in the Catholic subculture which created a large pool of voters available for changes in the party system. In Denmark, the sources of change are protest against high levels of taxation, disgruntlement over the similarity of policies pursued by different coalitions, and disagreements arising out of the Common Market issue. In Norway, the principal factors were divisions within established parties in the aftermath of the Common Market referendum and the emergence of a protest dimension, smaller in scale than in Denmark. In the United Kingdom, fragmentation reflects economic downturns, the apparent failure of essentially similar policies tried by both major parties, and the growth of Scottish nationalism.

The parties which have profited from the unfreezing of party alignments are as diverse as the sources of fragmentation. The beneficiaries include Poujadist-style protest parties (the Farmers' party in the Netherlands, the Progress party in Denmark, Anders Lange's party in Norway), fundamentalist parties in Scandinavia (Christian People's parties in Denmark and Norway), parties expressing communal claims (the Flemish and Francophone parties in Belgium, Scottish Nationalists), centre or 'progressive' parties (Democrats '66 in the Netherlands, the Liberals in Britain), right-wing Socialist parties (Democratic Socialists '70 in the Netherlands, the Centre Democrats in Denmark), and parties of the left (the Radical Political party in the Netherlands, the Socialist People's party in Denmark, the Socialist Electoral Alliance in Norway). This diversity reflects the variety of complaints in advanced industrial societies and the openness of the process under way. There is no automatic relationship between changes in social structure, and increased support for particular kinds of parties. Instead, the changes which occur depend on the structure of the electorate and on political activists, the concerns they articulate, the strategies they choose, and the ways in which parties and politicians respond.

16

MODELS OF CHANGE

SCOTT C. FLANAGAN AND RUSSELL J. DALTON

A single model is insufficient to describe the diverse changes occurring in contemporary party systems. The changes affecting these systems are too diverse, ranging from the emergence of new parties to growing anti-party sentiment. In most cases, however, recent examples of partisan change reflect one of two patterns—realignment or dealignment. A social cleavage model of politics attributes change in party systems to the rise and eclipse of social cleavages. The transition between electoral eras is marked by a *realignment*, as parties and their electorates adjust their positions along a new cleavage dimension. In contrast, a functional model evaluates party systems in terms of their relevance to social and political needs. This approach suggests that socio-economic trends are diminishing the relevance of parties to the political process and individual citizens, leading to a continuing pattern of partisan *dealignment*.

Realignment and the Social Cleavage Model

The first major framework for explaining electoral change revolves around the concept of realignment. Discussions of social group alignments and realignments are based on social cleavage theory which assumes that party systems are a reflection of a nation's pattern of social stratification and cleavage. If social cleavages structure the preferences of mass publics, the major social transformations that cause dislocation and conflict

Scott C. Flanagan and Russell J. Dalton, from 'Parties Under Stress: Realignment and Dealignment in Advanced Industrial Societies' reprinted by permission, from the seventh issue of West European Politics published by Frank Cass & Co. Ltd. Copyright Frank Cass & Co. Ltd.

may produce new cleavages which in turn may alter party alignments.

Over a decade ago, in their now classic essay, Lipset and Rokkan spelled out in some detail the historical linkages between social cleavages and party systems. Their analysis focused on two successive revolutions in the modernization of Western Europe—the National Revolution and the Industrial Revolution. In the course of the National Revolution, a number of *segmental cleavages*, revolving around religious, ethnic, and regional divisions, emerged as modernizing states struggled for national integration and the centralization of political authority. In many respects, differences in culture and values lay at the base of these conflicts, although they certainly had important ramifications for the distribution of wealth and economic power. By contrast, the later Industrial Revolution was primarily associated with *economic cleavages* between industrial sectors (primary and secondary industry) and between social classes (the middle and working classes).

Although most analysts have stressed the stability of the party systems that emerged from these cleavage alignments, in a longer-term perspective the social cleavage model also contains a dynamic element. In a number of European countries, for instance, many of the territorial, ethnic, and Church–State issues had been largely resolved prior to the advent of mass political parties in the early decades of the twentieth century. With the declining political salience of segmental cleavages, the party systems that emerged after the turn of the century primarily reflected economic cleavages. Furthermore, in the post-World War II period the religious cleavage underwent further alignment, as distinctly Catholic parties were replaced by more broadly-based Christian or conservative parties in West Germany, the Netherlands, Italy, and France.

These events point to an inherent cyclical pattern in any given social cleavage, especially with regard to how that cleavage is represented in a nation's party system. Sharp differentiation and polarization of a party system along a rising social cleavage is likely to be most intense when new parties representing formerly excluded groups gain entry into parliament and the political system, often after a prolonged struggle. During this formative period, the need to establish an identity separate from the established parties and mobilize a previously unpoliticized constituency induces the new parties to adopt a posture of principled opposition based on extreme, non-negotiable policy demands. Once inside the system, the party leadership is socialized into the realities and limitations of effecting political change and the need for compromise to achieve any progress. In time, the lures of power and effectiveness may prompt the party to moderate its platform and broaden its appeal to represent new kinds of issue interests and attract the marginal voter. The longer a party system remains frozen around a fixed set of institutionalized cleavages, the greater will be the tendency for party platforms to converge.[1]

The decline of party cleavages is generally accompanied by parallel changes in public values. Any given set of issues that provokes a particular pattern of social cleavage and party alignment will inevitably wane in salience over time. The institutionalization of an alignment pattern through organizational linkages and internalized party loyalties will prolong the representation of a cleavage in the party system. However, voters who are two or three generations removed from the issue conflicts which precipitated the original alignment should show little further commitment to those issues as they are resolved or lose their relevance.[2]

Thus, over time, the issues dividing the parties become less relevant to the electorate and the parties themselves become less differentiated on those issues. This latter phenomenon makes it more difficult for the voter to distinguish among the parties. These factors lead to an inevitable ageing of party alignment patterns. The result is a weakening of party attachments and increasing volatility in voting behaviour.

Throughout the post-war period the dominant partisan cleavage in most Western democracies distinguished between

[1] Allesandro Pizzorno, 'Interests and Parties in Pluralism', in Suzanne Berger (ed.), *Organizing Interests in Western Europe* (New York: Cambridge University Press, 1981), 270–1.

[2] Paul Allen Beck, 'A Socialization Theory of Partisan Realignment', in Richard Niemi and associates, *The Politics of Future Citizens* (San Francisco: Jossey-Bass, 1974), 199–219.

the working-class and bourgeois parties.[3] Recently, however, there have been increasing signs that this dominant class cleavage may also be moving into eclipse. A number of socio-economic changes associated with advanced industrialism may be encouraging a decay of the class cleavage. One of these is the homogenization of society and life-styles that has accompanied rising educational levels and growing affluence. The 'end of ideology', 'embourgeoisement' and 'middle mass' models of political change all suggest that as the income and life-style distinctions between the working and the middle classes become increasingly blurred, differences in values and interests between the classes are narrowed and class becomes a much less salient criterion in voting. At the same time, rising levels of social mobility are further blurring class alignments. To the extent that parental partisanship is inherited, class voting is weakened by social mobility. Finally, the class structure itself is changing. For example, a new middle class of salaried white-collar employees does not fit the traditional cleavage based on the self-employed versus the working class. The ambiguous social position of the new middle class has been associated with rising levels of unionization and declining levels of conservative voting within this occupational category in many advanced industrial societies.

The contributors to *Electoral Change*[4] assembled convincing evidence that the traditional middle-class working-class cleavage is weakening. Over the past several decades there has been a secular decline in social class voting throughout most of the Western world. For example, the Alford index of class voting in West Germany declined from a 30-point difference in 1953 to 10 points in 1983; a similar downward trend was observed in Britain, Norway, Sweden, and Denmark. Moreover, even the revival of economic problems in the late 1970s did not stimulate

---

[3] Arend Lijphart, 'Political Parties: Ideologies and Programs', in David Butler *et al* (eds.), *Democracy At The Polls* (Washington, DC: American Enterprise Institute, 1981); id., 'The Relative Salience of Socio-Economic and Religious Issue-Dimensions', *European Journal of Political Research*, 10/2 (1982), 201–11.

[4] [See Russell J. Dalton, Scott C. Flanagan, and Paul Allen Beck (eds.), *Electoral Change in Advanced Industrial Democracies: Realignment or Dealignment?* (Princeton: Princeton University Press, 1984).]

a renewal of class-based voting. The fact that a return to traditional economic issues has not reproduced traditional class alignments is strong evidence of a fundamental change in party politics.

Detailed case studies of the decline in the class cleavage suggest a realigning process much different from past historical patterns. Historically, most realignments have been linked to the rapid mobilization of new voters into the political process, thereby changing the partisan balance. For example, Lipset and Rokkan argued that European party systems were largely in place before the extension of the mass franchise. Thus, new voters were mobilized into this pre-existing framework.

Most contemporary democracies lack a large pool of non-voters that could have fuelled the decline in class voting. Instead, the findings of *Electoral Change* suggest that generational replacement has been a major driving force behind class voting trends, and evidence from several democracies documented a generational decline in class voting. Post-war generations are less concerned with economic issues and less likely to adopt a class-based framework in orientating themselves to politics. This provides further evidence of the ageing of the class cleavage. Indeed, in fully mobilized political systems the process of generational turnover may be one of the few means of recruiting new participants into politics, resulting in a secular realignment in voting patterns.

As the old class alignment weakens, cleavage theory also directs us to look for rising new social divisions as another contributory cause of the disruption of old alignment patterns. Perhaps the clearest expression of a predicted new cleavage has been presented by Erik Allardt. He argued that the party systems of today reflect the cleavage structure of the 1920s, but that in many ways these systems 'are obsolete and do not very adequately catch the actual cleavages and conflicts in society'.[5] He spoke of a third major transformation, the Educational Revolution, which is changing political orientations, particularly among the younger age groups in advanced industrial societies.

[5] E. Allardt, 'Past and Emerging Cleavages', in Otto Stammer (ed.), *Party Systems, Party Organizations, and the Politics of the New Masses* (Berlin: Free University, 1968).

As empirical evidence that such a third revolution is indeed under way, Ronald Inglehart has identified a new-issue agenda, signifying a division of the populations of advanced industrial societies along the lines of age and education.[6] Moreover, this new set of generational and educational cleavages cuts sharply across the old economic cleavages. A 'New Left' appears to be emerging from among the ranks of the younger age cohorts, and from the middle class rather than the working class. In addition, the late 1970s and early 1980s have witnessed the emergence of a conservative counter-attack arising from the issues raised by the New Left.[7] A new morality has given rise to a new set of conservative social issues, a reassertion of traditional values, and assaults on the welfare state.

In their separate contributions to *Electoral Change*, Inglehart, Sankiaho, and Flanagan made a factor analysis of group-affect thermometers and identified an emerging second dimension of group alignments. The first dimension is still defined primarily by the class conflict of unions and the established Leftist parties versus big business and the established Rightist parties. The second dimension aligns various establishment institutions such as the bureaucracy, the police, and occasionally the clergy, against rising new agents of social change such as radicals, student protesters, the women's movement, and minority groups. Moreover, Inglehart finds that while social class correlates more highly with the affect scores on the first dimension, post-material values correlate more highly with scores on the second dimension.

The precise form a new establishment anti-establishment cleavage might assume is still unclear, as is the question of whether it will ultimately replace or in some way be integrated into the present left–right party dimension. It does appear, however, that growing affluence in advanced industrial societies is associated with a decline in the salience of economic issues and a rise in the salience of non-economic value issues.

---

[6] R. Inglehart, *The Silent Revolution: Changing Values and Political Styles among Western Publics* (Princeton: Princeton University Press, 1977).

[7] Seymour Lipset, 'The Revolt against Modernity', in Per Torsvik (ed.) *Mobilization, Centre-Periphery Structures and Nation-Building* (Bergen: Universitetsforlaget, 1981).

This shift in the relative salience of these two broad types of issue has been reflected in two tendencies. The first is a revitalization of some of the traditional segmental cleavages which were not fully resolved, but which were largely eclipsed by economic issues throughout much of the twentieth century.[8] The past two decades have witnessed a resurgence of regional and ethnic conflicts in Britain, Belgium, France, and Spain. Religion has played a more prominent role in some countries with the political mobilization of fundamentalist groups in the United States and elsewhere, the revival of religious parties in Scandinavia, and the sectarian conflict in Northern Ireland. Racial issues also have become more salient in British and American politics.

A second development has been the emergence of non-economic value cleavages, based upon a new set of 'quality of life' and self-actualizing issues—environmental protection, the dangers of nuclear energy and nuclear war, sexual equality, consumer advocacy, human rights and the new morality. The environmental issue best typifies the development of this new cleavage dimension. This issue cuts across traditional class-based lines of political and party conflict. Thus, new ecologist parties have formed to represent these concerns in West Germany, Austria, France, Finland, and several other nations.[9] In other instances, the established parties have responded to these new issues, ranging from the Socialists in France, to the Centre in Sweden, to the Monarchists in Portugal—this is truly a cross-cutting issue.

Traditional cleavage theory would lead us to expect that eventually these issues or other emerging issues would coalesce into broad social movements which would realign the electorates and party systems of the advanced industrial societies around a new set of social cleavages. For example, in nation after nation we found a relationship between age and party choice. Furthermore, longitudinal analyses in West Germany

[8] Gordon Smith, 'Social Movements and Party Systems in Western Europe', in Martin Kolinsky and William Patterson (eds.), *Social and Political Movements in Western Europe* (New York: St Martin's Press, 1976).

[9] Ferdinand Mueller-Rommel, 'Ecology Parties in Western Europe', *West European Politics*, 5/1 (1982), 68–74.

and the Netherlands suggest that these sharp age differences first emerged in the early 1970s. In other cases, evidence of an emerging educational cleavage is also becoming visible.

The rising new-issue cleavages may assume a temporary generational form because of the rapid pace of the advanced industrial transformation and the fact that these new orientations are embraced most strongly by the post-war generations. Thus, after the post-industrial revolution has further progressed, the generational cleavage may eventually be replaced by more enduring social group cleavages. Cleavage theory predicts that the most virulent forms of conflict during this transitional period should emerge between the winners and losers in the social dislocations associated with post-industrial development. If knowledge becomes the primary resource in the emerging information societies, levels of education, knowledge, and specialized expertise may develop as a principal dimension of social stratification and cleavage. Alternatively, the issues of economic growth and nuclear energy have occasionally united management and unions against environmental groups. The issue of increased government social spending versus lower taxes is working to realign public sector workers against private sector workers. An anti-tax backlash has fuelled political conflict on both sides of the Atlantic.

At least to date, however, one distinctive feature of post-industrial conflicts is that they often involve value-sharing communities rather than economically or functionally defined social groups. As we shall see, this aspect of the new issue cleavages bears directly on the realigning potential of the post-industrial transformation.

Dealignment and the Functional Model

The social cleavage model suggests that the increasing signs of instability and volatility in contemporary party systems is a passing phenomenon. In this view, instability is a temporary phase, appearing only during the transition from one stable alignment to the next. However, a contrasting viewpoint argues that many of the changes associated with post-industrial development are fundamentally altering the context of political competition and the attitudes of citizens. A functional model of electoral change would interpret the growing signs of instability as a product of the loss of functions by political parties and the declining functional value of party identification to large numbers of citizens. A functional perspective suggests that contemporary dealignment may be a turning-point in the history of political parties—a permanent rather than a temporary condition. As the role of parties continues to decline, we may ultimately witness the eclipse or replacement of parties by other institutions that more effectively link the citizen and his government.

At the systemic level, many of the parties' traditional input functions either have become obsolete or have been largely taken over by other institutions. One of the parties' most central functions was the articulation and ordering of public interests. An explosion in the numbers of group demands and new issues has given the parties little hope of voicing this myriad of concerns. More and more groups, both large and small, have organized to press forward their own specialized interests. It is estimated, for instance, that in 1978, 6,000 interest groups were operating in Washington, DC, and a similar pattern undoubtedly exists in many European capitals. Modern technologies have made it efficient for these groups to educate the public on their pet issues and concentrate upon those demographic categories within the population most likely to lend support. Another method of expressing public interests is through the development of scientific survey sampling. A plethora of professional polling organizations now provides reliable information on popular support for all issues—large and small. Perhaps for the first time in the modern history of representative democracies, the general will can be assessed without relying on intermediary institutions such as parties.

Traditionally, parties have also performed a number of information and oversight functions—educating their constituents on the issues of the day and criticizing the actions of government. These communication and watchdog roles are vital for creating an informed electorate, capable of participating meaningfully in the political process. Increasingly, however, the media have taken over these roles, because they are considered unbiased providers of information and because the electronic media have created more convenient and pervasive delivery systems. Thus, there is a declining need for party newspapers, extensive grass-roots party organizations, and canvassing to inform voters.

Another input function of the parties is the programmatic function—the aggregation and screening of interests to provide the public with clear alternatives. The parties' ability to perform this function in recent decades has also declined. One source of this performance failure is found in the trend towards policy convergence among the parties on the economic and welfare issues associated with the traditional class cleavage. In addition, the new agenda of post-industrial issues often appears unsuited for mass political parties. Many of these issues, such as educational reform, minority rights, nuclear energy, or specific economic development projects, are too narrow to affect mass partisan alignments or realignments. The rise of single-issue interest groups and single-issue campaigns does not translate well into mass party politics. Typically, parties are reluctant to take clear stands on narrow issues because of the threat of losing more votes than they gain. Alternatively, many of the new issues, such as pollution, are valence issues or else involve choices among several positively valued goals. Again, parties tend to avoid clearly differentiated positions on these kinds of issue.

A final input function, and one that has been clearly dominated by parties, is recruitment to political office. Even here, however, there are signs of a weakening in the parties' role. The most advanced example would be the United States, where the introduction of open primaries and non-partisan elections has undermined the parties' hold on recruitment, but signs of a weakening party role in recruitment are also visible in some parliamentary systems. Several Icelandic parties initiated primaries in the mid-1970s, and Belgian parties have used a modified primary system to select parliamentary candidates. Such practices, if adopted in other parliamentary systems, might eventually result in parties that are organizationally weaker, less élitist, and more easily penetrated by new movements, organized interests, and currents of opinion within the electorate. Even without the primary, television is transforming campaigns into candidate, rather than party-focused, competitions.

If the mass media and interest groups have encroached increasingly on the parties' input functions, the bureaucracy in many countries has usurped much of their traditional output functions. Control over patronage and the spoils of office have, in many cases, been transferred to a professionalized civil service. Also, the parties' paternalistic distribution of benefits to constituents increasingly has been displaced by entitlement programmes which dispense benefits on the basis of apolitical bureaucratic criteria.

The parties have fared little better in the area of conversion functions. Parties emerged as *the* institution capable of asserting co-ordination and control over the authoritative decision-making process in modern mass democracies. Parties seemed to be the only vehicle that could control both the executive and legislative branches and bring coherence to government. However, with the increasingly technical nature of political issues and government programmes, the parties have been losing control of the policy-making process to the bureaucracy. Also, growing policy convergence among the parties and the resolution of many old class issues have left the parties in many nations without clear goals. Many of the goals that remain are more technical than political. To the extent that post-industrial societies have resolved the problem of chronic scarcity, the primary issue is no longer who will benefit, but what is the best means of ensuring continued economic growth and enhancing the quality of life.

A second systemic conversion function is authoritative decision-making, providing a mantle of legitimacy for the decisions of government. Parties, as the elected representatives of the people, have provided legitimacy for government policy decisions and have thereby assured the compliance of the masses. However, parties do not always legislate the will of the majority. With the expanded use of public opinion polling techniques, examples of issues in which the parties actually thwart majority opinion have become increasingly apparent to the public. The result has been a growing demand for plebiscites and referenda to enable the people directly to legislate their will. Even in Great Britain, the birthplace and bastion of party government, the first two nation-wide referenda occurred in 1975 and 1979. Studies have documented a rising incidence of national referenda in advanced industrial societies across the post-war period.[10]

In addition to direct participation techniques, there has been an increase in the direct role of interest groups in decision-making through Royal Commissions, advisory councils, and other public advisory bodies. In this 'neo-corporatist' decision-making model, peak associations representing business, labour, and/or other interested parties are appointed to an advisory body to hammer out policy decisions in a contested problem area. The party-controlled legislature simply ratifies the policy decisions made through direct negotiations among the concerned organized interests. There is evidence demonstrating that neo-corporatist decision-making lowers the level of citizen unruliness and protest activity, and increases the level of government fiscal effectiveness. In other words, in an era of hyperparticipation and the mobilization of a broad variety of competing interests and demands, parties may no longer be able to rule alone. Increasingly, neo-corporatist policy-making formulae may be utilized to aggregate egoistic demands, gain compliance for hard decisions, and resolve the problem of regime overload and ungovernability.

Not only do parties perform few system-level functions in advanced industrial societies, but party identification and party cues also are becoming less functional for citizens in these societies. W. Phillips Shively has argued that voters develop party identification as a crutch or short cut to help them handle difficult and often confusing political decisions.[11] By relying on decisional cues emanating from a party identification, the costs of participation are reduced.

Several social trends associated with post-industrialism have made party identification less necessary, and perhaps less relevant, for the voter. Rising levels of education have increased the voters' sophistication and ability to deal with the complexities of politics and reach voting decisions without relying on external cues. At the same time, the growing availability of

[10] David Butler and Austin Ranney (eds.), *Referendums* (Washington, DC: American Enterprise Institute, 1978).
[11] W. Phillips Shively, 'The Development of Party Identification among Adults', *American Political Science Review*, 73/4 (1979), 1039–54.

political information through the media has reduced the costs of making informed decisions. Moreover, the increasing instability of parties and party systems, the rise of new parties, and shifting party stands, have made long-standing party attachments less reliable guides. As noted above, the media themselves have reduced the relevance of party labels by highlighting candidate images and personalities. Finally, the shift in issues from broad cleavage-based issues to narrow special-interest issues, on which the parties generally have taken ambiguous stands, has reduced the relevance of party identification for the voters' decisions. For some voters it is becoming more feasible, and perhaps even more efficient, to identify individual candidates, form concrete images, and even to ascertain the positions of candidates on the salient issues.

In addition to the declining functional value of partisanship, a general process of value change also is weakening party identification.[12] Advanced industrialism has led to the development of post-material values which stress political participation and involvement in political decision-making. But in addition to these participatory norms, these values encourage self-directed political behaviour and independence from élite-controlled hierarchical organizations, such as political parties. Thus, value change should also promote the dealignment of mass politics.

CONCLUSION

Where are these changes leading contemporary party systems? We have noted that the forces of realignment and dealignment are intimately related to structural and attitudinal changes associated with post-industrial development. Hence, similar sources and processes of change are at work in all the advanced industrial societies. In other research, we have found that changes in the shape of party systems cannot be easily anticipated, because of the strong impact of intervening contextual

[12] Inglehart, *The Silent Revolution*; Russell Dalton, 'Cognitive Mobilization and Partisan Dealignment in Advanced Industrial Democracies', *Journal of Politics*, 46/1 (1984).

factors. For example, whether a new-issue cleavage is represented by the existing parties or new parties will depend, in part, on the established parties' response to the new issues. The structure and openness of an electoral system will also mediate the impact of realigning and dealigning forces.

However, both the cleavage and functional models do afford clearer predictions regarding the direction of development in the role and nature of political parties. While the role of parties is changing and declining, they are not likely to disappear in the foreseeable future. Parties provide a vehicle for limiting competition and choice that the myriad of interest groups cannot. Parties also provide stability for legislatures and executives, especially in parliamentary systems. Even if neo-corporatist formulae are increasingly introduced to negotiate policy agreements outside elected legislatures, there will remain a need for organized groups that can claim to represent the interests of the majority of the population and are able to oversee and ratify those agreements. Moreover, there will always be a need for some political groups to be in a position to make authoritative decisions free from the influences of special interests; this provides for the representation of interests not championed by any powerful national peak association. Finally, many voters still will lack the political information, cognitive sophistication or interest to participate in elections without the simplifying cues provided by political parties and partisan identifications.

If neither model predicts the disappearance of political parties, both point to a change in the types and roles of parties. With the narrowing of party functions and the shift of party support bases from broad, cohesive social groups towards a more diverse array of loosely organized issue groups, the context of party competition is changing. The parties that survive and flourish in the post-industrial era are likely to have a very different set of attributes than those traditionally envisioned in the responsible party model. Ideological parties or highly disciplined parties with stable and strongly articulated preferences are apt to be small. Of course, parties can accommodate themselves to the newly emerging political environment by fragmenting into a multitude of narrow-based parties. This type of party will probably also experience a more rapid cycle of growth, maturity, and decline than in the past. As we have seen, however, new organizational forms do not require a long start-up time, as is exemplified by the Social Democratic party in Britain.

For parties to command broad electoral support and be enduring, they will have to move away from the responsible party model and become more pragmatic, flexible, decentralized, and loosely structured, so that they are more receptive to new interests and more adaptable to local as well as national changes. Thus, the cohesion of large parties is likely to decline as legislators are encouraged to respond to constituency demands rather than those of party leaders. An increase in the use of party primaries is one solution to growing participation demands that would move parties in this direction.

Another means by which parties may adapt to a changing post-industrial environment is by abdicating to a continuing shift in decision-making authority to other sites. We have noted already the increasing reliance on various techniques of direct participation, such as the initiative and referendum and a growing trend towards neo-corporatist policy-making formulae. Parties may increasingly have to sanction such alternative decision-making procedures to avoid acquiring the popular image of obstructing rather than facilitating the public will. On the other hand, an increasing reliance on bureaucratic and technocratic modes of decision-making may frequently be necessary in some areas for nations to achieve the long-range planning and policy stability necessary to compete effectively in the international market-place. Thus, the forces of realignment and dealignment are not only destabilizing the party systems in advanced industrial societies; they are also likely to have a long-term impact on the role and type of parties that will emerge in the decades ahead.

17

THE NATURE OF VALUE CHANGE

RONALD INGLEHART

The basic value priorities of Western publics seem to be changing as their societies move into a Post-Industrial phase of development. This process of value change is likely to bring new issues to the fore. It may influence the public's choice of candidates and political parties. Ultimately, it will help shape the policies adopted by Western élites.

The process of change is not as ephemeral as the flow of events might suggest. Instead it appears to reflect a transformation of basic world views. It seems to be taking place quite gradually but steadily, being rooted in the formative experiences of whole generation-units. Its symptoms manifest themselves in a variety of ways; sometimes they are explosive, as was the case with the unexpected student rebellions of the late 1960s. But if, as we believe, the change is a basic, long-term process, we cannot rely solely on the more blatant manifestations such as these to give an accurate picture of the scope and character of value change among Western publics. Mass survey data offers a more systematic, if less sensational indication of what is happening. The evidence is still fragmentary, but a detailed examination of available data suggests that some profoundly important changes are occurring.

I. SOURCES OF VALUE CHANGE: SOME HYPOTHESES

Why is value change taking place? It seems to be linked with a cluster of socio-economic changes including rising levels of education, shifts in the occupational structure, and the development of increasingly broad and effective mass communications networks. But two phenomena seem particularly significant:

1. The unprecedented prosperity experienced by Western nations during the decades following World War II. Recent economic stagnation does not seem to have undone the effects of the twenty fat years from 1950 to 1970.
2. The absence of total war. The simple fact that no Western nation has been invaded for thirty years may have extremely significant consequences.

In short, people are safe and they have enough to eat. These two basic facts have far-reaching implications.

Our expectation that the value priorities of Western publics are changing is derived from two key hypotheses. The first is that people tend to place a high priority on whatever needs are in short supply. As a result of the two phenomena just mentioned, Western publics have for a number of years experienced exceptionally high levels of economic and physical security. Consequently, they have begun to give increasing emphasis to *other* types of needs.

If we wish to go beyond this simple explanatory scheme, the work of Abraham Maslow is particularly interesting, for it suggests a specific *direction* in which value change will move under given conditions. Maslow argues that people act to fulfil a number of different needs, which are pursued in hierarchical order, according to their relative urgency for survival.[1] Top priority is given to the satisfaction of physiological needs as long as they are in short supply. The need for physical safety comes next; its priority is almost as high as that of the sustenance needs, but a hungry man will risk his life to get food. Once an

---

[1] See A. H. Maslow, *Motivation and Personality* (New York: Harper, 1954); important efforts to apply Maslow's theory to political analysis include James C. Davies, *Human Nature and Politics* (New York: Wiley, 1963); id., 'The Priority of Human Needs and the Stages of Political Development', unpublished paper; Amitai Etzioni, *The Active Society* (New York: Free Press, 1968), ch. 21; and Robert E. Lane, *Political Thinking and Consciousness* (Chicago: Markham, 1970), ch. 2. A somewhat different analysis of human behaviour as goal-seeking activity following a regular hierarchy of needs is presented in Karl W. Deutsch, *The Nerves of Government* (New York: Free Press, 1963).

individual has attained physical and economic security he may begin to pursue other, non-material goals. These other goals reflect genuine and normal needs—although people may fail to give them attention when deprived of the sustenance or safety needs. But when at least minimal economic and physical security are present, the needs for love, belonging, and esteem become increasingly important; and later, a set of goals related to intellectual and aesthetic satisfaction looms large. There does not seem to be any clear hierarchy within the last set of needs, which Maslow called 'self-actualization needs'. But there is evidence that they became most salient only after an individual has satisfied the material needs and belonging needs.[2]

People have a variety of needs and tend to give a high priority to those which are in short supply. This concept is similar to that of marginal utility of the consumer in economic theory. But it is complemented by another equally important hypothesis: that people tend to retain a given set of value priorities through-out adult life, once it has been established in their formative years.

If the latter hypothesis is correct, we should find substantial differences in the values held by various age groups. One of the most pervasive concepts in social science is the idea that people tend to retain a certain basic character throughout adult life once it has been formed in childhood and youth. If there is any truth in this notion, older individuals should show value pri-orities which reflect the relatively insecure material conditions which prevailed during their formative years. On the other hand, during the thirty years that have passed since World War II, Western countries have experienced an unprecedented period of economic growth and they have all been free from invasion. Consequently, we might expect that younger groups,

[2] See Jeanne M. Knutson, *The Human Basis of the Polity: A Psychological Study of Political Men* (Chicago: Aldine, 1972). Allardt, however, questions whether there is any hierarchy among needs. He finds no relationship between income level and scores on subjective indices of Loving and Being; on the other hand, his data indicate that a sense of social support tends to be a prerequisite to emphasis on self-development. See Erik Allardt, *About Dimensions of Welfare: An Exploratory Analysis of a Comparative Scandinavian Survey* (Helsinki: Research Group for Comparative Sociology, 1973).

particularly those brought up since World War II, would place less emphasis on economic and physical security.

Let us see what light public opinion survey evidence sheds on the problem of value change. A rather exceptional data base is available for our investigation. In 1970 and again in 1971, the European Community carried out public opinion surveys in France, West Germany, Belgium, the Netherlands, and Italy; data for 1970 are also available from Great Britain. These surveys included a series of questions designed to indicate which values an individual would rank highest when forced to choose between security or 'Materialist' values such as economic and political stability; and expressive or 'Post-Materialist' values.[3] We hypothesized that those who had been socialized under conditions of peace and relative prosperity would be likeliest to have Post-Materialist values.

Representative national samples of the population over fifteen years of age were asked:

> If you had to choose among the followings things, which are the *two* that seem most desirable to you?
>
> —Maintaining order in the nation.
> —Giving the people more say in important political decisions.
> —Fighting rising prices.
> —Protecting freedom of speech.

Two choices were permitted; thus it was possible for a respondent to select any of six possible pairs of items.

Choice of the first of these four items ('order') presumably reflects a concern with physical safety; choice of the third item ('prices') presumably reflects a high priority for economic stability. We expected that people who chose one of these items would be relatively likely to choose the other item also: economic insecurity and physical insecurity tend to go together. If a

---

[3] In earlier publications, we used the terms 'Acquisitive' and 'Post-Bourgeois' to describe the two polar types on this value priorities dimension. These terms tend to overemphasize the purely economic basis of value change. Both our analytic framework and the way we have operationalized our measurement of value priorities give an equally important role to the importance of the safety needs. The term 'Materialist' should be understood to denote relative emphasis on *both* economic and physical security.

country is invaded, for example, there is likely to be both economic dislocation and loss of life. Conversely, economic decline is often associated with severe domestic disorder, as was the case in Weimar Germany.

Emphasis on order and economic stability might be termed a Materialist set of value priorities. By contrast, choice of the items concerning free speech or political participation reflects emphasis on two Post-Materialist values that, we expected, would also tend to go together. On the basis of the choices made among these four items, therefore, we can classify our respondents into six value priority types, ranging from a pure Materialist type to a pure Post-Materialist type, with four mixed categories in between.

Our first prediction was that the old would be likelier to have Materialist value priorities than the young; conversely, the Post-Materialist type should be more prevalent among the young. In both our 1970 and 1971 surveys, the relationship between age and value type clearly bears out our expectations. In France, for example, there is an immense preponderance of Materialists over Post-Materialists among those who are more than sixty-five years of age: 52 per cent are Materialists and a bare 3 per cent are Post-Materialists in our combined 1970 and 1971 data. As we move from older to younger age cohorts, the percentage of Post-Materialist types increases. When we reach the youngest cohort (those who were sixteen to twenty-four years old in 1971), the two types are almost equally numerous: 25 per cent are Materialist and 20 per cent Post-Materialist.

The same general pattern appears in each of the other five countries. In every case, the Materialists greatly outnumber the Post-Materialist type among the older age-cohorts, but the balance shifts in favour of the Post-Materialists as we move to the younger cohorts.

This pattern raises an important question. It could reflect historical change, as we hypothesized, or it could reflect a life-cycle effect. Conceivably, the young might tend to be relatively Post-Materialist simply *because* they are young, free from responsibilities, rebellious, idealistic, and so on; one might argue that when they become older, they will have the same preferences as the older groups. We must not ignore this possibility. The only way to be absolutely certain that long-term value change is taking place would be to measure a population's values, wait ten or twenty years, and then measure them again.[4]

[4] [See Chapter 19 below.]

18

DIMENSIONS OF IDEOLOGY IN EUROPEAN PARTY SYSTEMS

AREND LIJPHART

How can the contents and intensity of party ideologies and the ideological dimensions of party systems be identified? First, as Joseph LaPalombara states, 'we can get some clues to a party's collective ideology by looking at party statutes, platforms, special programmatic statements, proceedings of party congresses, press releases, and speeches by the party's leading figures'.[1] In addition, we can observe the actual policies pursued by a party when it is in power, or the policies promoted by a party when it shares governmental power with one or more partners in a coalition. *Ideologies and programmes must be distinguished from the characteristics of the voters that parties represent.* For instance, the fact that a party receives unusually strong support from Roman Catholic voters does not automatically make it a Catholic party and does not necessarily indicate that religion is an important dimension in the party system. On the other hand, it stands to reason that there is a mutual relationship between party programmes and the objective and subjective interests and needs of the party's supporters.

A second guideline for the identification of the ideological dimensions of party systems is that we should focus on the differences *between* parties rather than *within* parties. One or

Arend Lijphart, abridged from 'Political Parties: Ideologies and Programs', in David Butler, Howard R. Penniman, and Austin Ranney (eds.), *Democracy at the Polls: A Comparative Study of Competitive National Elections*, 1981. Reprinted by permission of the American Enterprise Institute for Public Policy Research.

[1] J. LaPalombara, *Politics within Nations* (Englewood Cliffs, NJ: Prentice-Hall, 1974), 534.

more ideological cleavages may divide parties internally instead of from each other, and these should not be confused with
those that divide the party system itself. Third, we should
restrict our analysis to the ideologies of and the ideological
differences between the *significant parties*, those parties that
Giovanni Sartori calls 'relevant': political parties that frequently participate in cabinets and are widely recognized as
acceptable coalition partners, or which are so large as to have
an important impact on the system even though they are not
considered acceptable governing partners. In Sartori's terminology, these are parties with either 'coalition potential' or
'blackmail potential'.[2] Finally, we should focus on the *durable
ideological dimensions* of party systems and ignore the more or less
programmatic differences that may emerge in one election but
fade away soon afterward.

The following ideological dimensions were present in many
democratic party systems in the 1970s and are likely to continue
in the 1980s:

1. socio-economic
2. religious
3. cultural–ethnic
4. urban–rural
5. regime support
6. foreign policy
7. post-materialism

The first six of these dimensions correspond quite closely with
the party system cleavages identified by a number of other
authors. Sartori's 'four basic cleavage dimensions' are left
versus right, secular versus denominational, ethnicity versus
integration, and democratic versus authoritarian divisions;
these are basically the same as the first, second, third, and fifth
dimensions listed above.[3] Michael Taylor and Michael Laver
use the equivalents of the first through the fourth and the sixth
dimensions of the list above in their study of West European

[2] G. Sartori, *Parties and Party Systems: A Framework for Analysis*, Vol. 1
(Cambridge: Cambridge University Press, 1976), 121–4.
[3] Ibid. 336. However, Sartori's left-right dimension also includes the
'constitutional left-right' cleavage which concerns 'how equal laws relate to
societal inequalities' (p. 337).

government coalitions.[4] Lawrence C. Dodd also uses the
Taylor–Laver dimensions but adds the regime support item
and drops the urban–rural division.[5] Robert Harmel and Kenneth Janda propose six ideological continua, all of which they
label left–right dimensions, but only four of which correspond
with the socio-economic dimension of the list above; the other

TABLE 18.1. Ideological Dimensions of European Party Systems
in the 1970s

Country	Socio-Economic	Religious	Cultural–Ethnic	Urban–Rural	Regime Support	Foreign Policy	Post-Materialist
Austria	X	X					
Belgium	X	X	X				
Denmark	X			X			
Finland	X		X	X	X		
France	X	X			X	X	
West Germany	X	X					
Greece	X				X	X	
Ireland	X					X	
Italy	X	X			X	X	
Netherlands	X	X					X
Norway	X	X		X			X
Portugal	X				X	X	
Spain	X				X	X	
Sweden	X			X			X
Switzerland	X	X					
United Kingdom	X						

[4] M. Taylor and M. Laver, 'Government Coalitions in Western Europe',
European Journal of Political Research, 1/3 (Sept. 1973), 237–48. Their foreign
policy dimension is limited to the Republic of Ireland where it refers to
attitudes toward the Treaty of 1921. An additional dimension that these two
authors use is the federalist versus unitarist dimension; I shall return to this
point later with special reference to the Belgian party system.

[5] L. C. Dodd, *Coalitions in Parliamentary Government* (Princeton, NJ: Princeton University Press, 1976), 99. I have combined four of Dodd's dimensions
—linguistic conflict, cultural conflict, regionalism, and German nationalism
in interwar Austria—into the single cultural–ethnic dimension.

two are the secular–denominational conflict and divergent foreign policy outlooks (favouring international alignment with the 'Western bloc' versus the 'Eastern bloc' of nations).[6] To the dimensions identified by these various scholars I have added the cleavage between 'materialists' and 'post-materialists', which Ronald Inglehart has found to be of great, and probably growing, significance in industrialized societies.[7]

The incidence of these seven ideological dimensions in the party systems is indicated in Table 18.1. This table is based on my own, necessarily subjective, judgement, but I believe that the majority of my decisions are straightforward and non-controversial. On the other hand, there are a number of difficult cases, and I shall point these out as I discuss each of the ideological dimensions.

1. *The Socio-Economic Dimension*. The four leftist versus rightist party positions on socio-economic policy enumerated by Harmel and Janda provide a good summary of the basic components of the socio-economic dimension of ideology: (1) governmental versus private ownership of the means of production, (2) a strong versus a weak governmental role in economic planning, (3) support of versus opposition to the redistribution of wealth from the rich to the poor, and (4) the expansion of versus resistance to governmental social welfare programmes.[8] The first three of these components coincide with what Martin Seliger calls the three socio-economic 'core-issues' of the left–right dimension.[9] This dimension is listed first in Table 18.1 because it is the most important of the ideological dimensions and because it is present in all of the democratic party systems.

This conclusion appears to contradict the end-of-ideology theory, which is especially concerned with the socio-economic

[6] R. Harmel and K. Janda, *Comparing Political Parties*, Supplementary Empirical Teaching Units in Political Science (Washington, DC: American Political Science Association, 1976), 33–5.

[7] R. Inglehart, *The Silent Revolution: Changing Values and Political Styles among Western Publics* (Princeton: Princeton University Press, 1977).

[8] Harmel and Janda, *Comparing Political Parties*, p. 35.

[9] M. Seliger, *Ideology and Politics* (London: George Allen and Unwin, 1976), 214–16.

ideological dimension. In fact, as Leon D. Epstein points out, it is the end of *socialist* ideology that the theory focuses on.[10] However, we can speak of the *end* of ideology only when we use the ideal-type meaning of ideology. When the term 'ideology' is used in the broader sense, as an empirical category including various degrees of ideological thinking, we have to speak more modestly of a *decline* of ideology. This decline, fuelled by the unprecedented growth in economic prosperity of the Western democracies in the 1950s and early 1960s, occurred particularly with regard to the question of governmental ownership of the means of production. In addition, the leftist positions on economic planning, income redistribution, and social welfare programmes—and the rightist responses to these policy preferences—have become more moderate. Seymour M. Lipset, writing in 1964, argues that this convergence of socio-economic ideologies marks the development of the new ideological agreement of 'conservative socialism' which he calls '*the* ideology of the major parties in the developed states of Europe and America'.[11]

With the advantage of hindsight, this judgement—which was partly a description and partly a prediction—appears to have been premature. For one thing, the economic problems of the 1970s, have heightened left–right tensions. Moreover, even though the objective growth of the total economic pie makes its division among different groups and classes in society easier, the economic expectations of these groups inevitably remain subjective and relative. As Lipset himself emphasizes, 'as long as some men are rewarded more than others by the prestige or status structure of society, men will feel *relatively* deprived'.[12] There has also been a growing awareness that economic prosperity and the distribution of prosperity are to a large extent politically determined. Robert A. Dahl argues that 'since any particular allotment reveals itself more and more clearly

[10] L. D. Epstein, *Political Parties in Western Democracies* (New York: Praeger, 1967), 286.

[11] S. M. Lipset, 'The Changing Class Structure and Contemporary European Politics', in Stephen R. Graubard (ed.), *A New Europe?* (Boston: Houghton Mifflin, 1964), 362.

[12] S. M. Lipset, *Political Man: The Social Bases of Politics* (Garden City, NY: Anchor Books, 1963), 444–5.

nowadays to be a product of political decisions and less and less an act of God, nature, or the inexorable operation of economic laws, conflicts over the distribution of income might, if anything, become more numerous even if less intense'.[13]

The importance of political influences on economic policies and performance has been confirmed by a spate of recent studies of the political-economic nexus. It is especially interesting for the purposes of this chapter that these studies show significant differences between the socio-economic policies pursued by leftist-oriented and rightist-oriented governments. David R. Cameron, Edward R. Tufte, Frank Castles, and Robert D. McKinlay show that leftist governments have systematically produced a higher rate of growth of the public sector of the economy, larger central government budgets, more income equalization, and higher levels of performance with regard to educational expenditures and public health than rightist governments.[14] Douglas A. Hibbs, jun., finds that when a choice has to be made between price stability, favoured by the parties of the right, and full employment, favoured by the left, 'the macroeconomic policies pursued by left-wing and right-wing governments are broadly in accordance with the objective economic interests and subjective preferences of their class-defined core political constituencies'.[15] Hibbs's finding on price stability is disputed by Andrew T. Cowart, but the two authors agree on the greater sensitivity of leftist governments to the problem of unemployment. Cowart also argues that, in general, leftist governments have been considerably more interventionist in both monetary and fiscal policy making.[16] The evidence

[13] R. A. Dahl, *Political Oppositions in Western Democracies* (New Haven: Yale University Press, 1966), 398.

[14] D. R. Cameron, 'The Expansion of the Public Economy: A Comparative Analysis', *American Political Science Review*, 72/4 (Dec. 1978), 1243–61; R. Tufte, 'Political Parties, Social Class, and Economic Policy Preferences', *Government and Opposition*, 14/1 (Winter 1979), 18–36, esp. pp. 28–30; F. Castles and R. D. McKinlay, 'Does Politics Matter? An Analysis of the Public Welfare Commitment in Advanced Democratic States', *European Journal of Political Research*, 7/2 (June 1979), 169–86.

[15] D. A. Hibbs, jun. 'Political Parties and Macroeconomic Policy', *American Political Science Review*, 71/4 (Dec. 1977), 1467–87.

[16] A. T. Cowart, 'The Economic Policies of European Governments, Part I: Monetary Policy', and 'Part II: Fiscal Policy', *British Journal of Political Science*, 8/3, 4 (July, Oct. 1978), 285–311, 425–39.

can be summarized in the following statement by Tufte: 'The single most important determinant of variations in macro-economic performance from one industrialized democracy to another is the location on the left-right spectrum of the governing political party. Party platforms and political ideology set priorities and help decide policy.'[17]

2. *The Religious Dimension.* The second most important ideological dimension concerns party attitudes and policies towards religion and religious values. On this dimension, too, a decline of ideology has occurred. In the continental European countries with mixed Catholic–Protestant populations and histories of Catholic–Protestant antagonism, interreligious tensions have largely disappeared and the two groups have even tended to unite politically. The Christian Democratic Union of the Federal Republic of Germany was founded as a joint Catholic–Protestant party. In the Netherlands, the Catholic party and the two main Protestant parties presented a single list in the 1977 parliamentary elections and are planning to merge into a single party organization, the Christian Democratic Appeal. Only in Switzerland do the Christian Democrats remain an almost exclusively Catholic party. Moreover, both the explicitly religious parties and their anticlerical opponents have moderated their claims and counterclaims to a large extent. On the other hand, the religious and secular parties are still divided on a range of moral issues, such as questions of marriage and divorce, birth control, abortion, sex education, and pornography. These issues became especially prominent in the late 1960s and 1970s.

Most of the party systems with an important religious cleavage can be found in continental Western Europe, excluding Scandinavia. West Germany, Italy, Austria, Switzerland, Belgium, and the Netherlands all have major Christian Democratic or Social Christian parties. In France, the original Christian Democratic party, the MRP, and its several successors have lapsed into insignificance, but the Gaullists now occupy the position of a conservative pro-Church party.

---

[17] Tufte, 'Political Parties, Social Class, and Economic Policy Preferences', p. 35.

Spain and Portugal are problematic cases. It would have been logical to expect the formation of Christian Democratic parties in these countries after the restoration of democracy. However, partly as a reflection of the decline of ideology along the religious dimension in the 1970s, the politicians belonging to this persuasion decided to participate in broader centre-right political groupings: the Union of the Democratic Centre in Spain and the Centre Social Democrats in Portugal. Hence the religious cleavage affects intraparty rather than interparty relations.

The end-of-ideology proposition with regard to the religious dimension appears to be disconfirmed by the emergence of Christian Democratic parties in all of the Nordic countries, especially in the 1960s and 1970s. Such parties were founded in Finland in 1958, in Sweden in 1964, and in Denmark in 1970. The Finnish and Danish, but not the Swedish, parties have achieved parliamentary representation. However, none of these parties can be regarded as 'relevant' according to Sartori's criteria. Only the older Norwegian Christian People's party, established in 1933, has played a significant political role and has participated in three cabinets.

3. *The Cultural–Ethnic Dimension.* In their developmental theory of cleavage structures and party systems, Seymour M. Lipset and Stein Rokkan identify four basic sources of party system cleavages. These are, in addition to the left–right and religious dimensions, already discussed, cultural–ethnic cleavages and the divisions between rural-agrarian and urban-industrial interests.[18] The cultural–ethnic dimension does not appear as often as the religious dimension, because eleven of the sixteen countries are ethnically homogeneous or contain only small and insignificant minorities. Moreover, of the remaining five countries with potential cultural–ethnic divisions

[18] S. M. Lipset and S. Rokkan, 'Cleavage Structures, Party Systems, and Voter Alignments: An Introduction', in S. M. Lipset and S. Rokkan (eds.), *Party Systems and Voter Alignments: Cross-National Perspectives* (New York: Free Press, 1967), 1–64. See also R. Rose and D. Urwin, 'Social Cohesion, Political Parties and Strains in Regimes', *Comparative Political Studies*, 2/1 (Apr. 1969), 7–67.

between the parties, only two have clear interparty cleavage dimensions.

Switzerland is often regarded as the plural society *par excellence*, but its party system reflects mainly religious and left–right differences, and linguistic issues are virtually absent at the national level. Even the protracted discussions concerning the Jura Problem did not stimulate interparty divisions or the emergence of other linguistic controversies. In Spain, regionalist and autonomist parties won almost 10 per cent of the vote in the 1979 elections, but this vote was divided among several disparate groupings; the largest ethnic party is the Catalan Convergence and Union party with only 2.7 per cent of the vote and 9 out of 350 seats. One or more of these parties may acquire coalition potential in the future, like the small Swedish People's party in Finland, which is a very frequent coalition partner, but they do not possess the potential to participate in government at the present time.

In the United Kingdom, similarly, the Scottish National party and other minority parties are too small to have a significant impact on national interparty relations. When the Callaghan cabinet in its last two years (1977–9) had become a minority government, it was dependent on support from the Liberals, the SNP, and other small parties, but this unusual situation cannot be considered sufficient grounds to credit the SNP with coalition potential.

At the other extreme is the Belgian party system in which the cultural–ethnic dimension has become a sharp dividing line between the two communities and their parties. During the 1960s three explicitly linguistic parties established themselves as important actors on the Belgian political scene: the Volksunie in Flanders, the Walloon Rally in Wallonia, and the Francophone Democratic Front in bilingual but mainly French-speaking Brussels. Subsequently, between 1968 and 1978, the three national parties—the Christian Social, Socialist, and Liberal parties—split into autonomous Flemish and Francophone organizations. It may also be argued that there are two different cultural–ethnic dimensions in Belgian party politics: a dimension of Flemings versus French-speakers in which the linguistic parties are at opposite ends of the scale and the older, still more nationally oriented parties take a centre position, and a federalist–centralist dimension with the linguistic parties on one side and the traditional parties on the other.

4. *The Urban–Rural Dimension.* Differences between rural and urban areas occur in all democracies, but they constitute the source of party system cleavages in only a few. Even here, it is somewhat questionable whether these differences can be regarded as ideological or programmatic, although it should be remembered that they entail not only divergent industrial versus agrarian objective interests but also the subjective contrast between urban and rural style of living.

Where agrarian parties are found, mainly in the Nordic countries, they have tended to become less exclusively rural and to appeal to urban electorates, too, prompted by the decline of the rural population. A clear indicator of this shift is that the Swedish, Norwegian, and Finnish agrarian parties all changed their names to 'Centre party' between 1957 and 1965. The Danish Liberal party also originated as an agrarian party but now similarly tries to portray itself as a centre party.

5. *The Dimension of Regime Support.* This dimension occurs in democracies as a result of the presence of important parties that oppose the democratic regime or that, as in the case of the Gaullists during the French Fourth Republic, demand a drastic overhaul of the democratic form of government. In contemporary democratic systems, the dimension of regime support is significant mainly when there are sizable Communist parties: in France, Italy, Spain, Portugal, Greece, and Finland.

With regard to this dimension, too, a decline of ideology appears to have developed. Especially in Italy, France, and Spain, 'Eurocommunism' has been adopted, signalling basic changes in Communist attitudes towards both democracy and foreign policy. However, the debate about the nature of Eurocommunism is not about whether these Communist parties have changed. The crucial question is whether they have changed sufficiently and whether their new outlook can be regarded as stable and durable. Table 18.1 is based on the cautious judgement that it is still too early to be sure that a fundamental and permanent reorientation has taken place.

It may also be argued that a few of the six party systems with a significant regime-support dimension of cleavage should be classified in this way because of anti-regime challenges not only from the left but also from the right. In particular, the Italian Monarchist party and neo-fascist Social Movement and the Francoist parties in Spain (the Popular Alliance in the 1977 election and the Democratic Coalition in the 1979 election) are such right-wing authoritarian parties. However, these parties have been weaker than the Communists in the two countries; they have no coalition potential; and their strength is not really sufficient to give them blackmail potential.

6. *The Foreign Policy Dimension.* The Eurocommunism and decline-of-Communist-ideology debates also concern the question whether the Communist parties have undergone a truly fundamental shift in their traditionally pro-Soviet or pro-Chinese attitudes. Table 18.1 reflects the same judgement on this dimension as on the dimension of regime support. The only exception is Finland, whose neutralism with a slight pro-Soviet tilt is broadly supported by the Communist and non-Communist parties alike as well as by the government of the Soviet Union.

The French party system is characterized by a second foreign policy dimension which concerns the parties' attitudes towards European integration. It divides both the two main parties on the left, the pro-integration Socialists and the anti-integration Communists, and the two main parties on the right, the pro-integration Republicans and the anti-integration Gaullists. The same cleavage has appeared in the three new member states of the European Community—the United Kingdom, Ireland, and Denmark—as well as in Norway, which, after a divisive referendum, declined to join. In these countries, the cleavages were often more intense within some parties, particularly the British and Norwegian Labour parties, than between the parties, but there were also clear interparty differences, such as between the British Labour party on the one hand and the Conservatives and Liberals on the other and between the Irish Labour party and the other two main parties of Ireland. Nevertheless, these divisions may be only temporary, and they are therefore not marked in Table 18.1. The foreign policy dimension that is indicated for Ireland in Table 18.1 refers to the split between Fianna Fáil and Fine Gael on the Treaty of 1921. It is of mainly symbolic significance in contemporary Irish politics, but it does result in at least slightly different attitudes towards the Northern Ireland problem.

7. *The Materialist versus Post-Materialist Dimension.* One question prompted by the end-of-ideology theory is whether the ideological synthesis of 'conservative socialism' represents the end of the ideological dialectic or merely a new dominant thesis which will be challenged by a new antithesis. Two elements of such an antithetical ideology emerged as a reaction to conservative socialism in the 1960s and 1970s. One is the ideology of participatory democracy, which can be seen as a reaction to the impersonality, remoteness, and centralization of bureaucratic decision-making created by conservative socialism. Dahl predicted in 1966 that this rejection of the 'democratic Leviathan' would be one of the new dimensions of opposition in democratic regimes.[19] The other element of a new antithetical ideology is environmentalism, a reaction to the economic growth orientation of conservative socialism.

Both participatory democracy and environmentalism fit the cluster of values of what Inglehart terms 'post-materialism'. Inglehart found that especially among young middle-class people in Western democracies a high priority was accorded to goals like 'seeing that the people have more say in how things get decided at work and in their communities' and 'giving the people more say in important government decisions'. Moreover, in the richer nations the cluster of post-materialist values also included the objective of 'trying to make our cities and countryside more beautiful'.[20]

Post-materialism has so far not become the source of a new ideological dimension in many party systems. The only examples are Norway and Sweden, where the Centre parties have made a smooth transition from old-fashioned rural to modern environmentalist values, and the Netherlands, where two new

[19] Dahl, *Political Oppositions*, pp. 399–400.
[20] Inglehart, *The Silent Revolution*, pp. 40–50. The other post-materialist values are much vaguer ('progress toward a less impersonal, more humane society' and 'progress toward a society where ideas are more important than money') or not really new ('protecting freedom of speech').

parties, Democrats '66 and Radicals, have espoused participa-
tionist ideology. The two Dutch parties are relatively small, but
they were cabinet coalition partners from 1973 to 1977. The
Swedish and Norwegian Centre parties are larger; in fact, the
Centre party of Sweden was the largest non-Socialist party
from 1968 until 1979, and it supplied the prime minister for the
two coalition cabinets of Centrists, Conservatives, and Liberals
formed in 1976 and 1979. The Swedish case also shows the
salience of the environmentalist dimension, because it was on
the issue of nuclear energy that the first of these three-party
cabinets was split from the outset and on which it disintegrated
in late 1978.

   The limited impact of post-materialism is not really surprising because it is always difficult for new issue and cleavage
dimensions to become represented in an established party
system. In addition, the post-materialists are still only a small
minority. In Inglehart's 1970, 1973, and 1976 surveys in the old
Common Market countries and in Great Britain, the average
proportion of post-materialist respondents that he found was a
meagre 11.5 per cent.[21] Another obstacle to a post-materialist
breakthrough in the party system is that the post-materialist
activists have tended to work through the leftist parties
where their middle-class background has clashed with the
traditional working-class orientation of these parties, and
where the essentially conservative nature of the environmentalist ideology is not easily reconcilable with the leftist self-image
of progressivism.

[21] Ibid. 104.

19

FROM CLASS-BASED TO VALUE-BASED POLITICS

RONALD INGLEHART

In the long run there seems to be a tendency for the pursuit of economic self-interest itself to reach a point of diminishing returns in advanced industrial societies, and gradually give way to post-materialist motivation, including greater emphasis on social solidarity.[1] A large body of survey data, gathered during the past fifteen years, suggests that economic development makes a sense of economic deprivation less widespread among mass publics, and consequently, a less important cause of political conflict.

This conclusion is not surprising. After the fact, it may even seem self-evident. It is not: it has been hotly debated, and can not be viewed as conclusively proven even now. A quarter of a century ago, the End of Ideology school concluded that growing prosperity was giving rise to the 'Politics of Consensus in an Age of Affluence'; the subsequent explosion of protest in the late 1960s led many to conclude that this school had been completely wrong. In fact, their analysis of what had been happening was partly correct; like Marx, they simply failed to anticipate new developments. While economic cleavages become less intense with rising levels of economic development, they gradually give way to *other* types of conflict.

Ronald Inglehart, excerpted from 'Value Change in Industrial Societies', *American Political Science Review*, 81/4 (1987), 1289–303. Reprinted by permission of The American Political Science Association.

[1] R. Inglehart, 'The Silent Revolution in Europe: Intergenerational Change in Post-Industrial Societies', *American Political Science Review*, 65 (1971), 991–1017; id., *The Silent Revolution: Changing Values and Political Styles among Western Publics* (Princeton: Princeton University Press, 1977).

TABLE 19.1.   Support for the Classic Economic Policies of the Left by Level of Economic Development, 1979–1983

Nation (ranked by per capita Gross Domestic Product)	GDP/capita in European currency units, 1982	Percentage in favour of:			Mean issues:
		1. Reducing income inequality	2. More government management of the economy	3. More nationalization of industry	
1. Greece	3,958	95%	82	80	86
2. Ireland	5,408	90	72	64	75
3. Italy	6,287	88	68	36	64
4. Northern Ireland	6,852	76	65	57	66
5. Belgium	8,735	87	53	42	61
6. Great Britain	8,755	73	64	46	61
7. Luxembourg	9,407	82	60	31	58
8. Netherlands	9,830	78	64	32	58
9. France	10,237	93	63	44	67
10. Germany	10,927	80	52	41	58
11. Denmark	11,194	71	57	19	49

Source: Based on combined results from Euro-Barometer #11, #16 and #19; respective N's are 8,884 for 1979, 9,909 for 1981 and 9,790 for 1983. Data on GDP/capita are from Eurostat, *Structural Data*, Luxembourg, 1985.

The evidence suggests that at high levels of economic development, public support for the classic economic policies of the Left tends to diminish. Table 19.1 sums up the responses of eleven Western publics to a set of questions dealing with three key issues underlying the classic Left–Right polarization. These questions were asked in Euro-Barometer surveys carried out in 1979, 1981, and 1983, in the ten member nations of the European Community (Greece, not yet a member, was not surveyed in 1979). The questions deal with redistribution of income, government control of the economy, and nationalization of industry—the central elements of the traditional Left's prescription for society. They were worded as follows:

> 'We'd like to hear your views on some important political issues. Could you tell me whether you agree or disagree with each of the following proposals? How strongly do you feel?'
>
> (1) 'Greater effort should be made to reduce income inequality.'
> (2) 'Government should play a greater role in the management of the economy' (in 1983, this item was reversed, to refer to 'a smaller role'; its polarity has been recoded accordingly).
> (3) 'Public ownership of industry should be expanded.'

Though a majority support greater income equality in every country, while further nationalization of industry is rejected by majorities everywhere except in Greece and Ireland, the *relative* levels of support for these three policies among the publics of given nations show impressive consistency—both across items and across time. Taken together, the results add up to a remarkably clear picture of which publics are most favourable to the classic Left economic policies—and the picture does not correspond to conventional stereotypes.

Everyone knows that Denmark is a leading welfare state, with advanced social legislation, progressive taxation, a high level of income equality, and well over half the GNP going to the public sector. Obviously, the Danish public must be relatively favourable to these traditional policies of the Left. Conversely everyone knows that Ireland is a largely rural nation, with a modest public sector and no significant communist or socialist movements. Clearly, Ireland must be a bastion of conservatism on the classic Left–Right issues.

In fact, the conventional stereotypes are dead wrong on both counts. The stereotypes reflect patterns that were true in the past, but precisely *because* Denmark has now attained high levels of social security—and very high levels of taxation—the Danish public has little desire for further extension of these policies. Instead, support for the classic economic policies of the Left tends to reflect a nation's level of economic development. As Figure 19.1 demonstrates, Greece is by far the poorest country among the eleven societies surveyed in 1979–83; and the Greek public has by far the highest level of support for

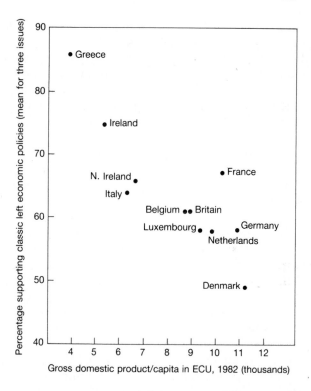

FIG. 19.1.   Support for the Classic Economic Policies of the Left by level of Economic Development, 1979–1983. Based on responses to three items, asked in three surveys.

nationalization of industry, more government management of the economy, and reducing income inequality. Ireland is the second poorest country, and overall Ireland ranks second in support for these policies. At the opposite end of the spectrum, Denmark is the richest country—and has the lowest level of support for these policies. West Germany ranks next to Denmark in economic level—and also in support for the classic Left policies.

The French show more support for these policies than their economic level would suggest—which may be linked with the fact that France also has an incongruously high level of economic inequality. But France constitutes the only significant anomaly. The other ten societies show an almost perfect fit between level of economic development and support for the classic economic policies of the Left.

These findings suggest that the principle of diminishing marginal utility applies at the societal level, as well as the individual level. Greece is an economically underdeveloped country, with many living in extreme poverty and a small affluent élite. In such a context, the balance between rich and poor can be redressed only by strong government intervention. Denmark, on the other hand, is a rich country that has long since developed some of the most advanced social welfare policies in the world—and one of the world's highest rates of taxation. Almost 60 per cent of her GNP is spent by the government; she is approaching the point where it becomes impossible to move much farther in this direction (even in the Soviet Union, the government's share probably isn't over 75 per cent). In Denmark, further redistribution by the government seems less urgent than in Greece—and the costs of government intervention impinge on a larger share of the population. The incentives to press farther with the traditional economic policies of the Left become relatively weak, and public resistance relatively strong.

In this sense, the policies that dominated the agenda of the Left throughout most of this century are running out of steam. Increased state intervention was desperately needed to alleviate starvation and social upheaval in the 1930s; was essential to the emergence of the welfare state in the post-war era; and still makes sense in some areas. But in others, it has passed a point of diminishing returns. The renewed respect for market forces that has emerged throughout most of the industrial world recently, reflects this reality.

The neo-conservative claim that the classic welfare state policies have failed is false, however. Quite the contrary, in countries like Denmark these policies have largely solved the problems they are capable of solving—and have thereby reduced the demand for more of the same. In so far as they *succeed*, they reach a point of diminishing returns, and begin to cede top priority to problems that have *not* been solved.

Any attempt to turn back the clock to the savage *laissez-faire* policies of the early twentieth century would be self-defeating, ultimately leading to a resurgence of class conflict in all its former harshness. But the fundamentalists of the Left are equally self-defeating in their rigid adherence to a traditional programme based on class conflict and state ownership and control of the means of production.

This does not mean that economic factors are no longer politically important. On the contrary, some of the most significant recent research in political science has demonstrated strong linkages between fluctuations in the economies of Western nations, and support for the incumbent political party.[2] But this research has also produced a surprising finding: while support for the incumbents *does* reflect the performance of the national economy, it does *not* seem motivated by individual economic self-interest. The electorates of advanced industrial societies do not seem to be voting with their pocketbooks, but instead seem primarily motivated by 'sociotropic' concerns: rather than asking 'What have you done for me lately?' they ask 'What have you done for the *nation* lately?'[3] Recent research carried out in France, West Germany, Italy, and Great Britain confirms that there—as in the United States—the linkage

---

[2] G. H. Kramer, 'Short-term Fluctuations in US Voting Behavior, 1846–1964', *American Political Science Review*, 65 (1971), 131–43; E. R. Tufte, *Political Control of the Economy* (Princeton: Princeton University Press, 1978); D. A. Hibbs, R. D. Rivers, and N. Vasilatos, 'The Dynamics of Political Support for American Presidents among Occupational and Partisan Groups', *American Journal of Political Science*, 26 (1982), 312–32.

[3] D. R. Kinder and D. R. Kiewiet, 'Sociotropic Politics: The American Case', *British Journal of Political Science*, 11 (1981), 129–61.

between the economic cycle and support for the incumbents is overwhelmingly sociotropic.[4]

In short, economics remains an important influence on electoral behaviour—but it reflects sociotropic motivations rather than class conflict. The politics of advanced industrial societies no longer polarize primarily on the basis of working class versus middle class; and the old issues, centring on ownership of the means of production, no longer lie at the heart of political polarization.

POLITICAL CHANGE AT THE INDIVIDUAL LEVEL

The argument presented above is implicit in the Materialist/ Post-Materialist value change thesis; it is new only in its application to the societal level. In this section we examine political change at the individual level. Here, we have a rare opportunity: the chance to test a set of predictions about social change that were published years before the data by which they are tested came into existence.

At the individual level, our hypothesis concerning the diminishing role of economic factors, is supplemented by a second basic hypothesis: that early-instilled values tend to persist throughout a given individual's life. In context with the unprecedented economic development of the post-war era, these hypotheses imply a shift from Materialist towards Post-Materialist values. At the individual level, we should find sizeable and persisting differences between the value priorities of young and old, reflecting their differing formative experiences; but at the societal level, this shift will manifest itself only gradually, as one generation replaces another. Moreover, because this shift involves basic goals, it implies a gradual change in the types of issues that are most central to political conflict, and in the types of political movements and parties people support. Finally, it also implies a decline in social class-voting and increasing polarization over non-economic values.[5]

The intergenerational value differences these hypotheses

[4] M. Lewis-Beck, 'Comparative Economic Voting: Britain, France, Germany, Italy', *American Journal of Political Science*, 30 (1986), 315–46.
[5] Inglehart, 'The Silent Revolution in Europe'; id., *The Silent Revolution*.

predict have now been explored extensively, in twenty-six different nations. Survey after survey reveals dramatic differences between the goals emphasized by old and young. Moreover, cohort analysis demonstrates that there is no tendency for given birth cohorts to become more Materialist as they age, as they would if these differences reflected life cycle effects. In 1985, given birth cohorts were fully as Post-Materialist as they had been fifteen years earlier. There were significant short-term fluctuations, reflecting period effects linked with inflation.[6] But by 1985, inflation had subsided almost to the 1970 level. With period effects held constant, there is no sign of the gradual conversion to Materialism that would be present if a life cycle interpretation were applicable. When short-term forces returned to normal, a substantial net shift towards Post-Materialism was manifest—most of it due to intergenerational population replacement.[7]

The predicted intergenerational value shift seems to be confirmed by a massive amount of empirical evidence, but the predicted changes in prevailing types of political cleavages have barely been touched on. Let us examine the relevant evidence.

FROM CLASS-BASED TO VALUE-BASED POLITICAL POLARIZATION

The idea that politics is a struggle between rich and poor can be traced to Plato. But unquestionably the most influential modern version of this idea has been Marx's argument that throughout industrial society, social class conflict is the central fact of political life, and the key issue underlying the Left–Right polarization is conflict over ownership of the means of production. Marx's influence is reflected not only in a vast literature of

[6] Inglehart, 'New Perspectives on Value Change', *Comparative Political Studies*, 17 (1985), 485–532; id., 'Aggregate Stability and Individual-Level Change in Mass Belief Systems: The Level of Analysis Paradox', *American Political Science Review*, 79 (1985), 97–116.

[7] P. R. Abramson and R. Inglehart, 'Generational Replacement and Value Change in Six West European Societies', *American Journal of Political Science*, 30/1 (Feb. 1986), 1–25.

social criticism, but also in the existence of an entire family of political parties that were inspired by his writings and, in varying degrees, purport to be guided by his analysis. The rise of Post-Materialism makes this analysis less adequate today. Let us consider why.

The Post-Materialist outlook is linked with having spent one's formative years in conditions of economic and physical security. Hence it is more prevalent among the post-war generation than among older cohorts, and tends to be concentrated among the more prosperous strata of any given age group.

The political implications are significant and at first seem paradoxical. Post-Materialists give top priority to such goals as a sense of community and the non-material quality of life, but they live in societies that have traditionally emphasized economic gains above all, even at the expense of these values. Hence, they tend to be relatively favourable to social change. Though recruited from the higher income groups that have traditionally supported the parties of the Right, they tend to shift towards the parties of the Left.

Conversely, when Post-Materialist issues (such as environmentalism, the women's movement, unilateral disarmament, opposition to nuclear power) become central, they may stimulate a reaction in which part of the working class sides with the Right, to reaffirm the traditional Materialist emphasis on economic growth, military security, and domestic order.

The rise of Post-Materialist issues, therefore, tends to neutralize political polarization based on social class. Though long-established party loyalties and institutional ties link the working class to the Left and the middle class to the Right, the social basis of *new* support for the parties and policies of the Left tends to come from middle-class sources. But, at the same time, the Left parties become vulnerable to a potential split between their Post-Materialist Left, which seeks fundamental social change, and their Materialist constituency, which tends to take a traditional stance on the new issues raised by Post-Materialists.

A long-standing truism of political sociology is that working-class voters tend to support the parties of the Left, and middle class voters those of the Right, throughout Western society.

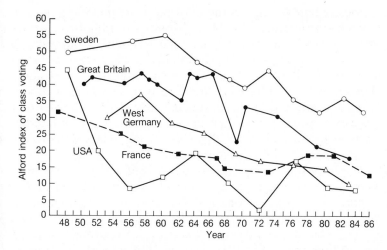

FIG. 19.2. The Trend in Social Class Voting in Five Western Democracies, 1947–1986. Adapted from S. M. Lipset, *Political Man* (2nd edn., Baltimore: Johns Hopkins University Press, 1981), 505; updated by present author with results from recent elections and French elections

This was an accurate description of reality a generation ago, but the tendency has been getting steadily weaker. As Figure 19.2 illustrates, social class voting has declined markedly during the past few decades. If 75 per cent of the working class voted for the Left, and only 25 per cent of the middle class did so, one would obtain an Alford class voting index of 50 (the difference between the two figures). This is about where the Swedish electorate was located in 1948, but by 1985 the index had fallen to 31. Norway, Sweden, and Denmark have traditionally manifested the world's highest levels of social class voting, but all have shown declining levels of social class voting during the past three decades.[8] In the United States, Great Britain, France, and West Germany, in the late 1940s and early 1950s, working-class voters were more apt to support the Left than were middle-class voters, by margins ranging from 30 to

[8] O. Borre, 'Critical Electoral Change in Scandinavia', in R. J. Dalton, S. C. Flanagan, and P. A. Beck (eds.), *Electoral Change in Advanced Industrial Democracies* (Princeton: Princeton University Press, 1984), 352.

45 percentage points. In the most recent national elections in these countries, this spread had shrunk to the range from 8 to 18 points. In the most recent national elections (from 1983 to 1986) class voting fell to or below the lowest levels ever recorded to date, in Britain, France, Sweden, and West Germany. Though long-established political party loyalties tend to maintain the traditional pattern, it is being eroded by the fact that (1) new support for the Left increasingly comes from middle-class Post-Materialists; and (2) by working-class shifts to the Right, in defence of traditional values.[9]

It is important to note that the class-conflict model of politics is not a mere straw man: a few decades ago it provided a fairly accurate description of reality. But that reality has changed, gradually but pervasively, to the point where today, class voting in most democracies is less than half as strong as it was a generation ago. This change seems linked with intergenerational population replacement: throughout Western Europe, social class voting indices are about half as large among the post-war birth cohorts as among older groups.

We have argued that Western politics are coming to polarize according to social class less and less, and according to values more and more. We have just seen evidence of the former. Now let us examine evidence of rising polarization according to Materialist/Post-Materialist values. Figure 19.3 sums up voting intentions by value type from almost 95,000 interviews carried out in Britain, France, Germany, Italy, the Netherlands, and Belgium, from 1970 to 1985. A vast number of nation-specific events took place in these six nations during fifteen turbulent years, which we will not attempt to discuss here. The overall pattern is clear, however: from 1970 to 1985, there was a trend towards increasing polarization on the basis of Materialist/Post-Materialist values.

In 1970, 61 per cent of the Materialists intended to vote for parties of the Right and Centre, as compared with 40 per cent of the Post-Materialists. Materialists were likelier than Post-Materialists to vote for the Right by a ratio of almost exactly 1.5 to one. This already was a sizeable difference—but it has grown

---

[9] Inglehart, *The Silent Revolution*; S. M. Lipset, *Political Man* (2nd edn., Baltimore: Johns Hopkins University Press, 1981).

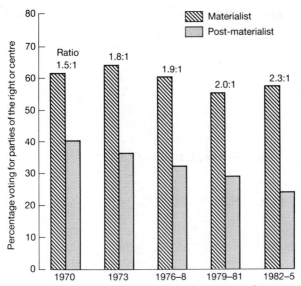

FIG. 19.3. Percentage Voting for Political Parties of the Right or Centre, by Value Type in Britain, France, Italy, West Germany, Belgium and the Netherlands, 1970–1985

steadily larger since 1970. In 1973, the ratio had increased to 1.8 to 1. In 1976–8, it grew to 1.9 to 1. By 1979–81 it was slightly more than 2 to one. And in 1982–5, the ratio had risen to 2.3 to one. This changing ratio was mainly due to a loss of Post-Materialist votes by the parties of the Right. In 1970, 40 per cent of the Post-Materialists supported parties of the Right and Centre; in 1982–5, only 25 per cent did so; 75 per cent were voting for the Left.

But which Left? In order fully to understand the significance of what has been happening, we must differentiate between various forces *within* a changing and divided Left. There has been only a modest increase in the proportion of Post-Materialists voting for the two major long-established parties of the Left, the Socialists and Communists. In 1970, they drew 48 per cent of the Post-Materialist vote; in 1982–5, they got 53 per cent. The major gains have been made by New Politics—above all, Ecologist—parties. In 1970 these parties won 13 per cent of the Post-Materialist vote. In 1982–5, they obtained 22 per cent. The New Politics gains reflect two countervailing trends: (1)

stagnation or decline of the Marxist New Left parties of the 1960s and early 70s; and (2) spectacular growth of Ecology parties, having a distinct and still evolving ideology concerning the quality of the physical and social environment. They have grown from almost nothing in the mid-1970s, to being the largest component of the New Politics parties. In the last few years, Ecology parties have won representation in the national parliaments of Belgium, Luxemburg, and West Germany, and in the delegations to the European Parliament elected in 1984 from Belgium, Germany, Italy, and the Netherlands. Their future potential may be even more than meets the eye, as we will see below.

The rapid growth of the Ecologists and the decline of the New Left parties of the 1960s reflect an important characteristic of both sets of parties: they have not yet developed strong voter loyalties or party organizations. Whether they ever will, is an open question. If they don't, in the long run their electorates will probably be absorbed by larger parties that modify their ideological stance sufficiently to present an attractive alternative, just as the Socialist party has absorbed much of the New Left electorate in the Netherlands—partly capturing it, and partly being captured *by* it. We will not attempt to forecast the fate of given parties in given countries; it is influenced by the party's leadership, the strategies they adopt, and by nation-specific events, as well as by the values of the electorate. Figure 19.3 makes one thing clear, however: since 1970 there has been a growing tendency for electoral behaviour to polarize on the basis of the Materialist/Post-Materialist value cleavage.

Post-Materialists have become increasingly likely to vote for the Left but this trend has become increasingly *selective*, with the Post-Materialist vote going to parties that have distinctive programmes tailored to Post-Materialist concerns. One striking consequence is that the Communists have lost their relative appeal to Post-Materialists. In the early and mid-1970s, Post-Materialists were about 2.5 times as likely to vote for the Communists as were Materialists. By the mid-1980s, there was little difference between the two groups.

When Post-Materialism emerged as a significant political force in the 1960s, its proponents tended to express themselves in Marxist slogans, which were then the standard rhetoric of protest in Western Europe. To a large extent the term 'Left' *meant* the Marxist parties, and it was natural for the Post-Materialists to assume that they were Marxists. But in fact there were profound and fundamental disparities between the goals of the Post-Materialists and those of the Marxist Left, as the Post-Materialists gradually discovered. These disparities became apparent in France earlier than in other countries —partly because the crisis of May–June 1968 brought to light the basic contradiction between the bureaucratic and authoritarian materialism of the French Communist party, and the Post-Materialist desire for a less hierarchical, more human society, in which the quality of life was more important than economic growth. Even there, ideological reorientation took many years. But today, a Left has evolved in France that is increasingly non-Marxist, and increasingly independent of the Soviet Union. The French Communist party, on the other hand, has remained one of the most authoritarian and Moscow-oriented parties in the West—with disastrous electoral consequences. After winning 20 to 25 per cent of the vote in most French elections from 1945 to 1978, the Communists suffered a sharp decline in the 1980s, falling to 16 per cent of the vote in 1981, then to 11 per cent in 1984, and dropping below 10 per cent in the 1986 election. Though the degree varies from country to country, by the 1980s Communism had lost its disproportionate appeal to the growing Post-Materialist constituency in Western Europe.

With this has come the decline of the Communist's relative appeal to youth. For decades it had been axiomatic that the young were disproportionately likely to vote Communist: 'If a man isn't a Communist when he's 25, he has no heart; if he's still a Communist when he's 45, he has no head.' This linkage between youth and the Communist party, however, was not a biological constant; it was based on the belief that the goals of a specific younger generation converged with those of the Communist party.

That belief persisted until recently. As Figure 19.4 demonstrates, the two post-war cohorts among the West European publics were markedly more likely to support the Communist party than were their elders in each of the Eurobarometer surveys carried out during the 1970s. But the differences were

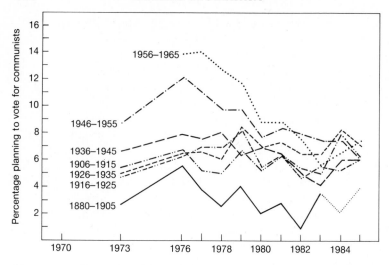

Fɪɢ. 19.4.   Percentage Voting for Communist Party in Nine European Community Nations, by Age Cohort, 1973–85. Based on representative national samples of publics of Britain, France, West Germany, Italy, Belgium, Netherlands, Luxemburg, Denmark, and Ireland, weighted according to population of given nation. Includes data from Euro-Barometer surveys 5 through 23, plus 1973 European Community survey.

growing weaker in 1978 and 1979. In the early 1980s, Communist support among the two post-war cohorts continued to decline, falling to, or even *below* the level of older cohorts. The young and the Post-Materialists had shifted to other parties.

Where did they go? For the most part, *not* to the parties of the Right, despite a good deal of recent talk about the growing conservatism of youth. The old Left clearly *is* in decline, which presents an opportunity for enterprising and adaptive parties of the Right and Centre. But given the option, younger voters gravitate towards New Politics parties, above all the Ecologists, rather than towards the Right.

As Table 19.2 demonstrates, support for the Communists no longer bears much relationship to age. The Socialists and Social Democrats have also lost their special appeal for the young, in most countries. Nevertheless, support for the parties of the Right and Centre is substantially *weaker* among the three post-war cohorts than among all of the older groups. There is

TABLE 19.2. Support for Traditional Left and New Politics Parties by Age Cohort in Britain, France, West Germany, Italy, Denmark, Ireland and Benelux, in 1984–5

Birth Years	Communists	Socialists & Soc. Dems.	Ecologists & Other New Politics Parties	Right & Centre	N
1966–1970	5%	31%	19%	45%	(1,026)
1956–1965	8	36	17	39	(3,782)
1946–1955	8	40	9	43	(3,692)
1936–1945	7	38	6	50	(3,143)
1926–1935	8	36	4	52	(2,810)
1916–1925	6	40	3	51	(2,886)
1906–1915	7	35	2	56	(1,732)
Before 1906	3	30	1	66	(421)

Post war [1956–1965, 1946–1955]

Source: Combined data from Euro-Barometers 21, 22 and 23 (April 1984, November 1984 and April 1985) weighted according to population of each nation (total number reporting a voting intention = 19,492)

no overall trend to the Right. Instead, the slack is taken up by a pronounced rise in support for the Ecologists and other New Politics parties. Consequently, the relative strength of the Communists and the New Politics parties has shifted dramatically among the young. Among the cohorts born before World War II, Communist support outweighs New Politics support by as much as 2:1 or 3:1. Among the cohort born in 1946–55, the New Politics parties are slightly stronger than the Communists. And among the two youngest cohorts, support for the New Politics parties outweighs support for the Communists by margins of 2:1 and nearly 4:1.

Neither the young nor the Post-Materialists automatically vote for any party that claims to represent the Left. They are influenced by past loyalties, like other voters. But when they abandon these loyalties, they do so in order to support the party that seems most likely to attain their goals—which are not necessarily those of the old Left, and emphatically not those of rigidly authoritarian parties such as the French Communist party. The old Left parties are losing ground among the young: they win the support of only 44 per cent of the 1945–65 cohort, and only 36 per cent of the 1966–70 cohort. But the Right need not win them by default. When an option is available that addresses the Post-Materialists' concerns, they tend to take it. The evidence indicates that the Left can win the young *provided* it develops programmes that appeal to the Post-Materialists, as well as the old Left constituency—clearly not an easy task, but not an impossible one.

PART IV

TYPOLOGIES OF PARTY SYSTEMS

20

THE TWO-PARTY SYSTEM AND THE
MULTIPARTY SYSTEM

MAURICE DUVERGER

A study of the distribution of the two-party system in time,
following the description of its distribution in space, leads to the
conclusion that since the nineteenth century three types have
succeeded one another. The property franchise first gave rise to
a 'bourgeois' two-party system, with the characteristic opposition between Conservatives and Liberals, whose social and
ideological sub-structure varied somewhat from country to
country. In general the Conservatives found their support
chiefly amongst the aristocracy and the peasantry; the Liberals
theirs amongst the trading, industrial, and intellectual middle
classes in the towns. However, this summary distinction is no
more than approximate: the line of demarcation in practice is
much more complicated and subtle. In some countries, in
Scandinavia for example, the Conservative aristocracy was
grouped in the towns; in consequence the tendencies towards
Liberalism first made their appearance in the countryside: it
would be more accurate to say that an Agrarian Liberalism
grew up in opposition to the more intellectual and industrial
Liberalism of the towns, which turned the fundamental two-
party tendency into a three-party system. From the point of
view of doctrines the Conservatives preached the virtues of
authority, tradition, and submission to the established order;
the Liberals, being individualist and rationalist, claimed de-
scent from the American and French revolutionaries and the
ideas of liberty and equality that they had trumpeted to the

Maurice Duverger, excerpted from *Political Parties: Their Organization and
Activity in the Modern State* (1954), Book II, Chapter 1. Reprinted by permission
of Methuen & Co. Published in the United States by John Wiley & Sons Inc.

world; yet many of them showed some timidity on the question of universal suffrage, and especially over the social changes demanded by the working classes. In Protestant countries the two-party system was not on the whole complicated by religious antagonisms; in Catholic countries the *de facto* linking of the clergy with the *ancien régime* gave the Conservatives the air of a party supported by the Church and threw Liberals into the anticlerical camp: the political struggle became in some cases a religious struggle, particularly acute over the schools question (e.g. in France and Belgium).

In the second half of the nineteenth century the development of Radicalism seemed to threaten the reign of the two-party system; but in fact this proved to be rather an internal division amongst the Liberals, whose moderate elements witnessed the growth of a left-wing tendency opposing them. In most cases this left-wing tendency remained within the party or joined it again or else disappeared; however, a viable Radical party seceded from the Liberals in the Netherlands in 1891, and in Denmark in 1906; the creation of the French Radical party in 1901 corresponds to a different situation. The development of Socialism, on the contrary, provoked the general modification of this first two-party system. In some countries Socialism was long held back by the restriction of the franchise, with the result that dualism still held the field in parliament, whereas in the nation there were three parties in the field: the franchise often being wider at the commune and local level, Socialist representatives gained a foothold in town and village councils without being able to enter parliament (except in very small numbers). A coincidence is therefore frequently to be observed between the establishment of universal suffrage (or the extension of a limited suffrage) and the appearance of Socialist parties at the parliamentary level. In Belgium the electoral reform of 1894 allowed twenty-eight Socialists to enter the Chamber, thus replacing the traditional two-party by a three-party system and reducing the Liberals to third place; in the Netherlands the first Socialist deputies appeared when the Van Houten law was brought into force (increasing the electorate from 295,000 to 577,000); in Sweden the electoral law of 1909 doubled the number of Social Democratic representatives in the Riksdag. Elsewhere (Germany, Great Britain, France,

Norway, and so on) since universal suffrage existed prior to the burgeoning of Socialism, the latter was therefore able to develop without hindrance.

The birth of Socialist parties was an almost universal phenomenon in Europe and the British Dominions at the turn of the century. However, the two-party system was not everywhere destroyed. As a matter of fact only one of the countries in which a two-party system flourished previously was unable to re-establish it: Belgium, because of the electoral reform of 1899. Everywhere else the two-party system suffered a period of eclipse of varying duration, to be reborn later in a new guise approximately in conformity with the class-struggle pattern of Marxist doctrine: opposition between a Bourgeois and a Socialist party. The former is sometimes the product of a fusion between two older parties, Conservative and Liberal, as is the case in Australia and New Zealand. In other countries the Conservative party has remained alone in opposition to the Socialists, the Liberals having been eliminated (e.g. Great Britain); but the converse has not occurred (Conservatives eliminated to the advantage of Liberals). This last feature can be explained on natural grounds: the Liberals at that time had realized the essentials of their programme and so found themselves constrained to adopt a conservative attitude: the appearance of a Socialist party naturally took from them a section of their left-wing support, whilst fear of the 'Reds' threw another section into the arms of the Conservatives; finally, the operation of the simple-majority ballot (which in fact was in force in the countries being considered) is unfavourable to Centre parties.

What we are considering is much more a 'Conservative-Labour' than a 'Conservative-Socialist' dualism. The new two-party system was established only in countries with Socialist parties based on trade unions, indirect in structure, with little doctrinal dogmatism, and of reformist and non-revolutionary tendencies. The last feature is fundamental: a two-party system cannot be maintained if one of the parties seeks to destroy the established order. At least it cannot endure unless that party remains always in opposition. Today the question no longer arises in the case of Socialist parties, which have all become reformist parties, direct and indirect alike. There would, for example, be no danger if Western Germany attained the two-party system (Christian Democrats—Social Democrats) towards which its present development is visibly leading it. But the question assumes a new urgency with the appearance of a third type of two-party system which as a matter of fact has nowhere so far come into existence, but which is already obviously developing in some countries, as for example in Italy: the opposition of the Communist party and a 'Western' party. The adoption of the simple-majority single-ballot system would undoubtedly bring it into being, but this event would be catastrophic. The first task of a Communist party in power would obviously be the suppression of its rival; in consequence the first duty of its rival once in power would be to take the initiative to prevent the establishment of a dictatorship of the Soviet type. This would be equivalent to setting up a dictatorship of a different type. It is therefore necessary to distinguish between two kinds of dualism: technical dualism, where the difference between the two rivals concerns only secondary aims and means, whilst a general political philosophy and the fundamental bases of the system are accepted by both sides, and metaphysical dualism, where the rivalry between parties concerns the very nature of the regime and the fundamental concepts of life and so assumes the aspect of a veritable war of religions. Only the first type is viable. This is equivalent to saying that the two-party system is inconceivable if one of the two parties is totalitarian in structure.

None the less the two-party system seems to correspond to the nature of things, that is to say that political choice usually takes the form of a choice between two alternatives. A duality of parties does not always exist, but almost always there is a duality of tendencies. Every policy implies a choice between two kinds of solution: the so-called compromise solutions lean one way or the other. This is equivalent to saying that the centre does not exist in politics: there may well be a Centre party but there is no centre tendency, no centre doctrine. The term 'centre' is applied to the geometrical spot at which the moderates of opposed tendencies meet: moderates of the Right and moderates of the Left. Every Centre is divided against itself and remains separated into two halves, Left-Centre and Right-Centre. For the Centre is nothing more than the artificial grouping of the right wing of the Left and the left wing of the

Right. The fate of the Centre is to be torn asunder, buffeted and annihilated: torn asunder when one of its halves votes Right and the other Left, buffeted when it votes as a group first Right then Left, annihilated when it abstains from voting. The dream of the Centre is to achieve a synthesis of contradictory aspirations; but synthesis is a power only of the mind. Action involves choice and politics involve action. The history of Centre parties would provide examples in support of this abstract argument: take, for example, the fortunes of the Radical party under the Third French Republic, the fortunes of the Socialists or the MRP under the Fourth. There are no true Centres, only superimposed dualisms, as we shall see: the MRP is politically Right, socially Left; the Radicals are Right in economics, Left in mystique.

The idea of a natural political dualism is to be encountered moreover in widely differing sociological conceptions. Some writers contrast the radical temperament (in the nineteenth-century sense; today we should call it the revolutionary temperament) with the conservative temperament. It is a summary and approximate view but not altogether inaccurate. It is true that some find themselves completely at home amongst commonplace ideas, accepted traditions, and conventional habits, whereas others experience the compelling need to change everything, to modify everything, and to innovate in all domains. The expression 'Better the folly of our ancestors than the wisdom of our children' epitomizes the conservative temperament. It has been suggested that the two tendencies could be identified with different ages, youth being 'radical' and maturity 'conservative': legislators have long been familiar with this fact; they raise the qualifying age for voters to favour the Right and lower it to favour the Left. Marxism re-establishes this deep-seated Manichaeism in a modern and different form, that of the opposition between the bourgeoisie and the proletariat, which is given approximate expression in the present-day two-party system of the Anglo-Saxon countries. Contemporary studies in political science reveal a duality of tendencies in countries that are to all appearances most divided politically: underlying the multiple and diverse parties of the French Third Republic François Goguel has succeeded in demonstrating the permanence of the conflict between 'order' and 'movement'. In

small French villages public opinion spontaneously distinguishes between 'Whites' and 'Reds', 'clerical' and 'anticlerical'; without bothering with the more varied official labels,
it seizes on the essential. Throughout history all the great
factional conflicts have been dualist: Armagnacs and Bur-
gundians, Guelphs and Ghibellines, Catholics and Protestants, Girondins and Jacobins, Conservatives and Liberals,
Bourgeois and Socialists, 'Western' and Communist: these
antitheses are simplified, but only by neglecting secondary
differences. Whenever public opinion is squarely faced with
great fundamental problems it tends to crystallize round two
opposed poles. The natural movement of societies tends
towards the two-party system.

MULTIPARTISM

Multipartism is often confused with absence of parties. A
country in which opinion is divided amongst several groups
that are unstable, fluid, and short-lived does not provide an
example of multipartism in the proper sense of the term: it is
still in the prehistoric era of parties; it is to be situated in that
phase of general development at which the distinction between
bipartism and multipartism is not yet applicable because there
are as yet no true parties. In this category we can place many
Central European countries between 1919 and 1939, most of
the young nations in Africa, the East, and the Middle East,
many Latin-American states, and the great Western states of
the nineteenth century. However, some of these countries
might be better classified in an intermediate category: in them
there are to be found authentic parties possessing a minimum of
organization and stability in juxtaposition to inorganic and
unstable groups. In this case the line of demarcation between
multipartism and absence of parties is blurred, all the more
so because vestiges of inorganic groups subsist inside many
countries that have organized parties: in France, for example,
that whole sector of opinion to the right of the Radicals is almost
entirely without true parties and consists rather of the fluid
groups which are characteristic of an earlier phase of
development.

In this sense multipartism is fairly characteristic of Western Europe, Great Britain excepted but Ireland included. It is of course true that some of these states have had experience of the two-party system at some periods in their history: Belgium was dualist until 1894; contemporary Germany is very near to being dualist. Other states have had experience of single-party systems: Italy from 1924 to 1945, Germany from 1933 to 1945, Spain and Portugal at the present day. It may also be thought that the European multiparty system is today in peril and that its future is uncertain. None the less in 1951 the multiparty system continues to hold sway throughout continental Western Europe; it seems too to correspond to the most general of her political traditions.

Formation of Multipartism. The typology of the multiparty system is difficult to establish: innumerable varieties can be imagined ranging from three parties to infinity, and within each variety innumerable patterns and shades of difference are possible. Post-Liberation tripartism in France has nothing in common with Belgian traditional tripartism; Scandinavian quadripartism is fundamentally different from Swiss quadripartism; the dispersal of the French Right means something quite different from the splitting of parties in pre-war Czechoslovakia or Republican Spain: each national organization seems to retain its own extraordinary and unique characteristics which prevent it from being classified in any general scheme. However, we can discover some traits that they have in common if we consider the ways in which multiparty systems come into being. In this connection we can construct a theoretical pattern which fits most of the facts if we take as our point of departure the idea that the two-party system is natural, and then consider this fundamental tendency to be subject to modification as a result of two different phenomena: internal divisions of opinion and their overlapping.

Take for example a two-party system like that in Britain in 1950. In the Labour party there was a fairly clear distinction between the moderates who supported the Attlee Government and a more radical, more extremist group which was sometimes at odds with Ministers and which followed its own line on some important questions, notably foreign affairs. Inside the Conservative party the divisions were less clear because the party was restricted to the role of opposition: when it came to power the differences became more obvious, as in pre-war days. We may proceed to generalize from this particular example: inside all parties there are moderates and extremists, the conciliatory and the intransigent, the diplomatic and the doctrinaire; the pacific and the fire-eaters. The cleavage between reformers and revolutionaries in European Socialist parties at the beginning of this century was simply one particular instance of a very general tendency. In fact the sociological distinction between 'radical' and 'conservative' temperaments should be complemented by a second distinction contrasting the 'extremist' temperament with the 'moderate'; each is complementary to the other, for there are extremist conservatives and moderate conservatives, extremist radicals and moderate radicals (e.g. Jacobins and Girondins). So long as this second distinction is limited in its effects to the creation of factions and rivalries inside parties produced by the first distinction, the natural two-party system remains unchanged. If, however, the factions become exasperated and can no longer meet on common ground the basic tendency to dualism is thwarted and gives way to multipartism. It was in this way that the split in Switzerland between Radicals and Liberals breached the original 1848 two-party system (Conservatives v. Liberals) and created a three-party system that the Socialists later transformed into a four-party system. The same is true of France: the gradual formation of the Radical party split the Republicans, with the result that by the end of the nineteenth century there were three basic tendencies visible: Conservatives, Moderate Republicans (Opportunists), and Radicals. In Denmark and Holland the birth of the Radical party was the product of an identical tendency: a split over the opinions common to moderates and extremists. About 1920 there were many cases in Europe of an increase in the number of parties due to splits between Communists (revolutionaries) and Socialists (reformers).

Such splits give rise to Centre parties. It has already been shown that there exists no Centre opinion, no Centre tendency, no Centre doctrine separate in kind from the doctrines of the Right or of the Left—but only a dilution of their doctrines, an attenuation, a moderate doctrine. If an old Liberal party (on the Left in a two-party system) splits into Liberals and Radicals, then the former become a Centre party. The same happens when a Conservative party divides into Moderates and Extremists. Such is the first method by which Centre parties are created (the second is a consequence of 'Leftism' and will be considered later). In theory an authentic Centre party would presuppose that right-wing Moderates and left-wing Moderates, breaking away from their initial tendencies, had united to form a single party; in practice, however, the origin of the central party is of little account; its very position and the contradictory attractions that are exerted on its members produce inside it a fundamental cleavage: every Centre party is by its very nature divided. An exception occurs when two Centre parties coexist in a country: this was approximately the case in Denmark before proportional representation was set up—the Liberals represented the Right-Centre and the Radicals the Left-Centre; the attraction of the two extremes still proved stronger than the solidarity of the Moderates, for the Radicals co-operated with the Socialists and not with the Liberals, illustrating thereby a tendency which is very common in Scandinavia. In France the Radical-Socialists (Left-Centre) alternated throughout the Third Republic between Central solidarity (which produced the 'concentration') and Left-wing solidarity (which produced the Left-wing Cartel, the Popular Front, and so on): these different patterns in the political ballet will be met again when we come to define party alliances.

'Overlapping' is a phenomenon however that seems to be more widespread than the 'split'. It consists in the non-coincidence of a number of different dualisms of opinion with the result that their combinations produce a multipartite division. In France, for example, the old division of opinion 'Clerical' v. 'Anticlerical' does not correspond with the division between 'West' and 'East' or with that between 'Freedom' and 'Planning' (Fig. 20.1). By superimposing these bipartite divisions we can draw a diagram showing the main spiritual families in France: Communists (East, Planning, Anticlerical); Christian Progressives (East, Planning, Clerical); Socialists (West, Planning, Anticlerical); MRP (West, Planning, Clerical); Radicals (West, Freedom, Anticlerical); Right and RPF

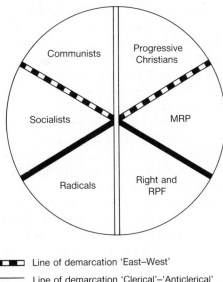

Line of demarcation 'East–West'
Line of demarcation 'Clerical'–'Anticlerical'
Line of demarcation 'Freedom'–'Planning'

FIG. 20.1.   Overlapping of Cleavages in France[1]

(West, Freedom, Clerical). Of course this classification is somewhat arbitrary and much oversimplified; none the less it corresponds on the whole to the main lines of cleavage in opinion as well as to the real division of parties (it gives too much importance to the Christian Progressives who are weak and too little to the RPF which exerts an influence beyond the frontiers of the Right). The multiparty system in France is a result of the non-coincidence of the main cleavages in opinion.

Here we see the limits of the field within which the two-party system is natural. All antitheses are by nature dualist where they involve rivalry between two points of view that are diametrically opposed (always remembering however that either can be defended with moderation or with zeal); if, however, there are various sets of antitheses and these are largely inde-

[1] The diagram takes no account of the strengths of the respective 'spiritual families': the Progressive Christians, in particular, are not numerous, though their intellectual influence is considerable.

pendent of one another, then one can adopt a viewpoint in one field and still be relatively free to choose one's point of view in other fields. Multipartism arises from the mutual independence of sets of antitheses. It necessarily presupposes that the different sectors of political activity are relatively isolated and sealed off one from the other: the distinguishing characteristic of every 'totalitarian' concept lies precisely in its establishment of a rigorous interdependence of all questions, with the result that an attitude to one necessarily involves a corresponding attitude to all others. Totalitarian ideologies may coexist, however, and produce a multiparty system on condition that they are not agreed upon the one supreme issue which determines for each of them the attitudes to be assumed on all other issues. If all Frenchmen were in agreement in holding that the antagonism East v. West took precedence over all others, then there would be only two parties: Communists and Anti-Communists. If they all accepted as fundamental the rivalry between freedom and planning, there would be only two parties: Conservatives and Socialists. If on the other hand they thought that the Clerical v. Anticlerical issue was basic, as is still held in some corners of France, then there would be only two parties: Catholics and Free-thinkers (there was a trend towards this at the beginning of the century). It is on the contrary the very fact that some emphasize the Freedom v. Planning issue, others the Clerical v. Anticlerical, and yet others the East v. West that maintains multipartism.

21

PARTY SYSTEMS AND PATTERNS OF OPPOSITION

ROBERT A. DAHL

Opponents of a government may display varying degrees of organizational cohesion; they may all be concentrated in a single organization, for example, or they may be dispersed in a number of organizations operating independently of one another.

Probably in no country, and certainly in no democratic country, are all the active opponents of government ever concentrated in one organization. If we concern ourselves with political parties, however, the situation is rather different. Because a political party is the most visible manifestation and surely one of the most effective forms of opposition in a democratic country, it is this particular form with which we have been most concerned in this book.[1] However, the extent to which opposition is concentrated depends on the party system of a country. Although genuine one-party systems probably cannot exist and certainly do not now exist except where governments prohibit opposition parties, in a few countries where key civil liberties are by no means wholly impaired, as in Mexico, a single party has enjoyed a near monopoly of votes, or, as in India, of parliamentary seats. In each of these countries, although some opposition is concentrated in small parties, a good deal of opposition operates as factions within the domi-

Robert A. Dahl, excerpted from 'Patterns of Opposition', reprinted from *Political Oppositions in Western Democracies* by Robert A. Dahl (ed.), pp. 332–8. Copyright © 1966 by Yale University, by permission of Yale University Press.

[1] [Dahl, *Political Oppositions in Western Democracies*, which includes essays on Britain, the United States, Norway, Sweden, Belgium, the Netherlands, Germany, Austria, France, and Italy, *PM*.]

nant party. The highest degree of concentration of opposition exists in two-party systems, where the out-party has a substantial monopoly of the opposition. In multiparty systems, opposition is likely to be dispersed among several parties.

In the English-speaking world, all thought about opposition has been dominated, at least in this century, by simple two-party models—to which multiparty systems are a kind of unsatisfactory and probably temporary exception. And this view, so confidently held in Britain and the United States, has often been accepted even outside the English-speaking world.

Yet the facts themselves are enough to discredit such a parochial notion. To begin with, the system of two dominant parties has not been much imitated outside the English-speaking world and its zones of influence. Of thirty countries having in 1964 opposition parties, widespread suffrage, and governments based on relatively recent elections, only eight would be considered 'two-party systems' in the usual sense.[2] Of these eight countries, all but two (Austria and Uruguay) are either English-speaking democracies or were launched politically under the influence of Britain or the United States.

Moreover, as our essays on Britain, the United States, and Austria make clear, even where there are only two dominant parties the patterns of opposition are often radically different. Indeed, in the English-speaking world, the British two-party system as we now understand it seems to exist only in Britain and in New Zealand. In Australia, one of the two major 'parties' is actually a coalition of two parties, while in Canada

[2] The eight countries are Australia, Austria, Panama, the Philippines, New Zealand, United Kingdom, the United States, and Uruguay. Even Australia is a highly doubtful case, since it can be included in the two-party class only if the coalition of the Liberal and Country parties is treated as a single party. The tests used to distinguish the two-party systems were somewhat arbitrary, but defensible. Two of the 30 countries, India and Mexico, were excluded because of one-party dominance. The other 21 countries were excluded because the proportion of third-party seats in one popularly elected chamber of the national legislature totaled more than 5 per cent. South Africa, which would have qualified as a two-party system by this test, was excluded from the list of 30 democratic countries because of its suffrage restrictions. A more carefully developed classification of party systems could not possibly change the size of the two-party category by much.

third parties have been much more significant than in either the United States or Britain. The United States is a paradoxical case. The relative weakness of third parties throughout American history makes the United States an even more clear-cut example of two dominant parties than Britain; yet within this framework of two parties, as we have seen, the American pattern of dispersed opposition has nearly as much in common with some of the European multiparty systems as it does with the 'concentrated' British pattern. Finally, as Allen Potter indicates in his essay, the British two-party system as we know it today has not existed for much more than the last four decades.[3] Thanks first to the Irish Nationalists and then to Labour, Britain could scarcely be classified as a genuine two-party system for the forty-year period from about 1880 to 1920; while in the middle decades of the nineteenth century, the British pattern was rather similar to that of the United States: two heterogeneous parties with an executive drawing support from sympathetic elements in both parties. Hence even in British experience the recent pattern is somewhat abnormal.

In sum, it might be reasonable to consider multiparty systems as the natural way for government and oppositions to manage their conflicts in democracies, while two-party systems, whether resembling the British pattern or the American, are the deviant cases. It is conceivable, of course, that the deviant cases represent superior forms; yet multiparty systems exist in Denmark, Norway, Sweden, the Netherlands, and Switzerland, countries widely thought to have handled their political, social, and economic problems with at least as much skill, justice, and social peace as any other democracies.

In addition to the number of important parties, concentration has yet another dimension. Parties themselves vary enormously in internal unity, as measured, for example, by the way their members vote in parliament; what is formally a single opposition party may in fact disintegrate into a number of factions. Since there are variations in the degree of unity and factionalism among parties even within a particular country, it is difficult to characterize whole systems; in Italy and France

---

[3] [In Dahl, *Political Oppositions*, PM.]

the Communists have been highly cohesive in their voting in the parliament, whereas in both countries the other parties are much more divided among themselves.

In order to consider the bearing of concentration on patterns of opposition in the ten countries treated in this volume, it is helpful to combine these two dimensions into four simple categories:

1. Two-party systems with a high degree of internal party unity, as in Britain.
2. Two-party systems with relatively low internal party unity, as in the United States.
3. Multiparty systems with relatively high internal party unity, as in Sweden, Norway, and the Netherlands.
4. Multiparty systems with low internal party unity, as in Italy and France.

To the extent that an opposition takes the party system of the country into account in selecting the strategy it will pursue, different party systems should be associated with different strategies. Thus an opposition confronted with a party system of the first type is likely to behave somewhat differently from an opposition confronted with one of the other kinds of party systems.

How competitive an opposition is depends partly on how concentrated it is. In this case 'competitive' does not refer to the psychological orientations of political actors but to the way in which the gains and losses of political opponents in elections and in parliament are related. On the analogy of an equivalent concept in the theory of games, two parties are in a strictly competitive (or zero-sum) relation if they pursue strategies such that, given the election or voting system, the gains of one will exactly equal the losses of another. Because in any given election the number of seats in a legislative body is fixed, whenever only two parties run competing candidates in an election they are necessarily engaged in a strictly competitive contest, since the seats gained by one party will be lost to the other. Applying the notion of strict competition to a legislative body presents some problems; but we can get around most of these by stipulating that two parties are strictly competitive in a legislature if they pursue strategies such that both cannot simultaneously belong to a winning coalition. As an empirical fact, of course, no legislature is strictly competitive all the time; some measures gain overwhelming or unanimous approval, while on others party leaders deliberately permit their followers to vote as they choose. In some legislatures, however, key votes are usually strictly competitive; votes on the formation of a government, votes of confidence, votes on the major legislative and budgeting measures submitted by the government, etc. We can regard parties as strictly competitive in parliament, then, if they are strictly competitive on key votes.

It might be conjectured that in a parliamentary or presidential system monopolized by two highly unified parties, competition would always be strictly competitive. The salient example is, of course, Britain. Yet the parties *could* deliberately decide to collaborate either in parliament or in elections, or in both. During most of two world wars the major parties in Britain agreed to substitute collaboration for competition: coalition cabinets were formed, and elections were delayed until after the end of the war. In Austria from 1947 onward, the People's party and the Socialist party formed a coalition government that left virtually no opposition in Parliament; yet at each election the two parties vigorously fought one another for votes.

Even in a system with two unified parties, then, strict competition is not inevitable. Yet the temptation to shift from coalition to competition is bound to be very great, particularly for the party that believes it could win a majority of votes. Hence coalition in a two-party system imposes severe strains and probably tends to be an unstable solution.

In the United States, the two major parties are strictly competitive during presidential elections and for the most part during congressional elections; but in Congress party cohesion is weak as compared with Britain, and elements within one party enter into winning coalitions with elements of the other party even on key votes. In multiparty systems strict competition is unlikely; in fact unless one party can form a majority by itself, strict competition is actually impossible; for unless two parties are willing to enter into a coalition, no majority can be formed. Moreover, parties may not be strictly competitive even during elections, for they may enter into electoral alliances that limit competition in various ways, for example by uniting in

TABLE 21.1. Competition, Co-operation, and Coalescence: Types of Party Systems

	Opposition in		
Type of system	Elections	Parliament	Examples
I. Strictly competitive	Strictly competitive	Strictly competitive	Britain
II. Co-operative-competitive			
A. Two-party	Strictly competitive	Co-operative and competitive	United States
B. Multiparty	Co-operative and competitive	Co-operative and competitive	France, Italy
III. Coalescent-competitive			
A. Two-party	Strictly competitive	Coalescent	Austria, wartime Britain
B. Multiparty	Co-operative and competitive	Coalescent	
IV. Strictly coalescent	Coalescent	Coalescent	Colombia

some districts around a single candidate, as in runoff elections in France.

Thus the competitiveness of opposition (in the sense in which the term is used here) depends in large measure, though not completely, on the number and nature of parties, i.e., on the extent to which opposition is concentrated. The possibilities we have discussed, and for which examples actually exist, extend from a system in which the opposition is concentrated in a party that is strictly competitive both in elections and in parliament, through various systems in which opposition strategies are both co-operative and competitive, to systems in which the minority party that would ordinarily constitute the opposition coalesces with the majority party both in elections and in parliament (see Table 21.1).

22

TYPES OF PARTY SYSTEM

JEAN BLONDEL

If undertaken on a world basis, the analysis of party systems would require a consideration of the number of parties, of their strength, of their place on the ideological spectrum, of the nature of their support, and of their organization and type of leadership. In the context of Western liberal democracies, it is possible to limit the analysis to the first three of these character-istics. With very few exceptions, Western parties can be deemed to be of the 'legitimate' mass type and to have a regularized system of leadership selection. Charismatic leader-ship is exceptional and, at the other extreme, Communist parties are becoming increasingly similar to other parties. Western parties appeal *nationally* to the electorate by trying to put across a general image; differences are more to be found in

TABLE 22.1.   Average Two-Party Vote, 1945–66 (percentage)

United States	99	Denmark	66
New Zealand	95	Sweden	66
Australia	93	Norway	64
United Kingdom	92	Italy	64
Austria	89	Iceland	62
		Holland	62
West Germany	80		
Luxemburg	80	Switzerland	50
Canada	79	France	50
Belgium	78	Finland	49
Eire	75		

Jean Blondel, excerpted from 'Party Systems and Patterns of Government in Western Democracies', *Canadian Journal of Political Science*, 1/2 (1968), 180–203. Reprinted by permission of the author and The Canadian Political Science Association.

the type of image than in the structural characteristics of the organization.

1. *Number of Parties in the System*

Two-party systems are rarely defined operationally. Yet, among Western democracies, four groups are clearly discernible (see Table 22.1). Five countries give on average more than 90 per cent of their votes to the two major parties. Second, five countries give between 75 and 80 per cent of their votes to the two major parties (though Belgium fell markedly below this level at the last election). In six countries, the two major parties obtain about two-thirds of the votes (though Holland is somewhat different, as we shall see). Finally, three countries give about half their votes to the two major parties, though, for the last two elections, France would have to be moved from the fourth to the third category: but as the French situation may well alter again after the end of the de Gaulle era, it is probably more realistic to draw conclusions from the average of the whole post-war period than merely from developments in the 1960s.

Countries belonging to the first group can be defined as two-party systems, though there is some ambiguity in the cases of Australia and Austria; in both these countries some governments depended for their constitution or maintenance on the support of more than one party. The five countries of the second group constitute the three-party systems, Germany having arrived at this status as a result of the operation of the electoral system as well as of the Adenauer tactics. The nine countries of the last two groups are the genuine multiparty systems, in which four, five, or even six parties play a significant part in the political process.

2. *Strength of Parties*

Little has to be said about countries of the first group, in which 90 per cent or more of the electors vote for, and 90 per cent or more of the seats are distributed between, the two major parties. It is interesting to note that discrepancies in strength between the two major parties are remarkably small, at least if averaged over the post-war period. While it could in theory be the case that one party might be permanently much larger than the other, no two-party system (i.e., no system in which the two parties obtain 89 per cent of the votes) gives to the larger of the two parties a permanent premium of over 10 per cent of its own electorate. Despite differences in social structure, for instance, between the United States, the United Kingdom, and Austria, the electorate distributes its preferences fairly evenly between the two parties. Although it cannot be stated with assurance that such a situation cannot exist in any type of social system (there are indeed examples of uneven distribution of party support among two-party systems outside Western democracies), it seems possible to hypothesize, in the absence of contrary evidence, that, in Western democracies, two-party systems show a tendency towards a relative equilibrium between the two parties.

Countries in the three-party system group also share several characteristics. First, disparities in strength between the two larger parties are generally much greater than among countries in the first group. They seem structural in that the swing of the pendulum does not, as among countries of the first group, diminish the gap, even if one considers a fairly long period: the average percentage point difference between the two major parties among the five countries of the first group is only 1.6 if all post-war elections are taken into account; it is 10.5 in

TABLE 22.2. Average Strength of the Two Major Parties in Two- and Two-and-a-half Party Systems (percentage votes cast)

Two-party systems				Two-and-a-half party systems			
			Difference				*Difference*
United States	49	50	1	Germany	45	35	10
New Zealand	48	47	1	Canada	36	43	7
Australia	47	46	1	Belgium	43	35	8
United Kingdom	45	47	2	Eire	46	29	17
Austria	46	43	3				
Average disparity between the two major parties		1.6					10.5

countries of the second group (excluding Luxemburg where data for all elections were not available) [see Table 22.2]. The often stressed phenomenon of the German SPD, which has not been able to achieve equality of strength with the CDU, is thus a general phenomenon among countries of this group. It can therefore be stated that in countries in which about 80 per cent of the votes go to two parties the distribution of the support tends to be uneven.

Three-party systems also have another, and converse, characteristic. They all have two major parties and a much smaller third party. While it would seem theoretically possible for three-party systems to exist in which all three significant parties were of about equal size, there are in fact no three-party systems of this kind among Western democracies: all the three-party systems are in the second group; all systems of the third group have more than three significant parties. It can thus be stated that, while theoretically possible, a genuine three-party system is not a likely type of system among Western democracies: countries of the second group should therefore be more strictly labelled as 'two-and-a-half-party systems'. It may indeed be permissible to add, after considering the evolution of party systems, particularly in the early part of the twentieth century, that genuine three-party systems do not normally occur because they are essentially transitional, thus unstable, forms of party systems.

The situation arising out of the 1965 Belgian election was thus of particular interest, since the upsurge of the Liberal party and the decline of the two major parties was such that Belgium appeared to have moved into the exceptional and seemingly transitional position of a 'genuine' three-party system. If the proposition advanced earlier is correct, it would seem that in the next few years Belgium will move to one of three types of further changes. The Liberals could return to their 'normal' position of small party; they could displace one of the two major parties (an unprecedented development in Western Europe since all the movements happened in the other direction); a split could occur among the supporters of one or both of the major parties and Belgium might move from the second group of countries (two-and-a-half party systems) to the third or fourth (multiparty systems). From the experience of other Western democracies the first and third of these three outcomes appears more probable than the maintenance of a genuine three-party system.

We included Holland among the countries which constituted the third group, composed of those countries in which the two largest parties obtained about two-thirds of the votes of the electorate. But if we consider the relative strength of the two major parties, the five other countries of the group differ markedly from Holland, in that they have one very large party, which might be defined as dominant as it obtains about 40 per cent of the electorate and generally gains about twice as many votes as the second party. In fact, in both Norway and Sweden, the mechanics of the electoral system have sometimes enabled this dominant party to obtain the absolute majority of seats in the Chamber. But these countries are at the same time multi-party systems as they all have four or five significant (and often well-structured) parties playing a crucial role in the operation of the political system. Four of the five Scandinavian countries are included in this group (the fifth being Italy), though in Iceland the dominant party is not the Socialist but the Conservative (Independence) party. The Fifth Republic, at least under de Gaulle, appears to be moving towards this pattern of party system, though the characteristics of the Gaullist party are such that it seems unreasonable to predict that the present party configuration is likely to survive de Gaulle. Thus, alongside two-party systems and two-and-half-party systems, the third group should be defined, not so much as a multiparty system in which two parties obtain about two-thirds of the votes of the electorate, but as a multiparty system with a dominant party which obtains about two-fifths and less than half of the votes.

Finally, the last four countries (if Holland is included and France maintained in the group in the view of the past and possible future performance of that country) constitute the 'genuine' multiparty systems: they have no dominant body and indeed seem to show a pattern of political behaviour in which three or four parties are equally well placed to combine or form coalitions. Recent electoral movements in Holland appear to bring that country gradually nearer towards this model: the slow decline of the Labour party and the patterns of governmental formation have tended to conform fairly closely to those which have been customary of Finland.

3. *Ideological Spectrum and Party Strength*

Western democracies can therefore be divided into four groups, if both numbers and strengths are taken into account: five are in the two-party system group, five in the two-and-a-half-party system group, five in the group of multiparty systems with dominant party, and four in the group of multiparty systems without dominant party. But the party system can only wholly be defined if we take into account the position of parties on the ideological spectrum, particularly when the system does not have a 'symmetrical' character.

Even in Western democracies, parties are difficult to categorize accurately. The United States and Eire always had parties which do not fit in any easily recognizable typology. The French Gaullists are not ordinary Conservatives, though they may have to be lumped with Conservatives for comparative purposes. The other multi-party system countries all have parties of a somewhat peculiar type, such as the two Conservative parties in Holland, the Swedish party in Finland, and the party of the Peasants, Artisans, and Bourgeois in Switzerland. In all these cases, certain rough approximations have had to be made.

Table 22.3 shows the panorama of party strengths within the ideological spectrum. Group 1, except for the United States, is fairly homogeneous: the four other countries in the group have a large Socialist party and a large Conservative or Christian party, together with a small other group, whose position in the centre is perhaps sometimes problematic. Countries of group 2 have two types of party systems: Belgium, Germany, and Luxemburg resemble countries of group 1, except that the centre party is stronger and, as we noted earlier, this increased strength is mainly at the expense of one only of the two major parties (in fact the Socialist party). The other two countries of the group (Canada and Eire) are different: the small party is not the centre, but the left-wing, party and, probably not quite accidentally, the right-wing party is not Christian but Conservative. In the early part of the twentieth century, it would

TABLE 22.3. The Ideological Spectrum of Parties in Western Democracies

	Comm.	Soc.	Lib./Rad.	Agr.	Christ.	Cons.
Group 1						
Two-party systems						
United States			L L			
New Zealand		L	e			L
Australia		L	e			L
United Kingdom		L	e			L
Austria		L	e?		L	
Group 2						
Two-and-a-half-party systems						
Germany		L	s		L	
Belgium		L	s		L	
Luxemburg		L	s		L	
Canada		s	L			L
Eire		s	L			L
Group 3						
Multiparty systems with one dominant party						
Denmark		L	s/m	s		s/m
Norway		L	s	s	s	s/m
Sweden		L	s/m	s		s/m
Iceland	s/m	s/m	M			L
Italy	m	s	s		L	s
Group 4						
Multiparty systems without dominant party						
Netherlands		M	s		M	s
Switzerland		M	M		M	s
France	M	s/m	s		s	M
Finland	M	M	s	M		s

L = large party (about 40 per cent)
M = medium-sized party (somewhat over 20 per cent)
s/m = small to medium-sized party (about 15 per cent)
s = small party (about 10 per cent or even less)
e = very small party (only mentioned in relation to two-party systems)

probably have been argued that both these countries were still in a transitional stage: Canada has a party system not unlike that of Britain in 1906. But it must by now be recognized both that the two-and-a-half-party system is stable (Belgium and Germany have had for long periods the British party system of the 1920s and do not appear to move further towards a two-party system) and that the two-and-a-half-party system is stable even if the left-wing party is the small party. Neither the Irish Labour party nor the Canadian NDP appear to be in a position to overtake the centre party in the near future: their position of small party seems stable. The reasons for the stability of the Canadian model of two-and-a-half-party system are probably to be found along lines similar to those which account for the stability of the American parties, which have remained in existence despite earlier predictions to the contrary.

Two types, and not more than two types, of multiparty systems with a dominant party can be found. Three Scandinavian countries have a dominant Socialist party; Iceland and Italy have a dominant Conservative or Christian party. In the latter two cases, we encounter for the first time countries with a really large Communist party. In Iceland and Italy (as in Finland and even France) the Communist party remained fairly stable throughout the whole period; the Socialist party is therefore correspondingly weak and the left is divided; as is well known, the converse occurs in Norway, Denmark, and Sweden. In these three countries, though the agrarian party is not placed symmetrically in relation to the Communists on the political spectrum, it probably plays the same divisive part. The absence of religious divisions might have led one to expect the three Scandinavian countries which do not have a large Communist party to have two-and-a-half-party systems, but the apparent feelings of identity of the agricultural community have created permanent cleavages on the right which have produced a party system in many ways 'symmetrical' to that of Iceland and Italy.

Countries of the fourth group have no dominant party: party strengths are therefore fairly evenly spread across the ideological spectrum, though Holland and Switzerland, with weak Communist parties, display somewhat less spread than France and Finland. This latter country combines the splintering characteristics of left and right of the Scandinavian countries: the divisions of Iceland are superimposed on those of Sweden.

There are thus six types of party systems in Western democracies. At one extreme are the broadly based parties of the two-party system countries: the United States is the most perfect case of this type, but four other countries closely approximate this model and they only diverge inasmuch as they have a small centre party and are divided ideologically between conservatives and socialists. At the other extreme, the votes of the electors are spread fairly evenly, in groups of not much more than 25 per cent and in many cases much less than 25 per cent over the whole ideological spectrum, as in Holland, Switzerland, France, and Finland. Between these two poles, one finds four types of party systems: five countries have two-and-a-half-party systems: among them, three have a smaller centre party, while the other two have a smaller left-wing party. The five remaining countries are multiparty systems with a dominant party, three of them having a dominant socialist party opposed by a divided right, largely because of the presence of an agrarian sentiment in the countries concerned, while the other two have a strong right-wing party opposed by a divided left, largely because of the presence of a substantial Communist party.

A number of types of party systems, which are theoretically possible, do not appear to exist. There are no three-party systems, as we saw; there are no 'unbalanced' two-and-a-half-party systems, out of the three which might have existed. Dominant parties in multiparty systems tend to be of the right or left, not of the centre. Patterns of party systems in Western democracies are thus limited in number. There are discrete points at which party systems are to be found: not only social structures but balance and equilibrium have surely to be taken into account in an analysis of the real world distribution of Western party systems.

23

THE ELECTORAL BALANCE

STEIN ROKKAN

The salient differences in the structure of electoral alternatives can be brought out through a crude classification by type of contest: this is attempted for the smaller democracies in Table 23.1.

None of our eleven democracies have experienced extended periods of straight alternation between two major parties: the typical 'ins-outs' politics characteristic of Britain, the United States, and some of the white Commonwealth countries. Austria and Ireland, and during some periods Belgium, have come closest to what German commentators have called the two-and-a-half party system: two large parties running neck and neck for the majority point but generally thwarted in their endeavours by the persistence of one small above-threshold party. This was the situation in Austria practically from the first republican election: the Nationalist camp was just strong enough to prevent one of the two large parties from gaining a safe majority. The Irish party system came close to this model in the late twenties but the Republican Fianna Fáil party was soon to take the lead and left the pro-Treaty Fine Gael well behind in election after election. In fact, the Irish constellations of the fifties and sixties are almost halfway between the German-Austrian system and the Scandinavian: one large party near the majority point and several middle-sized parties competing for the next places. Belgium enjoyed a two-party system during the *régime censitaire* but has since oscillated between the Austrian-Irish constellation and what we shall call the 'segmented pluralism' model.

Stein Rokkan, excerpted from *Citizens, Elections, Parties: Approaches to the Comparative Study of the Processes of Development* (1970), Chapter 3. Reprinted by permission of the Norwegian University Press.

TABLE 23.1. A Classification of the Party Systems of the Smaller European Democracies after World War I: By the Likelihood of Single-Party Majorities and the Distribution of Minority Party Strengths

Country	Period	Total seats (lower house)	Largest party: distance from majority point		Two next parties: seats below first party				Other parties: total seats	
					Second party		Third party			
			Min.	Max.	Min.	Max.	Min.	Max.	Min.	Max.
I. The British-German '1 vs. 1 + 1' System										
AUSTRIA	I. Rep.	159–183	− 1	− 11	2	16	45	67	0	3
	II. Rep.	165	+ 2	− 9	1	11	60	(none)	0	5
IRELAND	1922–32	128, 153	− 5	− 30	3	23	25	65	17	40
	1933–44	153, 138	+ 8	− 2	21	46	50	68	7	24
	1944–65	147, 144	+ 4	− 9	15	38	46	66	3	34
II. The Scandinavian '1 vs. 3–4' System										
SWEDEN	1921–32	230	− 11	− 25	17	46	58	76	28	39
	1936–44	230	+ 19	− 3	68	92	76	106	26	41
	1948–64	230, 233	− 2	− 10	48	74	64	82	25	45
DENMARK	1920–29	139, 148	− 13	− 23	3	18	20	37	19	22
	1932–57	148, 175	− 6	− 26	8	40	22	44	21	36
	1960–66	175	− 12	− 19	34	38	35	44	25	37
NORWAY	1921–30	150	− 16	− 28	6	29	14	30	27	38
	1933–57	150	+ 10	− 6	34	62	45	64	21	31
	1961–65	150	− 1	− 7	37	45	50	58	31	33

III. Even Multiparty Systems:
'1 vs. 1 vs. 1 + 2–3'

		Period									
1. Scandinavian 'Split Working Class' systems	FINLAND	1919–39	200	−15	−47	1	38	18	62	33	67
		1945–66	200	−44	−50	1	6	1	18	50	62
	ICELAND	1923–37	42, 49	+2	−6	2	8	10	19	0	5
		1942–63	49, 60	−5	−7	1	7	10	15	6	9
2. 'Segmented Pluralism'	NETHERLANDS	1918–37	100	−18	−22	6	12	14	18	29	36
		1946–56	100	−16	−20	0	5	18	24	23	28
		1959–67	150	−25	−33	1	7	25	35	34	54
	BELGIUM	1919–39	186, 202	−15	−31	1	9	39	55	9	48
		1946–65	202, 212	+2	−29	9	39	29	88	3	23
	LUXEMBOURG	1945–59	51, 52	0	−5	2	14	10	20	3	6
	SWITZERLAND	1919–39	187–198	−37	−44	2	17	8	17	42	53
		1943–63	194–200	−41	−47	0	9	3	13	46	50

In Sweden, Denmark, and Norway the first elections after the introduction of PR produced very even distribution among three to four parties, but the Social Democrats soon moved up to the Majority point and left the other contenders competing for the other half of the votes. This process went furthest in Sweden and in Norway: the Swedish Social Democrats entered the Executive as early as in 1917 and have managed to stay in power on majorities or near-majorities for over thirty years; the Norwegian Labour party had its first taste of ministerial Socialism in 1927 and stayed in power for thirty years from 1935 to 1965. The Danish Social Democrats never reached clear majorities: they have enjoyed long periods of Cabinet power but have either relied on *ad hoc* aggregations of support in Parliament or entered into coalition with minor partners. With the spectacular gain of the Left Socialists in 1966, the Danish system in fact moved closer to the other Scandinavian model: the type of structure produced in Finland and Iceland through the split between Communists and Social Democrats.

The Finnish constellation was quite similar to the Danish until the Second World War: one large Social Democrat party, one middle-sized Agrarian party, and a couple of parties (Finland: 3, Denmark: 2) in the 10–15 per cent range. With the legalization of the Communist party in 1944 the working class Left was split down the middle: the result was a '1 vs. 1 vs. 1 + 3' system doomed to some form of coalition government or, when coalitions could not be kept together, transitional admixtures of technocrats or even direct trade union representatives. There was a similar development in Iceland: before the war a period of majorities or near-majorities for the Conservative-Liberal and later the Independence party, later an even split among 3 to 4 parties.

This, of course, had been the typical constellation in the religiously and ethnically split countries along the Protestant–Catholic border belt across the Continent. In the Netherlands and in Switzerland no party was ever within shooting range of the majority point after the end of World War I. In Belgium the situation was very similar before World War II, but changed for a couple of periods after World War II. From 1949 to 1954 and again in 1958 the Catholics hovered close to the majority point and the system approached the '1 vs. 1 + 1' constellation we identified as Austrian-Irish: this, of course, came to an abrupt end with the politicization of the linguistic cleavages in the 1960s and the resurgence of the Liberals and the Flemish Nationalists.

This typology of party constellations is purely numerical: the decisive criteria of differentiation are the proximity to the majority and the evenness of the contests for the top position.

In our comments on the table, we have slipped into concrete interpretations of particular national cleavage structures, but the thrust of our argument is that the abstract numerical constellation is of critical importance in the comparative study of electoral behaviour: there is good reason to believe that it makes a difference, both in the style of party activity and in the behaviour of potential supporters, how close the system is to straight majority dominance and how much responsibility each competing party has had for central executive decision-making. This is an important field for detailed research across countries and across parties.

24

A TYPOLOGY OF PARTY SYSTEMS

GIOVANNI SARTORI

I. THE NUMERICAL CRITERION

1. *The Issue*

There are more than 100 states that display, at least on paper, some kind of party arrangement. The variety of these arrangements is as impressive as the number. How are we to order the maze? For a long time party systems have been classified by counting the number of parties—whether one, two, or more than two. By now, however, there is a near-unanimous agreement that the distinction among one-party, two-party, and multiparty systems is highly inadequate. And we are even told that 'a judgment as to the number of major parties . . . obscures more than it illuminates'.[1]

One reaction to the party-counting approach is simply to drop the numerical base, precisely 'on the assumption that the traditional distinction between two-party and multiparty patterns has not led to sufficiently meaningful insights'. Thus La Palombara and Weiner propose—for the competitive party systems—the following fourfold typology: (i) hegemonic ideological, (ii) hegemonic pragmatic, (iii) turnover ideological, (iv) turnover pragmatic.[2] The scheme is highly suggestive; but it is too sweeping. Another reaction is to let the data

Giovanni Sartori, excerpted from *Parties and Party Systems: A Framework for Analysis*, Volume 1, Chapters 5, 6, and 9 (Cambridge University Press, 1976). Reprinted by permission of the author.

[1] W. J. Crotty, 'Political Parties Research', in M. Haas and H. S. Kariel (eds.), *Approaches to the Study of Political Science* (Scranton, Penn.: Chandler, 1970), 282.

[2] J. LaPalombara and M. Weiner (eds.), *Political Parties and Political Development* (Princeton: Princeton University Press, 1966), 34, 36.

—especially the electoral turnouts—determine the classes, i.e., different clusters of party systems. This is the suggestion, for example, of Blondel.[3] A third reaction is to wonder whether we need classes at all, i.e., whether there is any point in classifying party systems. The argument is, here, that our universe is continuous and therefore that all we need is an index of fragmentation, or of fractionalization, or of linear dispersion, and the like. These suggestions will be taken up and discussed in due course. For the time being, let us simply note that almost every writer comes up with his own scheme. By now classifications and typologies of party systems are a plethora, and 'confusion and profusion of terms seems to be the rule'.[4]

We are seemingly entering, then, a vicious circle. On the one hand, we are on the verge of drowning in an *embarras de richesse*. On the other hand, this very proliferation attests that the universe of party systems badly and increasingly needs to be charted. But this appears to require further additions to the 'profusion and confusion'. The lesser evil is, perhaps, to backtrack and to review the case from the beginning. Was there something fundamentally wrong in the initial start, or have we gone astray somewhere along the way? It is not clear, in effect, where we stand on the issue. Do we mean that the number of parties is of little consequence? Or do we mean, instead, that our classifications fail to sort out these numbers?

To the first question I would reply that it does matter how many are the parties. For one thing, the number of parties immediately indicates, albeit roughly, an important feature of the political system: the extent to which political power is fragmented or non-fragmented, dispersed or concentrated. Likewise, simply by knowing how many parties there are, we are alerted to the number of possible 'interaction streams' that are involved. As Gunner Sjöblom points out, 2 parties allow for only 1 stream of reciprocal interaction, 3 parties allow for 3 streams of interaction, 4 parties for 6, 5 parties for 10, 6 parties

---

[3] Jean Blondel, 'Party Systems and Patterns of Government in Western Democracies', *Canadian Journal of Political Science*, 1/2 (1968), and his *Introduction to Comparative Government* (New York: Praeger, 1969), 155–60.

[4] Roy C. Macridis, 'Introduction', in Macridis (ed.), *Political Parties: Contemporary Trends and Ideas* (New York: Harper and Row, 1967), 20.

318 GIOVANNI SARTORI

for 15, and 7 parties for 21.[5] Since these possible interaction streams occur at multiple levels—electoral, parliamentary, and governmental—the indication clearly is that the greater the number of parties (that have a say), the greater the complexity and probably the intricacy of the system. For instance, from the vantage point of the electors a pairwise comparison between the programmes entails, for 8 parties, 28 comparisons, for 9 parties 36, and for 10 parties 45 comparisons. Furthermore, and in particular, the tactics of party competition and opposition appear related to the number of parties; and this has in turn, an important bearing on how governmental coalitions are formed and are able to perform.

All in all, the real issue is not whether the number of parties matters—it does—but whether a numerical criterion of classification enables us to get a hold of what matters. So far the answer is clearly no. And the preliminary reason is equally clear: No accounting system can work without counting rules. If we resort to counting, we should know how to count. But we are even incapable of deciding when one is one and when two is two—whether a system is, or is not, a two-party system. Thereupon we leap to infinity; that is, we give up counting altogether: Having failed to establish when two is two, we cover all the rest, in an exhausted mood, simply by saying more-than-two. It is no wonder, therefore, that the number-of-parties approach leads to frustration. Not only are three classes insufficient, but, as they stand, they do not sort out the cases.

The current state of the art is, plainly, that we have dismissed the numerical criterion of classification before having learned how to use it. And there are many reasons, I believe, for giving this criterion another try. For one thing, the number of parties is a highly visible element that provides 'natural' cutting points and reflects the real world terms of politics. Thus—regardless of our indexes—politicians and voters alike will continue to fight for, and argue about, more or fewer parties, whether the number of parties should be increased or reduced. On the other hand, let us not forget that parties are the coagulant, or the coagulation units, of all our measures. After all, the number of

[5] G. Söblom, *Party Strategies in a Multiparty System* (Lund: Studentlitteratur, 1968), 174–5.

votes and seats that each party wins at elections is our best and safest data base.

In the light of the foregoing I propose to begin with the counting rules and to explore, with the aid of these rules, the mileage afforded by a classification based on the number of parties. As will be seen, the numerical criterion can be put to efficient use. On the other hand, it will be equally seen that this efficient use is not unaided. At the beginning and for quite a long stretch it is fair to say that while not alone, the numerical criterion remains the primary variable. But the point is reached at which the pure and simple counting fails us.

2. *Rules for counting*

In a nutshell, the problem is: Which parties are *relevant*? We cannot count all the parties at face value. Nor can we settle the problem by counting them in an order of decreasing strength. True enough, *how many* relates to *how strong*. The question remains: How much strength makes a party relevant, and how much feebleness makes a party irrelevant? For want of a better solution we generally establish a threshold below which a party is discounted. But this is no solution at all, for there is no absolute yardstick for assessing the relevance of size. If this threshold is established—as is often done—at the 5 per cent level, it leads to serious omissions. On the other hand, the more the threshold is lowered, the greater the chances of including irrelevant parties. The relevance of a party is a function not only of the relative distribution of power—as is obvious—but also, and especially, of its position value, that is, of its positioning along the left-right dimension. Thus a party that ranges at the 10 per cent level may well count far less than a party that obtains only a 3 per cent level. A limiting, but eloquent case, is that of the Italian Republican party, whose average return over some twenty-five years has been around 2 per cent: Nevertheless it is surely relevant, for it has tipped the balance, over the whole period, of a number of governmental majorities.

Clearly, if the problem has a solution, it lies in stating rules according to which a party is to be counted or discounted. In substance we are required to establish a *criterion of irrelevance vis-à-vis* the smaller parties. However, since the bigness or smallness of a party is measured by its strength, let us first underpin this notion.

The strength of a party is, first of all, its electoral strength. There is more to it; but as long as we proceed with the numerical criterion, the base is given by this measure. However, votes are translated into seats, and this leads us to the strength of the parliamentary party. To avoid unnecessary complication we may thus settle for the 'strength in seats' —which is, in the final analysis, what really counts once the elections are over. Again for the sake of simplicity—but also of comparability—it is often sufficient to refer, in the bicameral systems, to the seats in the lower chamber—provided the other chamber does not have different majorities. It is permissible, then, to start with this measure: The strength of the parliamentary party is indicated by its percentage of seats in the lower chamber.

The next step is to shift the focus to the party as an instrument of government. This shift is of little interest with respect to two-party systems; but the more numerous the parties, the more we must inquire as to the *governing potential*, or the coalition potential, of each party. What really weighs in the balance of multipartism is the extent to which a party may be needed as a coalition partner for one or more of the possible governmental majorities. A party may be small but have a strong coalition-bargaining potential. Conversely, a party may be strong and yet lack coalition-bargaining power. The question now is whether a realistic estimate of the *coalition potential* of each party can be made on the sole basis of its strength. Clearly, the reply is no, for this criterion would lead us to consider all the possible numerical majorities, whereas we are interested in the *feasible coalitions*, which means only the ones that are ideologically consonant and permissible. Hence the rule for deciding—in a multiparty situation—when a party should, or should not, be counted, is the following:

Rule 1. A minor party can be *discounted as irrelevant* whenever it remains over time superfluous, in the sense that it is never needed or put to use for any feasible coalition majority. Conversely, a minor party must be counted, no matter how small it is, if it finds itself in a position to determine over time, and at some point in time, at least one of the possible governmental majorities.

This rule has a limitation, for it applies only to the parties that are governing oriented and, furthermore, ideologically acceptable to the other coalition partners. This may leave out some relatively large parties of permanent opposition—such as the anti-system parties. Therefore, our criterion of irrelevance needs to be supplemented—residually, or under special circumstances—by a 'criterion of relevance'. The question may be reformulated as follows: What size, or bigness, makes a party relevant regardless of its coalition potential? In Italy and France one finds, for instance, Communist parties that poll one-fourth, and even as much as one-third of the total vote but whose governmental coalition potential has been, for the past twenty-five years, virtually zero. Yet it would be absurd to discount them. We are thus led to formulate a second, subsidiary counting rule based on the power of intimidation, or, more exactly, the *blackmail potential*[6] of the opposition-oriented parties.

Rule 2. A party *qualifies for relevance* whenever its existence, or appearance, affects the tactics of party competition and particularly when it alters the *direction* of the competition— by determining a switch from centripetal to centrifugal competition either leftward, rightward, or in both directions—of the governing-oriented parties.

In summary, we can discount the parties that have neither (i) *coalition potential* nor (ii) *blackmail potential*. Conversely, we must count all the parties that have either a governmental relevance in the coalition-forming arena, or a competitive relevance in the oppositional arena.

These rules may appear unduly complicated and, in any case, difficult to operationalize. At the moment let us note, to begin with, that both criteria are postdictive, for there is no point in using them predictively. With respect to Rule 1 this means that the 'feasible coalitions', and thereby the parties having a coalition potential, coincide, in practice, with the parties that

---

[6] The label is not only drawn from but related to the blackmail party of Anthony Downs, *An Economic Theory of Democracy* (New York: Harper and Row), 1957, 131–2.

have in fact entered, at some point in time, coalition governments and/or have given governments the support they needed for taking office or for staying in office. In most cases, therefore, the rule is easily applicable—provided, of course, that we dispose of the very simple information it requires.

Turning to Rule 2, the objection could be that the direction of competition is no easy thing to assess. In theory this may be true—and will be seen at the end. But in practice the notion of blackmail party is mainly connected to the notion of antisystem party—and both the relevance and the anti-system nature of a party can be established, in turn, by a battery of ulterior indicators. If my rule brings to the fore the blackmail party of Anthony Downs, this is because party competition is very central to my overall argument. None the less, since the blackmail party generally coincides with an anti-system party (otherwise it would be comprehended, in all likelihood, under Rule 1) the assessment can well be pursued in the parliamentary arena. That is, the blackmail potential of the electoral party finds its equivalent in the veto potential, or indeed the *veto power*, of the parliamentary party with respect to the enactment of legislation. If there is any doubt as to whether a blackmail party should be counted or discounted, the matter can be pursued and checked on these grounds.

All in all, I submit that the difficulty of my rules resides either in the fact that scholars find it easier to deal with comparative politics without any substantive knowledge of the countries they cover, or in the fact that my rules demand data that are seldom systematically assembled. I have no remedy, I am afraid, for the first difficulty. As for the second difficulty, if my rules are more easily stated than applied, this is so because we never have the information we need until we ask for it. Let it be added that there is nothing 'softer' in the information required by my rules than in many of the data in which the social scientist currently places his unreserved confidence. On the other hand, it is simply not true that we dispose of better measures for the same thing: counting the number of 'relevant' parties with respect to their 'position value'. We do dispose of better measures—but for something else.

Thus far we know when three is three, four is four, and so forth; that is, we can sort out the *cases*. The next question is:

Does the numerical criterion also allow the sorting out of new *classes*? Until now we have been concerned with counting (according to rules). The new question raises, so to speak, a problem of intelligent counting. As a rule of thumb, few parties denote low fragmentation, whereas many parties indicate high fragmentation. However, as we count the parties we can also account for their strength. And there is one distribution that ostensibly stands out as a case by itself: When one party commands, alone and over time, the absolute majority (of seats). That is, intelligent counting is all we need for sorting out—just by looking—that distribution in which one party 'counts more' than all the other parties together: the class of the predominant-party systems. The advantage of sorting out this system is not only that four classes are better than three (unipartism, twopartism, and multipartism) but also that we now have a clean notion of fragmentation. Clearly, a predominant-party system can result from an excess of fragmentation of all the other parties—as in India. If we decide, however, that the salient property of the Indian party system is that the Congress party rules alone, then 'fragmentation' obtains a clear definition: A party system is declared fragmented only when it has many parties, none of which approaches the absolute majority point.

There is still another class that intelligent counting can sort out. If we leave the area of the competitive party systems and pass to the non-competitive, we may still find polities (e.g., Poland and, better still, Mexico) with more than one party in which the 'secondary parties' cannot be entirely dismissed as pure and simple façades. On the other hand, these secondary, peripheral parties do count less: They are, so to speak, licensed and permitted to exist only as subordinate parties. These are the systems I call hegemonic. And they can be detected by intelligent counting, which means, in this case, counting the hegemonic party first and the subordinate parties separately.

At this point the possibilities of the numerical criterion seem pretty much exhausted. I will enter shortly into the distinction between limited (moderate) and extreme (polarized) pluralism. But these classes cannot be identified and sustained on numerical grounds only. This is the point at which the number-of-parties variable becomes secondary and the ideology variable takes precedence.

3. *A Two-Dimensional Mapping*

A classification is an ordering based on mutually exclusive classes that are established by the principle, or criterion, chosen for that classification. A typology is a more complex matter: it is an ordering of 'attribute compounds', i.e., an ordering resulting from more than one criterion.[7] According to this distinction, up to now we have discussed a classification, not a typology; i.e., we have identified *classes*, not *types*, of party systems. And the numerical criterion can yield, I am suggesting, seven classes, indicated as follows:

1. one party
2. hegemonic party
3. predominant party
4. two-party
5. limited pluralism
6. extreme pluralism
7. atomized

With respect to the traditional threefold classification, two innovations are self-evident. First, I break down into three categories the traditional 'one-party lump' that brings together the most incongruent variety of heterogeneous phenomena, thereby allowing the reclassification of a number of polities erroneously identified as one-party into either the hegemonic or the predominant-party class. Second, I break down the traditional 'multiparty lump', under the assumption that the single-package treatment of the more-than-two party systems testifies only to the poverty of our counting rules.

As for my last category, the 'atomized' pattern requires little

[7] This is the definition of P. A. Lazarsfeld and Allen H. Barton: '. . . by "type" one means a specific attribute compound' ('Qualitative Measurement in the Social Sciences' in D. Lerner and H. D. Lasswell (eds.), *The Policy Sciences* (Stanford: Stanford University Press, 1951), 169). Whenever it is unnecessary to distinguish the classification from the typology, I shall use the term taxonomy. Strictly speaking, a taxonomy is an intermediate ordering between the classificatory and the typological (matrix-type) orderings. But this amount of detail is unnecessary for my purposes.

explanation: It enters the classification as a residual class to indicate a point at which we no longer need an accurate counting, that is, a threshold beyond which the number of parties—whether 10, 20, or more—makes little difference. The atomized party systems can be defined in the same way as atomistic competition in economics, that is, as 'the situation where no one firm [has] any noticeable effect on any other firm'.[8] This points up as well that the numerical criterion applies only to party systems that have entered the stage of structural consolidation.

Despite the overall analytical improvement, the first category is, very visibly, inadequate. One is just one, and under the numerical criterion the varieties and differences among the one-party polities totally escape recognition. At the other end, and still worse, it is unclear how the classes of limited and extreme pluralism are to be divided. The common-sense assumption underlying this distinction is that three-to-five parties, viz., limited pluralism, have very different interactions than six-to-eight parties, viz., extreme pluralism. But neither our counting rules nor intelligent counting can really sort out the two patterns. The reason is that when we enter the area of fragmentation—let us say from five parties onward—this fragmentation may result from a multiplicity of causal factors, and it can be underpinned only in the light of such factors. Briefly put, the fragmentation of the party system can reflect either a situation of *segmentation* or a situation of *polarization*, i.e., of ideological distance. It is evident, therefore, that there is something that counting cannot detect and yet is essential. This adds up to saying that we are peremptorily required to pass from the classification to the typology and, thereby, to implementing the numerical criterion with ideology as a criterion.

It will be recalled that I have already spoken of an ideology-to-pragmatism continuum.[9] In this reference the meaning of the word ideology is specified by its opposite, viz., pragmatism. But the connotation intended in the present context is more analytic. The term is used here first to denote an *ideological*

---

[8] Mancur Olson, *The Logic of Collective Action—Public Goods and the Theory of Groups* (Cambridge, Mass.: Harvard University Press, 1965), 49.

[9] [i.e. in *Parties and Party Systems: A Framework for Analysis*, p. 78.]

distance, that is, the overall spread of the ideological spectrum of any given polity, and second to denote *ideological intensity*, that is, the temperature or the affect of a given ideological setting. More precisely, the notion of ideological *distance* enters the apprehension of the more-than-one party systems, whereas the notion of ideological *intensity* is essential to the apprehension of the one-party polities.

Awaiting the full-fledged taxonomy that will emerge at the end of the inquiry, the foregoing considerations lead to a two-dimensional, preliminary mapping that might be called the modified classification. The modified classification leaves unsettled: how to dispose of 'segmentation'. The solution lies in having the segmented polities checked by the ideology variable. If they are fragmented but not polarized, they will be attributed to the type of (ideologically) *moderate* pluralism. If they are fragmented and polarized, they clearly belong to the type of (ideologically) *polarized* pluralism. The modified classification differs, then, from the numerical one only with respect to the classes of limited and extreme pluralism, which are replaced by the types that I call moderate and polarized pluralism. The expected correspondences are illustrated in the conversion scheme of Table 24.1.

Having laboured in the mapping, we might wonder whether the exercise is worth while. Does the modified classification yield insights? The contention could be, for instance, that the numerical criterion provides an indication, if only a very imperfect one, of the *distribution* of political power. The distribution is, however, a very tricky thing to assess. I would rather say, therefore, that what the mapping provides is a fairly good indication of the *dispersion*—either a segmented or a polarized dispersion—of power.

TABLE 24.1.   Patterns, Classes, and Types of Multipartism

Pattern	Class	Type
Low fragmentation (up to 5 parties)	⟶ Limited pluralism	⟶ Moderate pluralism
Segmentation ⟶	. . . .	
High fragmentation (above 5 parties)	⟶ Extreme pluralism	⟶ Polarized pluralism

To begin with, as it now stands the one-party case is clear: political power is monopolized by one party only, in the precise sense that no other party is permitted to exist. Then there is the case in which one party 'counts more' than all the others—but in two very different ways. On the one hand we find a hegemonic party that permits the existence of other parties only as 'satellite' or, at any rate, as subordinate parties; that is, the hegemony of the party in power cannot be challenged. On the other hand we find the predomininant-party system, that is, a power configuration in which one party governs alone, without being subjected to alternation, as long as it continues to win, electorally, an absolute majority. Two-party systems pose no problem, inasmuch as their power configuration is straight-forward: Two parties compete for an absolute majority that is within the reach of either. This leaves us with the power configuration of multipartism in general, which can be spelled out as follows: (i) No party is likely to approach, or at least to maintain, an absolute majority, and (ii) the relative strength (or weakness) of the parties can be ranked according to their respective coalition indispensability (or dispensability) and/or (iii) their eventual potential of intimidation (blackmail).

The number of parties, I have argued, matters. What remains to be explained is: Precisely with respect to what does it matter? When party systems are classified according to the numerical criterion, they are classified on the basis of their *format*—how many parties they contain. But the format is interesting only to the extent that it affects the *mechanics*—how the system works. In other words, the format is interesting to the extent that it contains *mechanical predispositions*, that it goes to determine a set of functional properties of the party system first, and of the overall political system as a consequence. Hence my subsequent inquiry will hinge on the distinction and relation between format and mechanics. This is tantamount to saying —in the light of my distinction between the classification and the typology of party systems—that we shall be exploring how the *class*, which denotes the format, relates to the *type*, which connotes the properties.

2. COMPETITIVE SYSTEMS

1. *Polarized Pluralism*

Our apprehension of party systems is very uneven. By and large, the systems that have been more adequately explored are the 'bipolar systems', the two-party systems and the systems that follow a similar dualistic logic, i.e., the systems that I call moderate pluralism. Extreme and polarized pluralism confronts us, instead, with a category whose distinctiveness has escaped attention. There are two reasons for this. One is the use of dualistic blinders, that is, the tendency to explain any and all party systems by extrapolating from the two-party model. These dualistic blinders have been proposed by Duverger as an almost 'natural law' of politics:

> We do not always find a duality of parties, but we do find almost always a dualism of tendencies. . . . This is tantamount to saying that the center does not exist in politics: We may have a center party, but not a center tendency. . . . There are no true centers other than as a crosscutting of dualisms.[10]

I will argue, contrariwise, that when we do not have a centre party, we are likely to have a centre tendency. For the moment let it just be pointed out that Duverger's dualistic blinders lead him—as subsequent developments have abundantly confirmed—to astonishing misperceptions, as when he finds that Germany and Italy are the two European countries that 'display a rather marked tendency' towards 'bipartism'.[11]

The second reason we already know well, namely, that the case of extreme pluralism can hardly be singled out unless we know how parties are to be counted. To this day, after having counted as far as two, what follows is 'polypartism'. But as soon as we establish an accounting system we can do better.

Since we need an operational demarcation, let us establish that the turning point is *between five and six* parties. It is well to repeat that the parties in question must be *relevant*, i.e., result

---

[10] Maurice Duverger, *Les Partis Politiques* (Paris: Colin, 1951), 245 and *passim*, 239–46, 251, 261–5.

[11] Ibid. 241, 269.

from discarding the parties that lack 'coalition use', unless their 'power of intimidation' affects the tactics of inter-party competition. Admittedly, my counting rules still leave room for arguing whether a small, marginal party should be counted or not and may still confront the classifier with some troublesome borderline cases. But this is hardly a tragedy. In the first place there is no magic in the numbers five and six; that is, their magic is an operational artefact only. In terms of substantive knowledge the threshold can—and indeed should—be expressed more loosely by saying that the interactions among more-than-five parties tend to produce a different mechanics than the interactions among five-or-less parties. In short, the border line is not *at* five (or at six), but *around* five (or six). In the second place, and in any event, we have a control variable: ideological distance. Therefore, while accounting discrepancies may disturb the classification, they will not affect the typology.

I propose to discuss in the next section which countries actually enter the class, and especially the type, of extreme and polarized pluralism. For a preliminary orientation it will suffice to say that the analysis in this section basically draws on the experience of the German Weimar Republic in the twenties, of the French Fourth Republic, of Chile (until September 1973), and on the current case of Italy. In any event, with respect to a party system that has remained largely unidentified, the preliminary task is to analyse *in vitro* its distinctive features and systemic properties. In what follows these features will be presented in an order of visibility rather than of importance.

1. The first distinctive feature of polarized pluralism resides in the presence of relevant *anti-system parties*. The system is characterized by an anti-system opposition—especially of the Communist or of the Fascist variety, but also of other varieties. A party can be defined as being anti-system whenever it *undermines the legitimacy of the regime* it opposes [but] the broad definition contains a narrower, more specific connotation. A first approximation to this more specific connotation points to the fact that an anti-system party would not change—if it could—the government but the very system of government. Its opposition is not an 'opposition on issues' (so little so that it can afford to bargain on issues) but an 'opposition of

principle'. Thus the hard core of the concept is singled out by noting that an anti-system opposition abides by a belief system that does not share the values of the political order within which it operates. According to the strict definition, then, anti-system parties represent an *extraneous ideology*—thereby indicating a polity confronted with a maximal ideological distance.

2. The second distinctive feature of polarized pluralism resides in the existence of *bilateral oppositions*. When the opposition is unilateral, i.e., all located on one side *vis-à-vis* the government, no matter how many parties oppose it, they can join forces and propose themselves as an alternative government. In the polarized polities we find instead two oppositions that are mutually exclusive: They cannot join forces. In fact, the two opposing groups are closer, if anything, to the governing parties than to one another. The system has two oppositions, then, in the sense that they are *counter-oppositions* that are, in constructive terms, incompatible.

The two foregoing characteristics are the most visible ones and already suffice to identify the category. If there are more than five parties, if the system displays bilateral counter-oppositions (in the plural) which include parties that oppose the very political system, then this type is definitely far removed from the type of multipartism characterized by a unilateral opposition and the absence of relevant anti-system parties.

3. If one wonders how we pass from unilateral to bilateral oppositions, one is immediately alerted to the third feature: The systems of polarized pluralism are characterized by the centre placement of one party (Italy) or of a group of parties (France, Weimar). Granted that whether it is a unified or a fragmented centre makes a difference, all our cases have or had—until falling apart—a fundamental trait in common: Along the left-to-right dimension *the metrical centre of the system is occupied*. This implies that we are no longer confronted with bipolar interactions, but at the very least with triangular interactions. The system is multipolar in that its competitive mechanics hinges on a centre that must face *both* a left and a right. While the mechanics of moderate pluralism is bipolar precisely because the system is not centre based, the mechanics of polarized pluralism is multipolar and cannot be explained, therefore, by a dualistic model.

It is important to stress that when one speaks of a centre-based system, one is concerned only with a *centre positioning*, not with centre doctrines, ideologies, and opinions—whatever these may be.[12] The physical occupation of the centre is, in and by itself, of great consequence, for it implies that the central area of the political system is *out of competition* (in the dimension in which competition occurs). In other terms, the very existence of a centre party (or parties) discourages 'centrality', i.e., the centripetal drives of the political system. And the centripetal drives are precisely the moderating drives. This is why this type is centre-fleeing, or centrifugal, and thereby conducive to immoderate or extremist politics.

4. If a political system obtains anti-system, bilateral oppositions and discourages—by the very fact that its centre is physically occupied—centripetal competition, these traits add up to a polarized system. *Polarization* can thus be revisited in more detail as a fourth, synthetic characteristic. In the Italian and Chilean cases the 'pull' is (was) mostly at the left; in the Weimar case it became stronger, in the thirties, on the right; in the case of the Fourth Republic it was more evenly distributed at both ends. The fact remains that in all cases the spectrum of political opinion is highly polarized: Its lateral poles are literally *two poles apart*, and the distance between them covers a maximum spread of opinion. This is tantamount to saying that cleavages are likely to be very deep, that consensus is surely low, and that the legitimacy of the political system is widely questioned. Briefly put, we have polarization when we have *ideological distance* (in contradistinction to ideological proximity).

To be sure, the system is centre based precisely because it is polarized. Otherwise there would neither be a central area large enough to provide space for occupancy, nor would a centre placement be rewarding—for the centre parties capitalize on the fear of extremism. None the less, it should not escape our attention that we are confronted here with a vicious whirl. In the long run a centre positioning is not only a consequence

---

[12] Duverger's thesis that 'the centre never exists in politics' (ibid. 245) confuses the various aspects of the problem and should be reversed: a centre 'tendency' always exists, what may not exist is a centre party.

but also a *cause* of polarization, for the very fact that the central area is occupied feeds the system with centre-fleeing drives and discourages centripetal competition.

5. The fifth feature of polarized pluralism has already been touched upon. It is the likely prevalence of the *centrifugal drives* over the centripetal ones. The characteristic trend of the system is the enfeeblement of the centre, a persistent loss of *votes* to one of the extreme ends (or even to both). Perhaps the centre-fleeing haemorrhage can be stopped; still the centrifugal strains appear to counteract successfully any decisive reversal of the trend. The most eloquent cases to this effect have been the Weimar Republic and Chile; but the French Fourth Republic also displayed a centre-fleeing trend. Until October 1947 the Communists entered the various post-war governments, and at the other extreme no adversary movement had emerged in the electoral arena. By 1951, however, the Gaullist reaction (tellingly labelled RPF, *Rassemblement du Peuple Français*) swept the country, the four 'constitutional parties' located between the Communist and Gaullist extremes, which had polled in June 1946 as much as 73.5 per cent of the total vote, had fallen to a bare 51.0 per cent, and the major losses (from 28.1 down to 12.5) were of the Christian Democrats, one of the two pivotal parties of the centre area. At the subsequent and last election of 1956 the centrifugal tendency appeared lessened in terms of electoral returns, but the Gaullist surge was replaced, if only in part, by the Poujade surge, by all standards a right-wing anti-system protest.

6. The sixth feature of polarized pluralism is its congenital *ideological patterning*. When one finds a large ideological space, it follows that the polity contains parties that disagree not only on policies but also, and more importantly, on principles and fundamentals. We are thus referred to a more substantive meaning of ideology. As noted earlier, 'ideology' may signify, (i) a highly emotive involvement in politics and (ii) a particular mentality, a *forma mentis*. In monistic polities the emphasis will be on the first element, on 'ideological heating'. But in pluralistic systems the emphasis should be laid on the second, on the 'mentality', that is, on ideology understood as a way of perceiving and conceiving politics, and defined, therefore, as a distinctly doctrinaire, principled, and high-flown way of focusing

political issues. This ideological *approach*, and indeed *forma mentis*, springs from the very roots of a culture (not merely of the political culture) and typically reflects the mentality of rationalism as opposed to the empirical and pragmatic mentality. This is not to say that given a rationalistic culture, ideologism necessarily follows. I simply mean that a rationalistic culture is the most favourable soil for the cultivation of ideological politics, whereas an empirical culture makes it difficult for an ideological approach to take root.

Due attention should be paid to the fact that the very configuration of the party system maintains and upholds the ideological patterning of the society. Objective socio-economic cleavages may no longer justify ideological compartmentalization, and yet denominational, Marxist, and nationalistic parties are able to maintain their appeal and to shape the society according to their ideological creeds. When a party system becomes established—passing beyond the stage of atomization—parties become built-ins, they become the 'natural' system of channelment of the political society. And when there are several built-in, established parties, the system acquires a vested interest in fostering an ideological type of canalization—for at least two reasons. The first is that if so many parties are to be perceived and justified in their separateness, they cannot afford a pragmatic lack of distinctiveness. The second reason is that in a situation of extreme pluralism most parties are relatively small groups whose survival is best assured if their followers are indoctrinated as 'believers'; and a law of contagion goes to explain why the largest party (or parties) is likely to follow suit.

7. The seventh feature of polarized pluralism is the presence of *irresponsible oppositions*. This feature is closely related to the peculiar mechanics of governmental turnover of the centre-based polities. On the one hand, the centre party (or the leading party of the centre) is not exposed to alternation: Being the pivot and the very backbone of any possible governmental majority, its destiny is to govern indefinitely. On the other hand, the extreme parties, the parties that oppose the system, are excluded almost by definition from alternation in office: Under normal circumstances they are not destined to govern. Under these conditions we cannot have, therefore, *alternative*

coalitions, the swing of the pendulum from one group to another group of parties. We find, instead, a *peripheral turnover*—peripheral in that the access to government is limited to the centre-left and/or the centre-right parties only. Differently put, alternative coalitions presuppose a system in which *all* the relevant parties are governing oriented and acceptable as governing parties. Contrariwise, peripheral turnover consists of permanently governing parties that merely change partners in their neighbourhood.

8. The final feature of polarized pluralism is the extent to which the polity displays a pattern that I call *politics of outbidding*, or of overpromising, which is very different from what is meaningfully called competitive politics. Competitive politics consists not only of competitiveness, that is, of how close the competitions are to each other; it consists also of *rules of competition*. The notion of competitive politics comes from economics, and when we have recourse to analogies, we should see to it that the analogy does not get lost along the way. Economic competition is made possible by two conditions: first, that the market escapes monopolistic control; second, and no less important, that the goods are what they are said to be. In the field of economics this latter condition is satisfied by legal control. If fraud were not punished and if producers could easily get away with selling something as something else—glass as diamonds, yellow paint as gold, water as medicine—a competitive market would immediately founder.

Similar, if less stringent, conditions apply to political competition. Competitive politics is conditioned not only by the presence of more than one party but also by a minimum of fair competition (and of mutual trust) below which a political market can hardly perform as a competitive market. Admittedly, in politics we must be less exacting, and political fraud is more difficult both to detect and to control than economic fraud. Yet the distinction between responsible and irresponsible opposition allows an equivalent distinction between fair and unfair political competition. If a party can always light-heartedly promise heaven on earth without ever having to 'respond' to what it promises, this behaviour surely falls below any standard of fair competition. And I submit that under these conditions 'competitive politics' is both an inappropriate choice of vocabulary and a misunderstanding of the facts. Actually, the political game is played in terms of unfair competition characterized by incessant escalation. And the politics of outbidding results—to revert to the economic analogy—in something very similar to *inflationary disequilibrium*: a situation is which competitors 'strive to bid support away from each other by stronger appeals and promises', so that the competition for the available supply increases while the supply does not.[13]

2. *Moderate Pluralism and Segmented Societies*

Limited and moderate pluralism is demarcated, at one boundary, by the two-party systems and, at the other, by extreme and polarized pluralism. The *class* basically encompasses, then, from three to five relevant parties—and this is why I call it 'limited' (in contradistinction to extreme) pluralism. Clearly, moderate pluralism is entitled to separate recognition to the extent that its systemic properties are neither the ones of twopartism nor the ones of polarized pluralism.

Vis-à-vis the properties of twopartism, the major distinguishing trait of moderate pluralism is coalition government. This feature follows from the fact that the relevant parties are at least three, that no party generally attains the absolute majority, and that it appears irrational to allow the major or dominant party to govern alone when it can be obliged to share its power. Thus minority single party governments do materialize, but they do so either as a result of miscalculated Indian wrestlings, or on the basis of a precise calculus (such as shedding unpopular, if necessary, policies), and otherwise as disguised coalitions and transitional caretaker governments. In any case, minority single party governments are—in the context of limited and moderate pluralism—'feeble' governments, even though they may not be shortlived.

Thus the formula of moderate pluralism is not alternative government but governing in coalition within the perspective of *alternative coalitions* (which does not necessarily mean actually

---

[13] H. V. Wiseman, *Political Systems* (New York: Praeger, 1966), 115. Wiseman draws from Harry C. Bredemeier, R. M. Stephenson, *The Analysis of Social Systems* (New York: Holt, 1962).

alternating coalitions). Aside from this major difference, in most other respects the mechanics of moderate pluralism tends to resemble and to imitate—albeit with a higher degree of complexity—the mechanics of twopartism. In particular the structure of moderate pluralism remains *bipolar*. Instead of only two parties we generally find bipolar alignments of alternative coalitions. But this difference does not detract from the fact that competition remains centripetal and thereby from the fact that the mechanics of moderate pluralism is still conducive to *moderate politics*.

While the distinguishing characteristics of moderate pluralism may not appear impressive *vis-à-vis* the two-party systems, they stand out neatly with respect to the systems of polarized pluralism. First, moderate pluralism lacks relevant and/or sizeable anti-system parties. Second, and correlatively, it lacks bilateral oppositions. To put it in the affirmative, in a system of moderate pluralism all the parties are governing oriented, that is, available for cabinet coalitions. Hence all the non-governing parties can coalesce *qua* oppositions, and this means that the opposition will be 'unilateral'—all on one side, either on the left or on the right. Basically, then, moderate pluralism is *non-polarized*. That is to say that if we abide by the same yardstick, the comparison between moderate and polarized pluralism reveals that their respective ideological spreads are significantly, and indeed critically, different.

In synthesis, a system of moderate pluralism is characterized by (i) a relatively small ideological distance among its relevant parties, (ii) a bipolar coalitional configuration, and (iii) centripetal competition.

It would be redundant to specify how many consequences do *not* follow—this is simply a matter of putting the minus sign wherever polarized pluralism obtains the plus sign. It is worthwhile recalling, instead, that the characteristics of the type can also be used as control indicators, that is, for controlling whether a growing fragmentation of the party system corresponds to a growing ideological distance. Whenever the question is whether the numerical criterion is a reliable indicator, one can swiftly check by ascertaining whether or not a more-than-two party system contains anti-system parties and bilateral oppositions. If the system does not, we are definitely confronted with a case of moderate pluralism. The point may be generalized as follows. If the number of parties grows and yet all the parties still belong to the 'same world'—i.e., accept the legitimacy of the political system and abide by its rules—then the fragmentation of the system cannot be attributed to ideological polarization. In this case the fragmentation is presumably related to a multidimensional configuration: a *segmented*, polyethnic and/or multiconfessional society. Conversely, when the number of parties exceeds the critical threshold and we do find anti-system parties and bilateral oppositions, then it can be safely assumed that more-than-five parties reflect a degree of ideological distance that makes a bipolar mechanics impossible.

If the question is whether moderate pluralism is a distinct type and whether it can sort out the cases, I would answer yes. The ulterior question might be, however, whether it is convenient to distinguish, within this type, a 'segmented' subgroup. And the ultimate problem arising from the literature on the segmented and 'consociational' democracies is whether all the countries so qualified should not be gathered into a category of their own.[14]

---

[14] Concerning the terminology, Lijphart settles for 'consociational democracy'; Lehmbruch speaks of *Konkordanzdemokratie* (and of a system of *amicabilis composito*); and Lorwin says 'segmented pluralism' (in Dutch: *verzuiling*). The terms 'ghettoization', *Lagermentalitaet*, and 'compartmentalization' are also fitting, and frequently used, for the Austrian case. Reference is made to the following writings: Hans Daalder, 'The Netherlands: Opposition is a Segmented Society', in Robert A. Dahl (ed.), *Political Oppositions in Western Democracies* (New Haven: Yale University Press, 1966); Arend Lijphart, *The Politics of Accommodation: Pluralism and Democracy in the Netherlands* (Berkeley: University of California Press, 1968), and his article, 'Typologies of Democratic Systems', *Comparative Political Studies*, 1/1, (1968); Gerhard Lehmbruch, *Proporzdemokratie: Politische System und Politische Kultur in der Schweiz und in Österreich* (Tübingen: Mohr, 1967); Jurg Steiner, 'Conflict Resolution and Democratic Stability in Subculturally Segmented Political Systems', *Res Publica*, iv (1969); Val Lorwin, 'Segmented Pluralism: Ideological Cleavages and Political Cohesion in the Smaller European Democracies', *Comparative Politics*, 3/2 (1971); Hans Daalder, 'On Building Consociational Nations: The Case of the Netherlands and Switzerland', *International Social Science Journal*, iii (1971), and 'The Consociational Democracy Theme', *World Politics*, 26/4 (1974); Jurg Steiner, *Amicable Agreement Versus Majority Rule* (Chapel Hill: University of North Carolina Press, 1974).

footnote continued overleaf.

338   GIOVANNI SARTORI

So far the countries brought under the rubric of *segmented pluralism*—to follow Val Lorwin—are especially the Netherlands, Belgium, Luxemburg, Switzerland, Austria, plus Lebanon. However, the list could be easily extended to include most, if not all, of the societies otherwise identified as polyethnic, multiconfessional, and/or multidimensional. Surely, Israel would qualify, and India is also a highly plausible candidate. Furthermore, if Belgium is entered, under the segmentation criterion it is difficult to exclude Canada. In the end, should the suggestion become fashionable, it will quickly be found that it is difficult to draw a line between the segmented societies and those already characterized as 'culturally heterogeneous'. But even if we are content with the Netherlands and Switzerland, Israel and India, Belgium, Canada, and Austria, we have in the act pooled together all the conceivable competitive systems. Whatever else it may sort out, the criterion of Lorwin, Lijphart, and Lembruch does not sort out the party system. Nor—let me hasten to make clear—is this their claim. We are thus referred to my initial question, namely, whether the segmented polities should be subsumed, under my typology, as a distinct subgroup. Clearly, the question relates to all my types. It can be discussed best, however, under the case of moderate pluralism, among other reasons because multidimensionality and/or segmentation tend to be cancelled out by strong ideological tensions—viz., in the polarized polities —whereas they acquire prominence precisely in the nonpolarized systems.

Let us begin with the definition. In the wording of Lorwin, segmented pluralism is 'the organization of social movements, educational and communication systems, voluntary associations and political parties along the lines of religious and

---

footnote continued

A useful symposium is Kenneth D. McRae (ed.), *Consociational Democracy: Political Accommodation in Segmented Societies* (Toronto: McClelland and Stuart, 1974). [Note: The application of Sartori's model to segmented societies is also discussed in Giacomo Sani and Giovanni Sartori, 'Polarization, Fragmentation and Competition in Western Democracies', in Hans Daalder and Peter Mair (eds.), *Western European Party Systems: Continuity and Change* (London: Sage Publications, 1983), 329–37, *PM*.]

ideological cleavages'. Thus segmented pluralism is 'pluralist in its recognition of diversity . . . ; it is "segmented" in its institutionalization'.[15] It is immediately apparent that the notion points first to a state of society, and only derivatively to the state of the polity. In other words, segmented pluralism is primarily a structural construct of the socio-cultural variety. Fair enough—and I shall arrive also at the sociology of politics. However, if we do not identify first the political structures —and particularly the party structuring—we are likely to miss this crucial question: *How is it that similar socio-economic structures are not translated into similar party systems?* In the case in point—the segmented societies covered by Lorwin—Austria definitely has a two-party format and has recently displayed also a two-party mechanics; Belgium has unquestionably had a three-party format (and mechanics) for some eighty years; Switzerland and the Netherlands have, instead, a polyparty system. It appears, therefore, that the segmentation of these countries is either a word with multiple meanings, or a structure without necessary consequence on the party system.

3. *Two-Party Systems*

The two-party system is by far the best known category. This is because it is a relatively simple system, because the countries that practise twopartism are important countries, and because they represent a paradigmatic case. Even so, we are immediately blocked by this simple question: How many two-party systems are there in existence? According to Banks and Textor, 11 of the 115 countries covered by their survey fall under the two-party rubric.[16] But the figure is surely exaggerated, for it includes a country such as Colombia, which has what can hardly be considered a party system at all. Dahl reduces the figure to 8, a number that includes Panama, the Philippines, and Uruguay.[17] Blondel indicates—albeit with various

---

[15] Lorwin, 'Segmented Pluralism', p. 141. I select Lorwin because his brilliant article represents the most general treatment. The other writings (above, n. 14) are generally on one or two countries only.

[16] A. S. Banks and R. B. Textor, *A Cross Polity Survey* (Cambridge, Mass.: MIT Press, 1963).

[17] Robert A. Dahl, 'Patterns of Opposition', in Dahl, *Political Oppositions in Western Democracies*, p. 333.

cautions appended—no fewer than 21 two-party states.[18] Since every specialist provides a different list, let us say that popular opinion generally considers England, the United States, New Zealand, Australia, and Canada as the 'classic' two-party systems. If we enter Austria—a recent accession—we have six countries. However, Austria practised, until 1966, 'grand coalitions'; hence its two-party system of government can hardly be considered, as yet, well established. On the other hand, Australia actually has three relevant parties; and Canada might appear even more anomalous than Australia. By a strict standard (thereby including a sufficient duration) we are thus left with three countries only: England, the United States, and New Zealand. And the final blow comes with the argument that English and American twopartism are so far apart that it makes little sense to classify them together.

We are seemingly approaching the paradox of having the most celebrated type of party system running out of cases. The paradox arises because—here as elsewhere—we confront two distinct problems that we generally attempt to solve in one blow. One is to decide when a country belongs to the two-party *class*, and this depends on the counting rules. The other problem is to decide whether we have a two-party *type* of system.

To the first question—when is it that a third party, or even third parties, should be discounted—the reply can be straightforward: We have a two-party *format* whenever the existence of third parties does not prevent the two major parties from governing alone, i.e., whenever coalitions are unnecessary. The reply implies that the format of twopartism must be assessed in terms of *seats*, not of electoral returns. The very obvious reason for this 'must' is that governments are formed, and perform, on the basis of their strength in parliament. The additional reason is that nearly all the polities under consideration (except Austria, which is a PR country) abide by a single-member district system which—as is well-known—turns relative into absolute majorities, and even upturns an electoral majority into a parliamentary minority.

The argument is more complex, however, as soon as we ask:

---

[18] Blondel, *Introduction to Comparative Government*, pp. 165–77.

What are the *properties* that characterize the two-party type of system? If the major characteristic of twopartism is that one party governs alone, we must immediately add: alone, but not indefinitely. If it is always the same party that remains in office election after election, we have a predominant, not a two-party, system. This is the same as saying that alternation in power is *the* distinguishing mark of the mechanics of twopartism. One may also say that 'two' differs from 'three' whenever third parties do not affect, in the long run and at the national level, the alternation in power of the two major parties. However, to avoid running out of cases neither the 'alternation' nor the 'governing alone' clause is rigidly applicable.

Alternation should be loosely understood as implying the *expectation* rather than the actual occurrence of governmental turnover. Alternation only means, then, that the margin between the two major parties is close enough, or that there is sufficient credibility to the expectation that the party in opposition has a chance to oust the governing party. In other words, the notion of alternation shades into the notion of competitiveness.

Turning to the *governing alone* clause, the matter is subject even more to flexibility in interpretation. That is, we must be very lenient with regard to the requirement that *both* parties should be in a position to win for themselves an absolute majority and hence to govern alone. The problem is especially posed by Australia, where the alternation in government occurs between the Labour party on the one side, and the alliance of the Liberal and Country parties on the other. Prima facie this is a three-party format, and the straightforward solution would seem to be to reclassify Australia as a three-party system, placing it with Belgium and West Germany. But no sooner do we bring these three countries together than we are alerted to their different mechanics. For one thing, the Germans have done something that is unthinkable in the logic of twopartism: They settled, in 1965, for a grand coalition between the two major parties. Moreover, and more important, the German and Belgian Liberals are free to change, and do change, coalition partners. Nothing of the kind happens in Australia. In particular, the permanent alliance between the Liberal and Country party is such that the two parties do not compete, in the constituencies, against each other: The two parties are, so to speak, symbiotic. Clearly, Germany and Belgium do not function according to the rules of two-partism, whereas Australia does. Therefore, we are justified in relaxing the 'governing alone' clause as follows: The turnover may be of one versus two, provided that 'two' is not a mere coalition but a coalescence.

The lenient conditions for a system that functions according to the rules of twopartism would thus be the following: (i) two parties are in a position to compete for the absolute majority of seats; (ii) one of the two parties actually succeeds in winning a sufficient parliamentary majority; (iii) this party is willing to govern alone; (iv) alternation or rotation in power remains a credible expectation.

I have conceded from the outset that the four conditions from which my definition of twopartism are contrived are lenient ones; and I have applied them as flexibly as possible. Even so, it turns out that two-party systems are rare. This is particularly evident in a longitudinal perspective: Austria is, so far, the only new Western entry in the category, and it is still somewhat soon to say whether the pattern inaugurated in 1966 will strike durable roots. It should also be recalled, in this connection, that the longevity of English twopartism is largely a myth. Only since 1885 is it appropriate to speak of a nationwide British party system; and since then the United Kingdom has displayed three different patterns. Between 1885 and 1910—when the major parties were the Conservatives and the Liberals—six out of eight general elections did not produce real single party government: The Conservatives needed the support of the Liberal Unionists (the Liberal split of Joseph Chamberlain), while the Liberals relied on the Irish Nationalists. During the interwar period (between 1918 and 1935) Labour became the second largest party, but the Liberals survived as a relevant third party, and the whole period was characterized by instability and coalitions. It turns out, therefore, that the British have abided by the classic rules of twopartism only for some thirty years.

The rarity of the case suggests that two-party systems are 'difficult'. But the emphasis is mostly on the view that two-party systems represent a paradigmatic case, an optimal solution. The claim has generally been—until recent discontents

—that two-party systems obtain beneficial returns for the polity as a whole. More precisely, two-party systems always 'work', whereas the more parties there are, the more we find 'less working' solutions and, ultimately, non-viable systems. The claim is not unwarranted; but it cannot be warranted by pointing to the countries in which twopartism happens to work. Indeed, these countries are so few that one may well argue that all of the more-than-two party systems are such precisely because the two-party solution either did not endure, or did or would prove to be unworkable. The retort could be, then, that twopartism generally fails or would fail if attempted.

By and large, two-party systems are explained along the lines formalized by the Downs model of party competition. The issue is simply: Under what conditions does twopartism work as predicted by the model? The model predicts that in a two-party system the parties will compete centripetally, soft-pedalling cleavages and playing the game of politics with responsible moderation. This happens, however, because centripetal competition is rewarding. Why is it rewarding? Presumably because the floating voters themselves are moderates, i.e., located between the two parties, somewhere around the centre of the spectrum of opinions. If the major group of floating voters were non-identified extremists, that is, extremists prepared to defect from an extreme left to an extreme right and vice versa, centripetal competition would no longer be rewarding. In short, twopartism 'works' when the spread of opinion is small and its distribution single peaked.

This is not to say that twopartism presupposes consensus, for it is equally true that the centripetal mechanics of twopartism *creates* consensus. Making the claim more modest, let us say that the competitive mechanics of the system paves the way to consensus in that it has a conflict-minimizing bent. The macroscopic example of this is the United States. The potentiality for conflict in American society is enormous. Yet it is not reflected at the level of the party system. The fact that the United States is the only industrial society that has not produced a working-class party is largely due to a set of peculiar historical circumstances but also to the nature of American twopartism. And the extent to which the party system is conflict minimizing is patently revealed not only by the very high percentage of

American non-voters, but especially by their being low-strata non-voters. The registration requirement would hardly be an impediment if politics had a salience for the non-voting strata —a salience it obviously does not have.

There is a systemic logic to all of this. Twopartism hinges, if not on actual turnover, on the expectation of alternation in government. Now the fact that two parties are nearly equal in strength can hardly be considered 'natural' or accidental. Clearly, the two-party type of balance and oscillation is obtained and maintained via the tactics of party competition. In twopartism, parties *must* be aggregative agencies that maintain their competitive near-evenness by amalgamating as many groups, interests, and demands as possible. It should not be taken for granted, therefore, that twopartism *presupposes* a set of favourable conditions—cultural homogeneity, consensus on fundamentals, and the like. If one reviews the development of the two-party countries historically, it appears that twopartism has largely *nurtured* and moulded such favourable conditions.

At any given point in time, however, it is clear that the smaller the spread of opinion, the smoother the functioning of twopartism. Conversely, the greater the ideological distance, the more a two-party format is dysfunctional. Therefore, it is misleading to assert that two-party systems always work. Rather, these systems represent an optimal solution only when they work, that is, whenever they presuppose and/or produce a highly consensual political society characterized by minimal ideological spread. Hence whenever a two-party format does not perform as required by the Downs model, we should expect the parties to become more than two and another type of party system.

4. *Predominant-Party Systems*

It bears repetition that my *predominant-party system* does not coincide, and indeed has very little in common, with the *dominant party* spoken of by a number of authors. The dominant party category was suggested more or less at the same time by Duverger and by Almond. Duverger's examples were the French radicals, the Scandinavian Social Democratic parties, and the Indian Congress party.[19] Probably in the wake of Almond's usage, Blanksten mentions a 'dominant non-dictatorial party' and offers, as clear-cut examples of the category, the Solid South in the United States, Mexico, and, as possible additional examples, Uruguay and Paraguay.[20] Over the years the list has grown, and so has the confusion.

As it stands, the category only obfuscates the systemic properties of the countries it sorts out. And the reason for this is not far to seek: Dominant party is a category that confuses *party* (in isolation) with party *system*. The shift is, with most authors, verbal. Their focus is, in effect, on the major party; but they then slip in the word system; and unwarranted inferences are thus made from the major party to the nature of the system. To be sure, the Italian DC, the Israeli *Mapai*, or the Danish Social Democrats are dominant parties: But it does not follow that Italy, Israel, and Denmark have dominant party 'systems'. In short, the notion of dominant party establishes neither a *class* nor a *type* of party system. It is correct, and telling, to say that certain parties are 'dominant'. But it has not been shown that this qualifier deserves the status of a category. What remains to be seen is whether the notion of dominant party can be utilized as a taxonomic category in conjunction with other criteria and, specifically, whether it belongs in the definition of the predominant-party systems.

The first point to be made with respect to the predominant-party systems is that they unquestionably belong to the area of party pluralism. Parties other than the major one not only are permitted to exist, but do exist as legal and legitimate—if not necessarily effective—competitors of the predominant party. That is to say that the minor parties are truly independent antagonists of the predominant party. Therefore, the predominant-party system actually is a more-than-one party system in which rotation does not occur in fact. It simply happens that

<hr/>

[19] Maurice Duverger, 'La Sociologie des Partis Politiques', in G. Gurvitch (ed.), *Traité de Sociologie* (Paris: Presses Universitaires de France, 1960), ii. 44; G. A. Almond, 'A Functional Approach to Comparative Politics', in G. A. Almond and J. S. Coleman (eds.), *The Politics of Developing Areas* (Princeton: Princeton University Press, 1960), 40–2.

[20] In Almond and Coleman, *Politics of Developing Areas*, p. 480.

the same party manages to win, over time, an *absolute majority of seats* (not necessarily of votes) in parliament.

Clearly, the crucial condition is the authenticity of such victories. Awaiting a more critical attitude towards, and inspection of, electoral statistics, let us state this condition as follows: The monopolistic permanence in office of the same party, election after election, cannot reasonably be imputed to conspicuous unfair play or ballot stuffing. In other words, we can close an eye to electoral irregularities as long as it can be reasonably assumed that in a situation of fair competition the predominant party would still attain the absolute majority of seats. The definition is, then, as follows: A predominant-party system is such to the extent that, and as long as, its major party is consistently supported by a winning majority (the absolute majority of seats) of the voters. It follows that a predominant party can cease, at any moment, to be predominant. When this happens, either the pattern is soon re-established or the system changes its nature, i.e., ceases to be a predominant-party system.

The foregoing definition has a virtue that weakens it and a feebleness that accrues to its virtue: It is too precise with respect to the threshold, and too vague about the duration. As the definition stands, a majority that is near-absolute but falls short of the 50 per cent mark is not a sufficient condition of 'predominance' as far as the qualification of the party system is concerned. This is correct in operational terms; but, at the same time, it is the feeble point of most, if not all, operational definitions related to precise thresholds and measures. My threshold is established at the 50 per cent mark under the assumption that constitutional government generally operates on the basis of the absolute majority principle. The facts of the matter are, however, that in Norway, Sweden, and Denmark, for instance, the 'conventions' of the constitution are different, as is testified by the longstanding performances, in these countries, of minority governments. Under this circumstance, my option is to sacrifice the neatness of operational precision. Hence the 50 per cent majority clause will be relaxed as follows: A predominant-party system is generally qualified by its major party obtaining the absolute majority of seats, with the exception of countries that unquestionably abide by a less-than-absolute majority principle. In these cases the threshold can be lowered to the point at which minority single-party governments remain a standing and efficient practice.

How long does it take for a predominant party to establish a predominant system? At this stage of the argument I am prepared to settle for the following criterion: Three consecutive absolute majorities can be a sufficient indication, provided that the electorate appears stabilized, that the absolute majority threshold is clearly surpassed, and/or that the interval is wide. Conversely, to the extent that one or more of these conditions do not obtain, a judgement will have to await a longer period of time to pass. Doubtlessly, this leaves the duration requirement fairly loose. But this is as it should be. At any given point in time a predominant-party system can cease to be such—exactly as can a two-party system. This is not to say, obviously, that the other party systems are not subject to change as well; it is only to say that the predominant and the two-party systems share a peculiar kind of fragility: Small differences in returns, or the mere changing of the electoral system, can more easily transform the nature of the system. On the other hand, the *over* time perspective can be different from the perspective *in* time. There is no contradiction in declaring that a given country does not function, *hic et nunc*, as a predominant type of system and yet displays an overall systemic record of predominance.

An additional clarification is perhaps redundant but not entirely superfluous. The predominant-party system is a *type*, not a class. This is to recall that the criterion here is not the number of parties but a particular distribution of power among them. Thus a predominant-party system can arise either from a two-party format (as in the limiting case of the American Solid South) or from a highly fragmented format, as is particularly the case of the Indian Congress party. It is only for the purpose of establishing a continuum that one may consider the predominant-party system as the variant of twopartism in which no alternation in power occurs (*de facto*) for a considerable length of time. For all other purposes it should be borne in mind that the predominant-party system can just as well be a variant of any multipartism.

5.   The Simplified Model

The *simplified model* (of the competitive system) [is] represented in Figure 24.1.

The first thing to note is that the upper right corner of the figure remains blank. Does this asymmetry point to a flaw? I think not, because the blank stands, in effect, for 'breakdown'. When a maximal ideological distance engenders a centrifugal competition, a two-party format is either blown up or paves the way to a civil war confrontation. Hence the figure suggests that extreme multipartism represents—under conditions of maximal polarization—the most likely outcome and, at the same time, the survival solution. The alternative might be, to be sure, a towering predominant party. But a strongly predominant party results from low competitiveness; and if the competitiveness is low, it follows that the variable 'ideological distance' does not carry much weight in the electoral arena.

The figure brings forcefully to the fore, in the second place, that my emphasis is on the *direction* of competition, not on

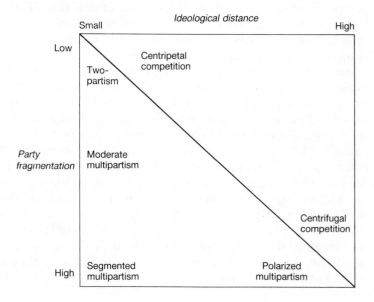

FIG. 24.1.   The Simplified Model

competitiveness. Since most authors neglect this aspect, it is appropriate to insist on its importance. To be sure, I also account for competitiveness. Thus a predominant-party system can be said to correspond—as I have just recalled—to low inter-party competitiveness. Likewise, the mechanics of two-partism hinges on high competitiveness. However, beyond this point the systemic consequences of competitiveness are not at all clear—as we know. Too much competitiveness—as measured by the closeness of the margins among the competitors—may be as unhelpful as too little competitiveness; or, alternatively, different degrees of competitiveness may not produce any detectable difference either in the behaviour of politicians or in the governmental outputs. And this is a first reason why I cannot follow the various attempts at construing 'competition' as an independent or central explanatory variable—even though I well understand what prompts these attempts, namely, that competition is a measurable variable and a very attractive one at that. But my major criticism is precisely that our measures cannot sort out the direction of competition and are therefore blind to the one element that surely is of decisive consequence on the overall performance of a polity.

NOTES ON CONTRIBUTORS

JEAN BLONDEL is Professor of Political and Social Sciences at the European University Institute, Florence.

HANS DAALDER is Professor of Political Science at the University of Leiden.

ROBERT A. DAHL is Professor of Political Science at Yale University.

RUSSELL J. DALTON is Professor of Political Science at Florida State University.

MAURICE DUVERGER is Professor of Political Science at the Sorbonne, University of Paris I.

SCOTT C. FLANAGAN is Professor of Political Science at Florida State University.

RONALD INGLEHART is Professor of Political Science at the University of Michigan, Ann Arbor.

OTTO KIRCHHEIMER was Professor of Government at Columbia University.

JOSEPH LAPALOMBARA is Professor of Political Science at Yale University.

AREND LIJPHART is Professor of Political Science at the University of California, San Diego.

S. M. LIPSET is Professor of Political Science and Sociology at Stanford University.

PETER MAIR, the editor of this volume, is Senior Lecturer in Government at the University of Manchester.

SIGMUND NEUMANN was Professor of Government and Modern History at Wesleyan University.

MOGENS N. PEDERSEN is Professor of Political Science at the University of Odense.

ALESSANDRO PIZZORNO is Professor of Political and Social Sciences at the European University Institute, Florence.

STEIN ROKKAN was Professor of Sociology at the University of Bergen.

RICHARD ROSE is Director of the Centre for the Study of Public Policy at the University of Strathclyde.

GIOVANNI SARTORI is Albert Schweitzer Professor of Humanities at Columbia University.

DEREK URWIN is Professor of Politics at the University of Warwick.

MAX WEBER was Professor of Economics at the University of Heidelberg.

MYRON WEINER is Professor of Political Science at the Massachusetts Institute of Technology.

STEVEN B. WOLINETZ is Associate Professor of Political Science at the Memorial University of Newfoundland.

SELECT BIBLIOGRAPHY

(See also the references in the Introduction)

I. THE DEVELOPMENT OF THE MASS PARTY

The literature on the development of political parties is enormous, and readers would be best advised to begin with the 'classics' in the field, extracts from some of which have been included in this reader:

DUVERGER, MAURICE [originally published in French in 1951], *Political Parties: Their Organization and Activity in the Modern State* (London: Methuen, 1954).

LAPALOMBARA, JOSEPH and WEINER, MYRON (eds.), *Political Parties and Political Development* (Princeton: Princeton University Press, 1966).

MICHELS, ROBERT [originally published in German in 1911], *Political Parties: A Sociological Study of the Oligarchical Tendencies of Modern Democracy* (New York: Free Press, 1962).

NEUMANN, SIGMUND (ed.), *Modern Political Parties: Approaches to Comparative Politics* (Chicago: University of Chicago Press, 1956).

OSTROGORSKI, M. I., *Democracy and the Organization of Political Parties*, 2 vols. (London: Macmillan, 1902).

SARTORI, GIOVANNI, *Parties and Party Systems: A Framework for Analysis*, Vol. 1 (Cambridge: Cambridge University Press, 1976).

For two useful surveys of the writing on parties and party systems in Western Europe, see:

URWIN, DEREK W., 'Political Parties, Societies and Regimes in Europe: Some Reflections on the Literature', *European Journal of Political Research*, 1/2 (1973), 179–204.

DAALDER, HANS (1983). 'The Comparative Study of European Parties and Party Systems: An Overview', in Hans Daalder and Peter Mair (eds.), *Western European Party Systems: Continuity and Change.* (London: Sage Publications), 1–28.

For some early criticisms of Duverger's approach, see:

ENGELMANN, FREDERICK C, 'A Critique of Recent Writings on Political Parties', *Journal of Politics*, 19/3 (1957), 423–40.

354   SELECT BIBLIOGRAPHY

LEYS, COLIN, 'Models, Theories and the Theory of Political Parties', *Political Studies*, 7/2 (1959), 127–46.

WILDAVSKY, AARON B., 'A Methodological Critique of Duverger's "Political Parties"', *Journal of Politics*, 21/2 (1959), 303–18.

For a more general overview of the development of Kirchheimer's ideas, see:

BURIN, F. S. and K. L. SHELL (eds.), *Politics, Law and Social Change: Selected Essays of Otto Kirchheimer* (New York: Columbia University Press, 1969). This collection includes, inter alia, the two essays listed below and the essay in LaPalombara and Weiner (1966).

KIRCHHEIMER, OTTO, 'The Waning of Opposition in Parliamentary Regimes', *Social Research*, 24/2 (1957), 127–56.

—— 'Germany: The Vanishing Opposition', in Robert A. Dahl (ed.), *Political Oppositions in Western Democracies* (New Haven: Yale University Press, 1966), 237–59.

Finally, examples which emphasize the importance of the way in which parties could encapsulate their supporters can be found in the following highly readable studies:

BAKVIS, HERMAN, *Catholic Power in the Netherlands* (Kingston and Montreal: McGill-Queens University Press, 1981).

DIAMANT, ALFRED, 'The Group Basis of Austrian Politics', *Journal of Central European Affairs*, 18/2 (1958), 134–55.

ROTH, GUENTHER, *The Social Democrats in Imperial Germany: A Study in Working-Class Isolation and National Integration* (Totowa, N.J.: Bedminster Press, 1963).

II. THE STABILIZATION OF PARTY SYSTEMS

The key analysis in this context is clearly the seminal essay by Lipset and Rokkan, a shortened version of which is included in this reader. For a more general overview of Rokkan's approach see:

ALLARDT, ERIK and HENRY VALEN, 'Stein Rokkan: An Intellectual Profile', in Per Torsvik (ed.), *Mobilization, Centre-Periphery Structures and Nation-Building: A Volume in Commemoration of Stein Rokkan* (Oslo: Universitetsforlaget, 1981), 11–38.

DAALDER, HANS, 'Stein Rokkan 1921–1979: A Memoir', *European Journal of Political Research*, 7/4 (1979), 337–55.

FLORA, PETER, 'Il Macro-Modello dello Sviluppo Politico Europeo di

Stein Rokkan', *Rivista Italiana di Scienza Politica*, 10/3 (1980), 369 –435.

ROKKAN, STEIN, *Citizens, Elections, Parties: Approaches to the Comparative Study of Political Development* (Oslo: Universitetsforlaget, 1970), Chapter 3 of which incorporates much of the argument of the Lipset and Rokkan essay.

SAELEN, KIRSTI THESEN, 'Stein Rokkan: A Bibliography' in Per Torsvik (ed.), *Mobilization, Centre-Periphery Structures and Nation-Building: A Volume in Commemoration of Stein Rokkan* (Oslo: Universitetsforlaget, 1981), 525–53.

Some methodological criticisms of Rokkan's approach are developed in:

ABRAMS, PHILIP, *Historical Sociology* (Ithaca, N.Y.: Cornell University Press, 1982).

ALFORD, ROBERT R. and ROGER FRIEDLAND, 'Nations, Parties, and Participation: A Critique of Political Sociology', *Theory and Society*, 1/3 (1974), 307–28.

III. THE TRANSFORMATION OF PARTY SYSTEMS

The literature on this theme has burgeoned in recent years. The following selection of titles offers a guide to further reading. First, for useful assessments of recent changes in individual countries, see the following collections of essays:

BARTOLINI, STEFANO and PETER MAIR (eds.), *Party Politics in Contemporary Western Europe* (London: Cass, 1984).

CREWE, IVOR and DAVID DENVER (eds.), *Electoral Change in Western Democracies: Patterns and Sources of Electoral Volatility* (London: Croom Helm, 1985).

DAALDER, HANS (ed.), *Party Systems in Denmark, Austria, Switzerland, the Netherlands and Belgium* (London: Pinter, 1987).

DALTON, RUSSELL J., SCOTT C. FLANAGAN and PAUL ALLEN BECK (eds.), *Electoral Change in Advanced Industrial Societies: Realignment or Dealignment?* (Princeton: Princeton University Press, 1984).

LAWSON, KAY and PETER MERKL (eds.), *When Parties Fail: Emerging Alternative Organizations* (Princeton: Princeton University Press, 1988).

MAIR, PETER and GORDON SMITH (eds.), *Understanding Party System Change: The West European Experience* (London: Cass, 1990).

WARE, ALAN (ed.), *Political Parties: Electoral Change and Structural Response* (Oxford: Blackwell, 1987).

WOLINETZ, STEVEN B. (ed.), *Parties and Party Systems in Liberal Democracies* (London: Routledge, 1988).

For more explicitly comparative assessments of the extent of electoral change in Western Europe, see:

BARTOLINI, STEFANO and PETER MAIR, *Identity, Competition, and Electoral Availability: the Stabilization of European Electorates 1885–1985* (Cambridge: Cambridge University Press, 1990).

ERRSON, SVANTE and JAN-ERIK LANE, 'Democratic Party Systems in Europe: Dimensions, Change and Stability', *Scandinavian Political Studies*, 5/1 (1982), 67–96.

SHAMIR, MICHAL, 'Are Western European Party Systems "Frozen"?', *Comparative Political Studies*, 17/1 (1984), 35–79.

For more analytic and methodological discussions of the problems of measuring and interpreting party system change, see:

DAALDER, HANS and PETER MAIR (eds.), *Western European Party Systems: Continuity and Change* (London: Sage Publications, 1983).

LYBECK, JOHAN A, 'Is The Lipset-Rokkan Hypothesis Testable?', *Scandinavian Political Studies*, 8/1–2 (1985), 105–13.

MAIR, PETER, 'The Problem of Party System Change', *Journal of Theoretical Politics*, 1/3 (1989), 251–76.

PEDERSEN, MOGENS N., 'On Measuring Party System Change: A Methodological Critique and a Suggestion', *Comparative Political Studies*, 12/4 (1980), 387–403.

SMITH, GORDON, 'A System Perspective on Party System Change', *Journal of Theoretical Politics*, 1/3 (1989), 349–63.

IV.   TYPOLOGIES OF PARTY SYSTEMS

Sartori's typology clearly represents the most extensive and elaborated attempt to understand the key elements which distinguish between competitive party systems, and has now gained widespread acceptance in the literature. For earlier versions of this typology, see:

SARTORI, GIOVANNI, 'European Political Parties: The Case of Polarized Pluralism', in Joseph LaPalombara and Myron Weiner (eds.), *Political Parties and Political Development* (Princeton: Princeton University Press, 1966), 137–76.

SARTORI, GIOVANNI, 'The Typology of Party Systems: Proposals for Improvement', in Erik Allardt and Stein Rokkan (eds.), *Mass Politics: Studies in Political Sociology* (New York: The Free Press, 1970), 322–52.

For further discussions of the relevance of the Sartori typology to the Italian case see:

DAALDER, IVO H., 'The Italian Party System in Transition: The End of Polarized Pluralism?', *West European Politics*, 6/2 (1983), 216–36.

FARNETI, PAOLO (1985), *The Italian Party System (1945–1980)* (London: Pinter, 1985).

SARTORI, GIOVANNI, *Teoria dei Partiti e Caso Italiano* (Milano: Sugarco Edizioni, 1982).

For more general discussions and qualifications, see:

BARTOLINI, STEFANO, 'Institutional Constraints and Party Competition in the French Party System', *West European Politics*, 7/4 (1984), 103–27.

DAALDER, HANS, 'In Search of the Centre of European Party Systems', *American Political Science Review*, 78/1 (1984), 92–109.

SANI, GIACOMO and GIOVANNI SARTORI, 'Polarization, Fragmentation and Competition in Western Democracies', in Hans Daalder and Peter Mair (eds.), *Western European Party Systems: Continuity and Change* (London: Sage Publications, 1983), 307–40.

Over and above the approaches already included as chapters in Section IV of this reader, discussions of other typologies can be found in the following:

JUPP, JAMES, *Political Parties* (London: Routledge and Kegan Paul, 1968), 5–21.

LAPALOMBARA, JOSEPH and MYRON WEINER, 'The Origin and Development of Political Parties', in Joseph LaPalombara and Myron Weiner (eds.), *Political Parties and Political Development* (Princeton: Princeton University Press, 1966), 3–42.

MACRIDIS, ROY C., 'Introduction: The History, Function and Typology of Parties' in Macridis (ed.), *Political Parties: Contemporary Trends and Ideas* (New York: Harper and Row, 1967), 9–23.

SMITH, GORDON, 'Western European Party Systems: On the Trail of a Typology', *West European Politics*, 2/2 (1979), 128–42.

Finally, although largely dealing with the classification of political systems rather than party systems *per se*, readers are also recom-

358   SELECT BIBLIOGRAPHY

mended to consult the seminal analyses of Almond and Lijphart, viz:

ALMOND, GABRIEL A., 'Comparative Political Systems', *Journal of Politics*, 18/3 (1956), 391–409.

ALMOND, GABRIEL A., 'A Comparative Study of Interest Groups and the Political Process', *American Political Science Review*, 52/1 (1958), 270–82.

LIJPHART, AREND, 'Typologies of Democratic Systems', *Comparative Political Studies*, 1/1 (1968), 3–44.

v.   ADDITIONAL TITLES (BOOKS ONLY)

1   *General Analyses*

BEYME, KLAUS VON, *Political Parties in Western Democracies* (Aldershot: Gower, 1985).

BUTLER, DAVID, HOWARD R. PENNIMAN and AUSTIN RANNEY (eds.), *Democracy at the Polls: a Comparative Study of Competitive National Elections* (Washington D.C.: American Enterprise Institute, 1981).

CASTLES, FRANCIS G. and RUDOLF WILDENMANN (eds.), *Visions and Realities of Party Government* (Berlin: de Gruyter, 1986).

EPSTEIN, LEON D., *Political Parties in Western Democracies* (New Brunswick, N.J.: Transaction Books, 1980).

JANDA, KENNETH, *Political Parties: A Cross-National Survey* (New York: The Free Press, 1980).

PANEBIANCO, ANGELO, *Political Parties: Organisation and Power* (Cambridge: Cambridge University Press, 1988).

SMITH, GORDON, *Politics in Western Europe*, 5th ed. (London: Heinemann, 1989).

SEILER, DANIEL-LOUIS, *De La Comparaison des Partis Politiques* (Paris: Economica, 1986).

WARE, ALAN, *Citizens, Parties and the State* (Oxford: Blackwell, 1988).

2   *Party Families in Western Europe*

BEYME, KLAUS VON (ed.), *Right-Wing Extremism in Western Europe* (London: Cass, 1988).

FOGARTY, MICHAEL P., *Christian Democracy in Western Europe, 1820–1953* (London: Routledge and Kegan Paul, 1957).

GIRVIN, BRIAN (ed.), *The Transformation of Contemporary Conservatism* (London: Sage Publications, 1988).

IRVING, R. E. M., *The Christian Democratic Parties of Western Europe.* (London: Allen and Unwin, 1976).

KIRCHNER, EMIL (ed.), *Liberal Parties in Western Europe* (Cambridge: Cambridge University Press, 1988).

LAYTON-HENRY, ZIG, *Conservative Politics in Western Europe* (London: Macmillan, 1982).

MCINNES, NEIL, *The Communist Parties of Western Europe* (Oxford: Oxford University Press, 1975).

MORGAN, ROGER and S. SILVESTRI (eds.), *Moderates and Conservatives in Western Europe* (London: Heinemann, 1982).

MUELLER-ROMMEL, FERDINAND (ed.), *New Politics in Western Europe: The Rise and Success of Green Parties and Alternative Lists* (Boulder Co.: Westview Press, 1989).

PATERSON, WILLIAM E. and ALASTAIR H. THOMAS (eds.), *Social Democratic Parties in Western Europe* (London: Croom Helm, 1977).

PATERSON, WILLIAM E. and ALASTAIR H. THOMAS (eds.), *The Future of Social Democracy* (Oxford: Oxford University Press, 1986).

ROGGER, HANS and EUGEN WEBER (eds.), *The European Right: A Historical Profile* (Berkeley: University of California Press, 1966).

ROKKAN, STEIN and DEREK W. URWIN (eds.), *The Politics of Territorial Identity* (London: Sage Publications, 1982).

URWIN, DEREK W., *From Ploughshare to Ballotbox: The Politics of Agrarian Defence in Europe* (Oslo: Universitetsforlaget, 1980).

WHYTE, JOHN H., *Catholics in Western Democracies: A Study in Political Behaviour* (Dublin: Gill and Macmillan, 1981).

WALLER, MICHAEL and MEINDERT FENNEMA (eds.), *Communist Parties in Western Europe: Decline or Adaptation* (Oxford: Blackwell, 1988).

For a general overview, see also:

SEILER, DANIEL-LOUIS, *Partis et Familles Politiques* (Paris: Presses Universitaires de France, 1980).

3 *Collections of Country Studies*

(See also under 'The Transformation of Party Systems')

BUDGE, IAN, DAVID ROBERTSON and DEREK HEARL (eds.), *Ideology, Strategy and Party Change: Spatial Analyses of Post-War Election*

Programmes in 19 Democracies (Cambridge: Cambridge University Press, 1987).

DAHL, ROBERT (ed.), *Political Oppositions in Western Democracies* (New Haven: Yale University Press, 1966).

HENIG, STANLEY (ed.), *Political Parties in the European Community* (London: Allen and Unwin, 1979).

HENIG, STANLEY and JOHN PINDER (eds.), *European Political Parties* (London: Allen and Unwin/PEP, 1969).

KATZ, RICHARD (ed.). *Party Governments: European and American Experiences* (Berlin: de Gruyter, 1987).

KOLINSKY, EVA (ed.) *Opposition in Western Europe* (London: Croom Helm, 1987).

MACKIE, THOMAS T. and RICHARD ROSE, *The International Almanac of Electoral History*, 2nd ed. (London: Macmillan, 1982).

McHALE, VINCENT and SHARON SKOWRONSKI (eds.), *Political Parties of Europe*, 2 vols. (Westport, Conn.: Greenwood Press, 1983).

MERKL, PETER (ed.), *Western European Party Systems* (New York: The Free Press, 1980).

RASCHKE, J. (ed.), *Die Politischen Parteien in Westeuropa—Geschichte —Programm—Praxis: Ein Handbuch* (Reinbek bei Hamburg: Rowohlt, 1977).

ROSE, RICHARD (ed.), *Electoral Behaviour: A Comparative Handbook* (New York: The Free Press, 1974).

INDEX